PHILMONT

PHILMONT

A History
of New Mexico's
CIMARRON COUNTRY

by

LAWRENCE R. MURPHY

ALBUQUERQUE

UNIVERSITY OF NEW MEXICO PRESS

PREFACE

This book is intended as a guide to the history of a large section of northeastern New Mexico, around the town of Cimarron and including most of the vast Beaubien and Miranda Land Grant that extended west into the Sangre de Cristo Mountains, north into Colorado, east onto the edge of the Great Plains, and south toward the Mora valley.

Because the most famous modern feature of this region is the Philmont Scout Ranch, even the United States Geological Survey publications now refer to this at times as the Philmont Country. Every year more than twenty thousand older Boy Scouts, Explorers, adult leaders, and their families visit Philmont Scout Ranch. An even greater number of tourists seek out the ghost camp of Elizabethtown, fish at Eagle Nest, or enjoy the historic scenes of the village of Cimarron.

To all such visitors, this study may provide insight into the process by which the American Southwest was settled. In the country around Philmont can be seen every phase through which the frontier passed on its way from wilderness to civilization.

I first learned of Philmont in 1961 and sought a position on its summer staff. My initial interest in the history of northeastern New Mexico was awakened that summer as I operated an outpost store of the Philmont Ranch, and this interest grew in succeeding summers at other outposts. My serious academic interest in the Philmont

country began in 1965 and led to completion of a master's thesis at
the University of Arizona dealing with the history of the Baldy
Mountain mining district. Later published in a very limited edition
by the National Council, Boy Scouts of America, that thesis forms
the basis of the mining chapters in the present book. From 1967
through 1970 I continued at Philmont, primarily concerned with
the development of their historically oriented programs.

Parts of Chapter 6 first appeared in the *New Mexico Historical Review*, and a portion of Chapter 10, on Stanley McCormick, originally
appeared in the *California Historical Society Quarterly*. The section
of Chapter 12 on the Cimarron and Northwestern railroad comprised three articles in the *New Mexico Railroader*. Each part has
been revised for this present book, but thanks are due to the respective journals for permission to reprint the material.

In the course of writing this history, I have become indebted to
more people than could be listed here. First and foremost, my thanks
to Ray H. Bryan, who first encouraged me to pursue the ranch's past
and who provided every assistance. Without his enthusiastic help
the work could never have been finished. Second, I am indebted to
the late Harry G. McGavran, M.D., who shared interviews and
manuscripts and provided financial assistance during the early stages
of research.

The entire professional staff at Philmont also cooperated fully:
the late A. J. "Skipper" Juncker and his successor Joe Davis shared
their knowledge, as did William C. Littrell of the ranch department.
Jack Blum and Kent Bush, successive directors of the Ernest Thompson Seton Memorial, opened their resources without reservation.
Among Philmont summer employees, Dr. Jerry Traut, Cynthia and
Nick Pisor, Mark Clayton, and Mike Glassow deserve special notice
for their patience and indulgence.

Dozens of others, listed in the bibliography, were interviewed or
wrote correspondence. Particular thanks are due to "Doc" and Viv
Leitzell of Cimarron, the Frank Alpers family in Raton, Elliott W.
Phillips at Valmora, and former Philmont director Minor Huffman,

now at Roswell. Among many library staffs who gave their time were those at the New Mexico State Records Center and Archives at Santa Fe; University of New Mexico's Zimmerman Library at Albuquerque; New Mexico Highlands University, Las Vegas; Arizona Historical Society Library at Tucson; Texas Christian University library and Amon Carter Museum of Western Art library, both at Fort Worth; the National Archives and Library of Congress, Washington; and the Western Illinois University Library, Macomb. My brother Steven C. Murphy prepared the maps, and Mrs. Beth Douthitt aided with proofreading and indexing. Finally I am grateful to the Helene Wurlitzer Foundation of New Mexico and its gracious director, Dr. Henry A. Sauerwein, Jr., for enabling me to spend a summer in Taos completing this study.

This volume is dedicated to the memory of four individuals, all now deceased, who typify the kind of man who transformed 137,000 acres of New Mexico wilderness into a paradise for Scouting. Without of the generosity and foresight of Waite Phillips and others like him much of Philmont's greatness could never have occurred. Harry G. McGavran, M.D., represented the devotion of volunteer Scouters; not only did he take time out of a busy professional life to teach each year at Philmont, but he played an active role on the committee which gives overall direction. A. J. "Skipper" Juncker was a professional Scouter, one of thousands in the Boy Scout movement, and typical of the able administrators at Philmont. Last, but certainly not least, Rick Garcia, whose life ended suddenly, typified the hundreds of younger men who put the Philmont program into action every summer. Each of these individuals contributed in his own way to Philmont's success. It is their story, as well as that of the land itself, which this volume attempts to tell.

LAWRENCE R. MURPHY

CONTENTS

ILLUSTRATIONS

MAPS

Natural Features

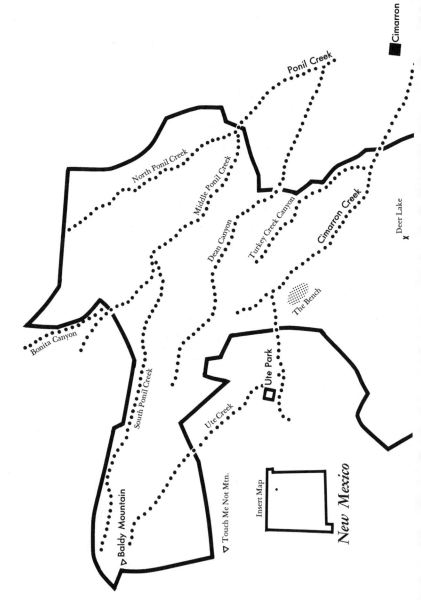

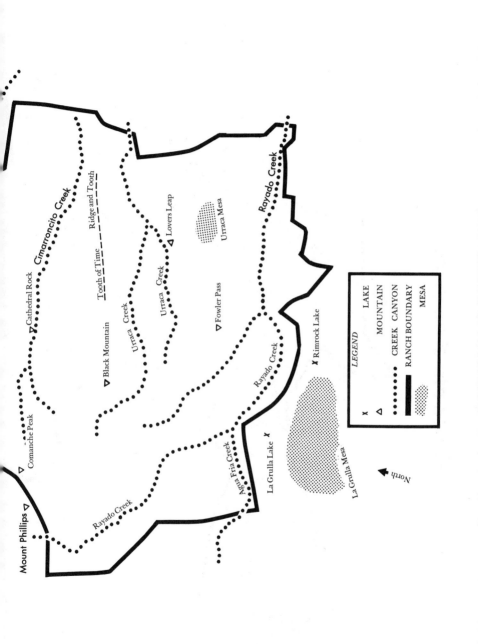

Historic Features

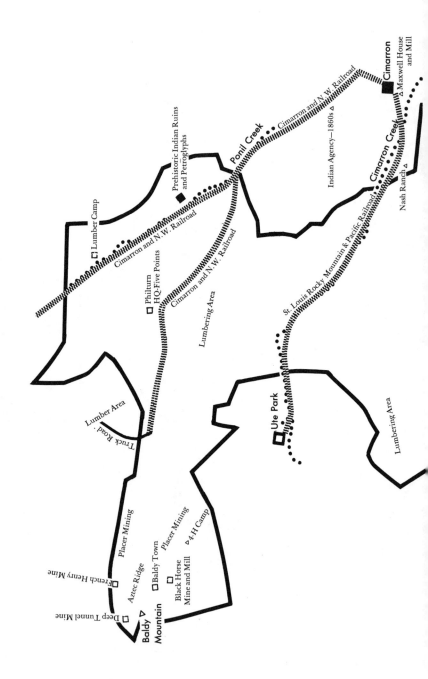

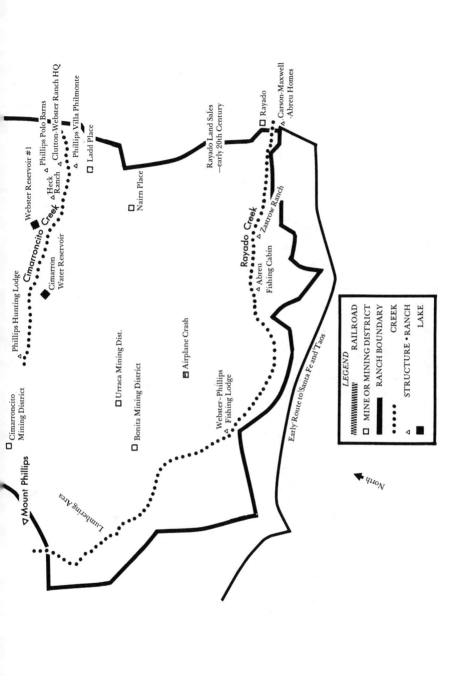

Philmont Scout Ranch

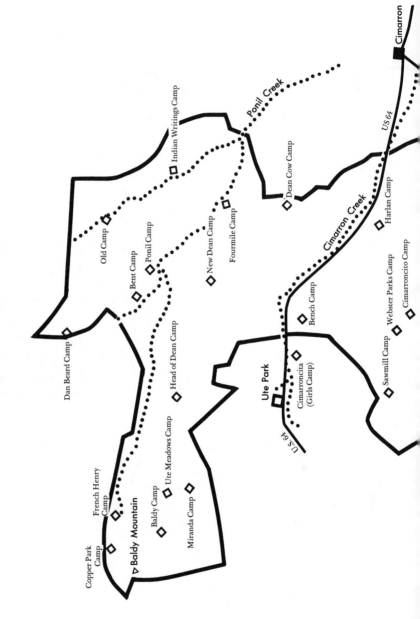

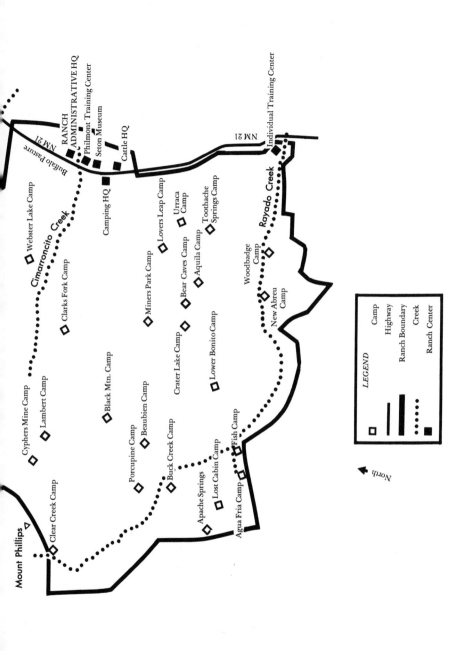

I

THE CIMARRON
COUNTRY

Long before man set foot on what is now Philmont, natural forces had molded the terrain, creating the mountains, valleys, and plains which have influenced subsequent historical development.[1] During time periods beyond man's comprehension, mountain ranges rose and receded, seas covered all of northern New Mexico and retreated, and coastal swamps, sandy deserts, and hilly plains replaced them. Each era contributed to the complex geological pattern that now underlies the area. Successive layers of sandstone and shale, lava, or strangely metamorphosed formations all testify to changing conditions.

These geological developments divided Philmont topographically into two parts split by the Cimarron River. Changes are also evident from east to west. At the southeastern corner of the ranch near historic Rayado, the low, gently sloping Las Vegas Plateau adjoins the flat-topped mesas and piles of accumulated rubble before ascending the heights of the Cimarron Range. Steep-sided, level-topped mesas such as La Grulla, Urraca, and Fowler are capped by a layer of basalt which has prevented erosion. Once an active volcano, Crater Peak has worn away until its crest is nearly flat. Depressions on top of these mesas have slowly filled with decayed plants, creating rich, black soil. Where drainage is poor, as on La Grulla, vast meadows (excellent for summer pasture) are interspersed by shallow lakes. Rayado, Urraca, and Bonito creeks, through countless ages of erosive action, have penetrated this volcanic cap, carving dramatic canyons throughout the region.

North and west of this basalt flow, ancient pre-Cambrian formations dominate a large portion of Philmont. Deeply scarred by the Rayado and Cimarroncito Creek systems, the impressive Cimarron Range is topped by the Waite Phillips, Black, and Bear peaks. Soil deposits only thinly cover the highest slopes, but forest and woodland growth at lower levels make this region a favorite for campers and hikers. Bonito Canyon, where alluvial deposits create grassy meadows, also attracts many outdoorsmen. From any mountaintop there are magnificent views of neighboring valleys and distant plains. Game animals and wild flowers thrive in this portion of Philmont's wilderness backcountry.

Further east and north of the Fowler Pass fault, dacite porphyry dominates an area complicated by frequent uplifting and the subsequent exposure of underlying formations. Straggling out onto the plains, the Tooth of Time Ridge is probably the Philmont region's most dramatic and most famous geographic feature. Weathered by countless centuries of erosion, the massive tooth itself towering over camping headquarters is a suitable symbol for the entire 137,000 acres; rugged and enduring, it has persevered where less sturdy rocks would long ago have worn away. Porphyry outcroppings also extend north along the Cimarroncito Valley, notably as Cathedral Rock and Lover's Leap. Porphyry also reaches northwest across the Cimarron Canyon toward the Baldy area where it has protected the top of Wilson Mesa and formed the Palisades.

That part of Philmont bordering the Cimarron Canyon is a transitional zone. For example, Deer Lake Mesa looks very similar to the mesas of southern Philmont, but it lacks the typical basalt cover. Instead, its cap is sandstone, shaped by wind and water erosion. Descending from this mesa, a series of benches drop into the Cimarron Canyon, which penetrates the entire ranch and slices the area through the middle. Along the stream's south bank, rock and dirt deposits worked loose from mountain peaks and slid downward, creating rounded hills. North of the canyon, however, only Bear and Turkey canyons penetrate steep sandstone walls typical of northern Philmont.

Not as high but just as rugged as the southland, the northern section of the ranch is an extension of the Park Plateau, a forty-mile-wide sandstone exposure stretching from southern Colorado to Ute Park, just west of Philmont. Here Ponil Creek and its tributaries have created a series of narrow canyons surrounded by steep-sided mesas and ridges. Steep trails climb the rugged walls and cross high ridges from which dramatic vistas extend in all directions. On the grassy valley floors, where most camping spots are situated, streams move slowly and frequently disappear below ground level.

West of the Ponil country, Baldy and Touch-Me-Not mountains top northern Philmont. On the western side of these peaks, various layers of sandstone folded upward and caused a complex repetition of exposed layers. Shales cap the upper elevations, only to be hidden by several types of sandstone at lower levels. A sheet of dacite porphyry several hundred feet thick separates all these sedimentary formations from an underlying basement of older pre-Cambrian origin. Frost weathering has broken the exposed sandstones and shales, leaving sharply edged pieces which give the mountains their stern, lifeless appearance and increase the difficulty of hiking on their upper slopes.[2]

Although the most scenic of Philmont's region, the high mountains have been of little economic significance except for mining and some grazing. Towns, ranches, lumber camps, and farms developed at lower elevations along the edge of the Cimarron Range. In the wide valleys where the Rayado, Urraca, Cimarroncito, Cimarron, and Ponil canyons leave the mountains, men successfully grew corn or wheat for themselves and their livestock; railroads easily penetrated the lower country to secure timber, but could never have traversed the steep mountains. The town of Cimarron grew up at the entrance to Cimarron Canyon, while Rayado occupied a similar position to the south. Many ranches were situated along the Urraca, Cimarroncito, and Ponil creeks.

Life Zones of the Philmont Area[3]

In addition to the geological variations throughout Philmont, a series of life zones appear as the mountains lift up from the treeless expanse of the Great Plains. Different trees and vegetation gradually replace one another, so that the trees and flowers common at one altitude are unknown at others. At the highest points on Philmont those few hardy plants which survive differ greatly from those on the flatlands thousands of feet below and from those in the dense woods in between.

Beginning at the lowest elevation, the Great Plains is Philmont's first life zone. An arid grassland devoid of trees, this area so repulsed early explorers that they termed it the "Great American Desert." Rainfall here averages fifteen inches or less a year, and even then frequent droughts alternate with sudden summer downpours to prevent full utilization of moisture. Intense winter cold, biting gusty winds, and poor drainage have prevented the growth of forests. On the high plains of northern New Mexico, where rain is often insufficient even to support grass, bunch-like vegetation appears. Once the area provided ideal grazing for the buffalo herds that roamed mid-America; now it serves primarily for raising cattle.

At Philmont, plains extend from the eastern boundary to the mountains throughout the southern half of the ranch but end at the Cimarron River. Flat, open valleys reach westward for considerable distances along the Cimarroncito Creek and Rayado River, where increased water and better soil make cultivation possible. Cimarron, which has an average annual rainfall of 15.35 inches, marks the extreme western edge of the Great Plains. Attempts to establish farms near Rayado and Miami failed, however, because of inadequate water. Unsuited for camping and hiking, most of Waite

Phillips's Great Plains properties were not given to the Boy Scouts but instead were sold to a commercial ranching company for raising livestock.

Philmont's foothill area is located in the piñon-juniper zone, characterized by scrub trees and widely separated open spaces. The most common vegetation is the piñon pine, a short, woody plant which reminded early visitors of "unpruned, ill-kept apple orchards."[4] Several varieties of juniper, scrub oak, mountain mahagony, and other generally worthless plants are often found with piñons. Philmont's piñon-juniper zone parallels the edge of the plains and in the southern sections climbs onto low mesas and ridges. To the north, it is the major type of vegetation in the lower Ponil Canyon. Camps at Ponil, Indian Writings, New Dean, Webster Lake, Stockade, and Rayado are all located in this typical Southwestern environment.

Ascending into larger, more dramatic forests, the ponderosa or Western yellow pine dominates the New Mexico mountains at altitudes of 7000 to 8000 feet. It is a tall, stately tree with red-brown bark and huge crowns. Because these trees cover less than twenty-five percent of the ground and because brush seldom grows in their shade, beautiful grassy parks typify a ponderosa forest.

At Philmont, ponderosas shade some of the most beautiful campgrounds. A broad belt extends in the south from Zastro and Abreu on the Rayado River, northward through Lovers Leap, Miners Park, Shaeffers Pass, Clarks Fork, and Cimarroncito camps, all well known for their scenic beauty. Much of the Ponil country and Dean and Turkey Creek canyons once contained stands of ponderosa, too, but loggers long ago removed most of it for lumber. Far to the west, gold seekers in the Moreno Valley cut ponderosas for mine props and firewood. Lumbermen today would welcome the opportunity to harvest Philmont's remaining trees, but ranch policies assure their preservation for the enjoyment of campers and hikers.

Above the ponderosa pine belt, a zone of dense alpine fir and Engelmann and blue spruce forest is found at an elevation of approximately 8500 to 10,000 feet. These trees are more pointed than the ponderosa, with limbs reaching almost to the ground. They grow in thick stands, sometimes so close as to be almost impenetrable. Humidity and precipitation are high, and deep snows often remain in the shade until late spring. During wet years, scattered patches of snow last throughout the summer. Normally, heavy rains protect these woods from fire, but when a spruce-fir forest is for any reason destroyed, fast-growing aspen normally replace it. Once these softwood trees have shaded the ground, conifers again take root and eventually crowd out the aspens.

Spruce-fir forests cover most of Philmont's mountainous back-country. Because of the natural beauty of these areas, many campers prefer the upper Rayado or Bonito canyons, Black Mountain, Red Hills, or Cyphers Mine camps. Especially popular are lush mountain meadows where, primarily because of poor drainage, forests have not developed. Instead, deep green grass and sedges, bespeckled with multicolored blossoms, provide unforgettable campsites. Aspen-spruce succession patterns are also common. At Beaubien Camp, for instance, the aspen groves which once dominated the area disappeared during the last decade as conifers matured and took over. Similar changes have occurred on the north-facing slopes near Fish Camp and at numerous other spots. The destruction of hundreds of acres of spruce-fir woodland near Porcupine and Apache Springs in 1965 will surely lead to the rapid growth of aspen groves in those regions.

Atop Philmont's loftiest ridges is a narrow zone called *Krumm-holz*, a German term meaning "crooked wood." Although it contains many of the same species found in lower forests plus the white and foxtail pines, everything in this area is noticeably deformed. Only hardy shrubs and trees survive. Scattered ridge tops in southern Philmont, including Comanche Peak and Waite Phillips Mountain, are covered with *Krummholz* vegetation. In the north, Aztec Ridge and the upper slopes of Baldy Mountain provide the best examples.

Highest of the Rocky Mountain life zones is the treeless Alpine tundra. Here every condition hinders plant growth. The poorly drained soil is full of gravel. Deep snows cover the area for eight or nine months each year; frost-free nights are few. As a result, only a few closely matted plants can survive. All are perennials and grow much smaller than plants of the same species at lower elevations. Alpine tundra is infrequently found in the southern Rockies and can be seen at Philmont only near the top of Baldy Mountain and on the saddle separating it from Touch-Me-Not Mountain.

The Wildlife

Visitors have often been impressed by the quantity and variety of animals found in northern New Mexico.[5] "There is probably no other extent of wilderness in the world so well supplied," exclaimed Augustus Storrs after traveling near the area in 1824.[6] On the plains, buffalo, antelope, rabbit, and prairie dogs lived in great quantity. Nearby mountains teemed with deer, bear, elk, turkey, mountain lion, and numerous lesser species. Mountain streams sheltered beaver and a wide variety of fish.

No animal more typifies the West than the American bison or buffalo. Vast herds of these huge, shaggy beasts once roamed the plains east of Philmont, stirring up dust clouds visible for hundreds of miles. Indian tribes based their entire subsistence on the buffalo, and the hunters, trappers, and Santa Fe traders depended on them for food.

Philmont probably marked the western limit of the main buffalo herds in the Southwest. Major Stephen H. Long, visiting the area in 1823, mentioned killing buffalo on Cimarron Creek; other hunters occasionally slaughtered them to the north in Ponil Park and as far west as the Moreno Valley. Indians reported finding a few there as late as 1863, but with the arrival of American miners and ranchers, the herds rapidly diminished. Waite Phillips, who wanted to preserve the vanishing species, began to purchase buffalo soon after he acquired Philmont. Included in his gift to the Boy Scouts, the herd is now one of the ranch's prized attractions.

The pronghorn antelope is also typical of the plains. This graceful brown and white animal depends on its speed and alertness for protection, and few animals can outdistance a healthy adult pronghorn. The thirty or so antelope that still inhabit the foothills along the eastern edge of Philmont and up the Rayado, Cimarroncito, and Ponil valleys can be spotted only by an observer with patience and keen eyesight.

Far more numerous than either buffalo or antelope are the deer which inhabit the Cimarron area in large herds. Mule deer, the most common, are large animals with protruding ears. Males carry handsome antlers. They are dark gray during the winter but turn to a reddish brown during the summer. A short white tail with a black tip and a large white rump patch make them easy to spot. A few white-tailed deer are found at lower elevations along the edge of the plains.

Deer, unlike most other animals, have increased in number during recent years. As man has exterminated native predators such as the coyote and the mountain lion, deer populations have increased until an estimated 3000 to 8000 now roam the Philmont backcountry. They are seldom seen during the day, but in early morning and evening deer graze on the rich grass or drink from cool streams throughout the ranch. Nightly they appear near camping headquarters as if on schedule. They have been known to enter campsites to lick unwashed dishes. Even mature bucks with impressive antlers may approach close enough for pictures.

Bear in large numbers also make up a part of Philmont's game population. Although the fierce grizzly once inhabited these mountains, only black bear (which range in color from blonde to brown and black) are now found. They eat almost anything but seem to prefer berries, acorns, or fruit. When these are unavailable, they venture into garbage pits, campsites, or even tents in search of food. In fact, most troublesome bears are merely looking for something to eat, even those which occasionally become such a bother they have to be trapped and transported to another section of Philmont. Campers tie food high out of reach, but hundreds are awakened suddenly at night by clattering pots and muffled growls. The bear has always been a nuisance to Philmont residents. Two of the earliest settlers, Tom Boggs and John Hatcher, grew so tired of chasing grizzlies out of their fields that they moved out, leaving the beasts to "roam unmolested through the deserted ranch." The black bear was so common in the Rayado area in 1890 that Charles Abreu killed four in two weeks, and Mrs. Mason F. Chase, wife of a pioneer rancher, chased, treed, and killed one by herself in 1913.[7]

Of all Philmont's game animals, the most impressive and most difficult to observe is the elk. The second largest of North American deer (only the moose is bigger), they are dark brown to buff colored. Males carry large antlers during most of the year. Few if any native elk remain in northern New Mexico; present herds probably descend from those introduced from Colorado. The territorial game warden purchased some which he released in 1911. Probably even earlier, George H. Webster, Jr., whose Urraca Ranch included the central portion of Philmont, introduced a small herd from Colorado.[8] Today three separate bands of elk inhabit the ranch: the largest, about fifty, grazes on the meadows of the upper Rayado and Buck creek areas; two smaller groups of twenty-five to thirty roam the slopes of Baldy and Tooth of Time Ridge.

Predators, too, are found in Philmont's backcountry. Among the most "cautious, secretive, and wary" of North American mammals is the mountain lion, which is seen so seldom that no accurate count is possible. Only the carcasses of the deer, sheep, or cattle killed by the mountain lions testify to their presence. Charles Abreu recorded the first kill in 1891, taking a massive trophy that measured nine feet from end to end. In response to a call from Waite Phillips a quarter of a century later, a government trapper tracked down and killed a lion described as the "largest any hunter in the biological service" had brought down. Two other smaller animals were taken on the same trip.[9] In the fall of 1966 a ranch employee shot a "good-sized" one in the Baldy area.

Even more hated by pioneer stockmen was the wolf, once common around Philmont. Sometimes cattlemen offered bounties as high as fifteen dollars for "scalps." Frequently they hired professional hunters to pursue these animals. Organized hunts not only eliminated predators but also became exciting social events. Charles Abreu killed a white wolf which he said resembled a white calf with angora goat hair. More common were the bobcat and the coyote, many of which still roam the Cimarron Mountains.[10]

Almost countless smaller animals inhabit Philmont. Squirrel and chipmunk scurry from one end of the ranch to the other. Only a few beaver remain, but muskrat, mink, and other related species are fairly common. The unwary camper may meet a skunk or porcupine. Cottontail and jackrabbit make their homes in many parts of the ranch. There are dozens of species of mice and bats. Almost every body of water abounds with fish: perch, bluegill, and bass in lakes and reservoirs, and rainbow trout in mountain streams. Finally, Philmont has tremendous numbers of birds that vary in size from the smallest hummingbird to great hawks and eagles.

II

PREHISTORIC INHABITANTS

Southeastward out of the Sangre de Cristo Mountains through Philmont flows the north fork of Ponil Creek. Midway on its descent to the plains, steep sandstone walls flank the stream. Along the narrow valley floor are many low terraces, created from deposits of rich alluvial soil. Here, protected from the icy winds and heavy snows of the plains, yet assured of a continuous water supply, primitive people could settle. And here Philmont's first inhabitants settled a thousand years or more ago. Nearby forests—today tragically destroyed by twentieth-century lumbermen—supplied wood and sheltered game. Corn grew tall in the fertile soil.

People of the Plains and the Pueblos

The first people in the area came even earlier. They were Asiatic nomads who roamed onto the Great Plains to hunt mammoths, those huge, tusked elephants that grazed the flatlands over 11,000 years ago. Campers have found mammoth bones at Philmont; perhaps early man even hunted along the foothills of the Sangre de Cristos. When the plains elephants were killed off, men turned to smaller game. Although numerous campsites and killing grounds have been discovered from Canada to Mexico, one of the most important was at Folsom, New Mexico, less than one-hundred miles northeast of Cimarron. Scientists believe that Folsom man lived in the area about 10,000 to 11,000 years ago. Unfortunately little remains except a distinctive spear point from which we can study the culture.

A great drought prevented large-scale occupation of the plains for many centuries. By 2500 B.C., however, conditions allowed Indians to live in the region, but a diminished animal supply forced them to gather seeds to supplement their diet. During this era, too, they learned to make pottery. Permanent multifamily dwellings became rather large. Probably the women tilled gardens along the wooded creek bottoms while their husbands hunted in nearby hills.[1]

A different people lived west of Philmont along the San Juan River and the Rio Grande. By the beginning of the Christian era, these "ancient ones" had established permanent settlements in southwestern Colorado and northern New Mexico. Hunting and planting much like their plains neighbors, they lived in permanent mud and wood houses. Beans enriched their diet of squash and corn. Excellent baskets and sandals reflected their high cultural level. They also wove high-quality cloth and made excellent pottery. Houses grew increasingly larger, until the people first called the "basketmakers" soon became the "pueblos."

By the time those first Indians settled in Philmont's canyons, Pueblo culture had reached a high stage of development. In place of small pole-and-mud homes, they built multistoried structures of rock and adobe. Special underground chambers called kivas were the sites of complex and colorful religious ceremonies. Ceramic wares improved in quality until they far excelled those of the plainsmen. Agriculture played an increasingly large role in their economy, but deer, bear, and rabbit remained important in the diet.

Cultural growth achieved its greatest height during the pueblo period which corresponded to the occupation of Philmont. Trends toward concentrated population continued; great communal dwellings of one to five stories dominated most Indian villages. Religion became more elaborate, with huge ceremonial kivas and smaller clan structures. Pottery became more artistic, with each area developing a distinctive type. Migration to the south led to the founding of new settlements along the Rio Grande, where Pueblo culture continued to flourish.[2]

The Ponil People

Located geographically between the Pueblos and the Plains groups, the culture of Philmont's Indians contained elements of both.[3] They hunted, using arrows and small spears to kill deer and rabbit for the meat. At the same time, however, Ponil residents also raised corn. They probably learned pottery making from the Pueblos, but their earthenware was considerably rougher than that of the more highly skilled Rio Grande people. Instead of either multistoried adobe homes or more primitive mud-and-stick structures, Philmont Indians lived in semipermanent rock or wooden buildings.

Determining where the Ponil Indians originated is a difficult problem for archaeologists. Many believe that about A.D. 1000 or 1100 a considerable expansion occurred among the Pueblo people who lived in the upper Rio Grande Valley. They theorize that some of these people moved east across the mountains to settle temporarily in the Philmont area. Once removed from their established homes and traditional agricultural ways, they built simpler homes and crafted poorer quality pottery. Perhaps because of contacts with the Plains tribes, hunting became more important while farming decreased in significance. A second group of scholars, however, believes that the Ponil people were westward stragglers from the plains who ventured into the mountains where they traded with the Pueblos and learned many of their skills. Still a third theory is that early Philmont inhabitants were "unspecialized hunting and gathering people" who, after contacting both eastern and western neighbors, selectively accepted or rejected traits from both groups. Because evidence for all these theories is scant and at times contradictory, the origins of the Ponil people remain uncertain.

We know considerably more about their dwellings. The crudest of the structures were natural rock overhangs eroded out of canyon walls and only slightly modified by the Indians. One such site is Lizard Cave, named for two "mummified" lizards found there. Located about 75 feet above the valley floor, it is nearly 50 feet long and approximately 11 feet deep. Although only 5½ feet high, it sheltered early Philmont residents adequately. The cave dwellers improved on the natural features by building a stone pavement to enlarge their living area and by erecting several rock partitions to create rooms.[4] Similar overhangs are known as Salt Lake Cave and Box Canyon Cave. In some cases stone walls protected residents from the weather. In caves used for storage they kept corn, yucca, sandals, baskets, arrow shafts, and other household goods.

Far more elaborate than these primitive natural shelters was the "slab house," probably built between A.D. 1100 and 1300. One three-room structure, which may be seen today, measures about 24 by 32 feet. Four large posts support the roof, with the walls formed by leaning beams against the edges. To provide additional support or to serve as partitions between rooms, the Indians set thinner posts throughout the building. The two smaller rooms were doubtlessly added to the original one-room building either to store perishable goods or to accommodate daughters who brought their husbands home to live. Rock slabs around the perimeter of the house supported walls made of sticks and branches woven together and covered with layers of mud.

Activity in this and all other Indian huts centered about the hearth. Here residents roasted chunks of venison or ears of corn. During the long, cold winters, the fire provided warmth. Centrally located in the principal room, the main fire pit was circular, about 3 feet in diameter. Adobe mud around it baked hard and turned fire red from frequent use. Perhaps a large broken *metate* (the stone tool used by Southwestern Indians to grind corn into meal) found on the east side of the room at Philmont was used as a heat deflector. It would have been placed behind the fire to direct heat wherever desired. In the southwest corner of the room the Indians had built a second, smaller fireplace.[5]

Scattered throughout the slab house when it was found were many household implements. Bits of plain pottery from broken utensils, scraps of deer bone, and stone chips flaked off as the men shaped their arrow or spear points remained on the floor for hundreds of years. Spearheads or arrowpoints, discarded when they became broken or dull, provide additional keys to the culture of these people.

Prehistoric Philmont Indians also used pit houses very similar to those found among the Pueblos. They dug a 15-foot-wide circular hole 3 to 4 feet into the surface of the ground. Inside, four main posts and several smaller ones supported a mud-and-brush roof. The artifacts found in a pit house help show its use. Archaeologists unearthed several kinds of pottery, small projectile points, stone household wares, and bone fragments. On the floor were two large earthen jugs, a cedar-bark mat, and portions of a large basket. Buried in the floor was the body of a young woman, evidently placed there while the building was still in use as a residence. Next to her chin was a small pot, probably a burial offering.[6]

Anyone in the future who wished to determine how Americans lived in the twentieth century would learn little by a mere examination of the architectural features in residences and business buildings. Their foundations alone would provide even less information. Similarly, although archaeologists have discovered much from dwelling sites in the Ponil Valley, they have obtained more information from the multitude of artifacts found in these dwellings or in nearby occupation areas. Fragmented yucca sandals, broken bits of pottery, discarded corn cobs or animal bones, rock tools, and worked stone implements have helped to describe the culture of these primitive people.

Fragments of pottery are the most important artifacts. Some found at Philmont, usually bowls which could have been easily transported through the mountains from Taos, were imported from the Pueblos. The names assigned to these types—"Taos gray," "Kwahe'e black-on-white," or "La Plata black-on-red"—describe both the source of the item and also its coloration. Such Rio Grande designs and the processes used in their manufacture changed through long periods of time, enabling scientists to use complicated dating processes to determine approximately when certain varieties were in vogue. When pottery with these designs is found in the Ponil, it can be very useful in determining just about when the Indians occupied a particular site.

A far greater proportion of the ceramics were made locally and are much inferior to contemporary Pueblo work. Instead of the smooth, well-tempered, strong Rio Grande wares, Ponil people made soft, easily crushed vessels. Tempering particles protruded visibly from the clay. Often the pots were left undecorated, but in neck-banded types, coils near the top served as decoration. Others that were formed inside baskets retained an intricate woven design after they were fired. In still another variety, the Indians drew parallel lines, diamond shapes, or herringbone designs in the moist vessel before it hardened. Lugs or handles sometimes made it easier to use larger pots.

By carefully examining the pottery at a site, archaeologists ascertain more than just the date of occupation. From the number of pieces found, for example, they can estimate the size of the population. Dietary habits are often expressed through the types of vessel used. The percentage of imported wares similarly demonstrates the amount of trade carried on with the Pueblos. In short, a sample of shaped, hardened clay tells the trained observer much about the people who made it.

Although more interesting to laymen, the worked stone tools found in the Ponil Valley provide less information to the scientific investigator than pottery. The exposed sandstone rock in the canyon was too soft for making flaked tools, and early residents had to import hornfels, chalcedony, obsidian, and other harder rocks from distant points. Perhaps because of the difficulty in securing proper materials, Indians manufactured uniformly small projectile points (arrow or spear heads). Usually they were less than 1-inch long. Still they killed the deer, rabbit, and other small game found along the creek. Scrapers and knives enabled them to butcher animals, prepare leathery yucca leaves for sandals or mats, or scrape hides for clothing and blankets. Drills and other specialized tools demonstrated the variety of stone implements developed. Expertly chipped from imported stone, these tools not only indicate the craftsmanship of the Philmont natives but also the attention they gave to hunting.

Another kind of stone implement was shaped by slow battering rather than chipping. Hammerstones were used to dislodge chunks of rock which could be flaked with antler points into scrapers, arrowheads, and the like. Frequently the *metates* and *manos* used for food preparation are found in home sites. Worn smooth by countless hours of pounding and scraping, they played just as important a role in the Indian household as did the earthen pots or arrowheads.

Other implements further illustrate the primitive ingenuity and skill of the Ponil people. For decorative purposes, they strung tiny rodent-bone beads and stone pendants on animal sinew. Colorful natural minerals were ground into powder and mixed with animal fat to make an excellent, if somewhat smelly, body paint. Olivella shells, probably secured from the Gulf of California via an elaborate Indian trade network, provided the basis for much of their jewelry. Pipes were made of fired clay or stone. Local weeds and grasses were woven into baskets and sturdy sandals were manufactured from the yucca plant.

Among the most interesting but least understood aspects of the Ponil culture are the petroglyphs or "Indian writings" found on major sandstone outcroppings along the canyon walls northeast of the slab, pole-and-mud, and pit houses. While some of these were evidently made after the abandonment of prehistoric valley sites, the Ponil people probably created most of them before 1400.

Archaeologists have spent little effort in determining what the petroglyphs mean, and it seems highly unlikely that they will ever be deciphered. Some have suggested that they had no meaning at all, but were merely abstract designs casually applied to convenient surfaces much as boys carve on trees or write on fences. It seems more likely, however, that the symbols had some supernatural or religious significance. Concentric circles were very common. Could they have represented the sun or some other revered power? Observers have interpreted other symbols as showing maps, corn stalks, bolts of lightning, and the like. Unfortunately, no definitive interpretation may ever be possible.[7]

Groups similar to those in the Ponil Canyon apparently lived along the edge of the Sangre de Cristos throughout northeastern New Mexico and southeastern Colorado. Random collections of ceramics and chipped stone from Nash Gulch and Horse Mesa suggest the existence of campsites or even semipermanent habitations in the foothills just west of Cimarron. Hunting parties probably left the two unbroken pots found near Miners Park Camp high in the mountains at an elevation of over 8000 feet, and metates, projectile points, and additional pots from the Urraca and Rayado areas demonstrate at least seasonal occupation of southern Philmont. Many other sites have been found in the Vermejo Canyon north of Philmont and around Trinidad, in southern Colorado.

Finally, archaeologists have asked what happened to the Indians who designed and executed the petroglyphs on the Ponil Canyon walls and left so many other evidences of their presence. As in discussing the origins of these people, many uncertainties arise. By 1300 the Pueblo Indians had stopped expanding out of the Rio Grande Valley. If the Philmont people were part of this movement, they might simply have returned to their homes. Or perhaps they left because of a great drought which caused widespread population shifts throughout the Southwest. Evidence that this dry spell ever reached the Philmont area is scant, however. If, as some scientists have postulated, the settlements were destroyed by enemy attacks, no bodies or ruined dwellings prove that there was such a massacre. The Indians may have lost their separate identity and merged into the expanding Plains tribes or into the Ute and Apache cultures which were just emerging in the region.

By 1400 at the latest, these interesting people had left their canyon homes, but new inhabitants soon arrived. Plains Indians ventured into the region to establish camps from which they could hunt the nearby game supplies. More important, the Indians soon heard stories of bearded men in shining armor who had been seen to the south. These conquerors, carrying the flag of Spain, soon marched northward through New Mexico, driving the natives from their retreats. Eventually they, too, would control the Philmont country.

III

INDIANS AND SPANIARDS

In the seventeenth century, new residents occupied the New Mexico wilderness that would someday become Philmont. Mounted troops carrying the Spanish flag marched northward seeking treasure and in the process establishing permanent settlements. Challenging these Europeans for control of the area were several Indian groups which had migrated into the region from the north and east. Comanche, Kiowa, Ute, and Apache battled each other over land, slaves, and plunder. The arrival of the Spaniards intensified hostilities which continued well into the 1800s.

Slowly the Spanish pioneers extended their control northward from Mexico. Their soldiers explored and mapped the territory. European towns replaced Indian villages, and new social and political institutions were introduced. The Catholic friars who accompanied the troops and settlers introduced the Indians to Christianity. Frequently the clergy persuaded the nomadic natives to settle in agricultural mission communities. When French explorers and Plains Indians threatened from the east, New Mexico officials even proposed the establishment of a permanent military fortification in the Philmont area. The idea was soon abandoned, however, and not until a hundred years later did Europeans secure a lasting foothold at the headwaters of the Canadian River.

The Indian Invasion

While European soldiers approached Philmont from the south, other people entered the area from the north and east. No selfish desire to find riches or humanitarian zeal to spread religion motivated them. Instead, during the sixteenth and seventeenth centuries, food shortages, population pressures, and the fear of aggressive neighbors forced many American Indians to resettle. For the first time since the departure of the Ponil Canyon people, new tribes moved into Philmont, where they camped, hunted, and fished. Varying widely in cultural characteristics, they were the sole permanent inhabitants of the area for more than 150 years. Only after a long struggle with Mexican and American settlers during the nineteenth century were they finally expelled, making way for the subsequent development of mining and agriculture along the edge of the Sangre de Cristos.

One of the earliest modern Indian tribes to reach Philmont was the Jicarilla Apache. Members of the extensive Athabascan language group that originally lived in central Canada, they left their traditional homes about 1200 to begin migrating southward. One segment followed an interior route through the highlands west of the Rocky Mountains. Eventually they became the Navajo and the Western Apache. More important to Philmont's history was a second subdivision which migrated through the Great Plains. They may have lived in Kansas, Wyoming, Nebraska, and Colorado before reaching New Mexico. They had certainly reached the Cimarron area by 1700, and may have come as much as 200 years earlier.[1]

In the course of their long move south, the Apache modified their way of life through contact with other Indians. From the Plains people they learned to use dogs as beasts of burden. A family's possessions could be loaded onto poles and hauled by a dog team from one place to another. They also depended on the buffalo for the skin tepees in which they sometimes lived, and for their clothing, food, and bone tools. The Jicarilla obtained Spanish horses, and when other tribes moved into the area, they learned to raid their neighbors, stealing food or horses and enslaving captives. Soon after reaching the Philmont area, the Apache also came into contact with the Pueblo Indians, especially those from Taos and Picuris where they frequently traded. From these Rio Grande people they learned to farm: corn and beans were their most important crops. Many of their religious ceremonies included Pueblo features. In addition to baskets, they began to make high-quality pottery. "Jicarilla culture," Dr. Morris Opler, the leading student of these Apache, has written, "can best be comprehended as a growth and modification of the basic southern Athabascan pattern in terms of Plains and Pueblo influences."

By the time Europeans first reported Apache at Philmont, they had developed a well-balanced, prosperous economy. Hunting was still important, but more attention was devoted to agriculture. The Indians cleared fields beside many of Philmont's rushing mountain streams, built dams and dug ditches to carry water to their crops, and developed crude tools to ease the chores of planting and harvesting. Although their principal crop was still corn, the Apache also grew beans, peas, pumpkins, cantaloupes, and tobacco.

Hunting and food gathering remained essential aspects of the Jicarilla economy. The men spent much of their time seeking game to feed their families. Sometimes they stalked their prey, often camouflaging themselves. They also learned to surround antelope and drive them into box canyons; smaller animals could be caught in snares placed around their holes. Several times a year the men ventured onto the plains to hunt buffalo. During the spring and summer, berries, roots, and stalks found in the area's high mountain meadows supplemented their diet.[2]

At Philmont the Jicarilla apparently lived first on the plains or near the edges of the several valleys reaching into the mountainous backcountry. Attacks from other Indians—especially the Ute and Comanche—pushed them slowly westward, further into the mountains. Early Spanish explorers reported them in the Rayado, Ponil, and Cimarron valleys of Philmont. Dr. James Gunnerson, an archaeologist from Northern Illinois University, has attempted to locate pieces of a distinctive pottery containing mica which the Jicarilla used. He found probable Apache sites in Ponil Canyon and on the Chase Ranch just east of Philmont's boundary. Gunnerson believed that the Apache occupied these areas during the early 1700s. They may also have been some of the same sites visited by the Spaniards. Other Apache homes were found in Nash Gulch, between Philmont's Cimarroncito Creek and the village of Cimarron.[3] Apache folk stories mention a whole series of campsites scattered across the Scout ranch's backcountry, many of them no doubt the same places where boys still camp.[4] Apache habitation was not limited to Philmont, however, and probably included an area near the base of the mountains along several hundred miles of northern New Mexico and southern Colorado.

A second group of Indians, who at first were the archenemies of the Jicarilla and later almost amalgamated with them, was the Moache (pronounced and sometimes spelled Mow-a-tsi) Ute.[5] Related by language to the Shoshonean people of the northeastern United States, they probably came to New Mexico from Utah, which was named for their people. For centuries, the rugged mountains, broad plateaus, and high deserts of the intermountain region had been the home of these nomads. But game shortages and pressure from other tribes pushed them slowly southward, just as the Apache had been pushed. By 1700, Philmont marked the southern edge of Ute civilization.

Perhaps because of their precarious economic base, the Ute were some of the most ferocious raiders in northern New Mexico and southern Colorado. Joining with the Comanche, fiercest of the High Plains tribes, they fought unending battles with the Jicarilla, raiding their settlements, burning their fields, and capturing their women and children. Frequently their attacks included the Spanish settlements along the Rio Grande. Much of the Spanish activity in the area resulted from efforts to protect the peaceful Jicarilla and Pueblo from these more warlike neighbors.

For reasons which are not wholly clear, the Ute altered their tribal affiliations about 1750. After enduring a series of Spanish attacks, they abandoned the alliance with the Comanche and made friends with the Jicarilla. Members of the two tribes intermarried until it became difficult to tell them apart. The Ute also helped the Spaniards fight Comanche and Kiowa raiders from the plains. By the time the first white immigrants from the East arrived in the Philmont area, the Ute had become peaceful and unaggressive. Bands made up of large families headed by the eldest male moved from camp to camp throughout the Philmont area according to the season of the year. High mountain meadows were ideal during the summer, but warmer, lowland sites were preferred during winter. Each Ute family followed a pattern so precisely determined by custom that everyone knew just where his neighbors would be camped at any time.

Life was never easy for the Ute. As beautiful as their new homeland might have been, it did not abound with food, and the struggle to survive was constant. Stalking antelope, deer, elk, and other animals filled a family's cooking pot only after strenuous effort. The women gathered berries, roots, and nuts to supplement the diet. Unlike the Apache, the Ute did not engage in regular farming. Only by spreading themselves out over a vast mountainous land could they provide an adequate food supply for each family. Probably fewer than 1000 people occupied all of southern Colorado and northern New Mexico.

The presence of Ute at Philmont contributed much to the history of the area. Ute Park, a beautiful green meadow astride Cimarron Creek, was a popular Ute campsite, as were many other mountain areas at Philmont. Huge scars on ponderosa pine trees resulted from the Indians' use of bark for medicinal purposes, especially, it is said, to induce abortions.

A third and very different group of Indians lived east of the Philmont area on the Great Plains. They were nomadic people who probably never resided for any length of time in the area, but for centuries news of an expected raid struck terror in the hearts of everyone in northeastern New Mexico. The Comanche, among the most warlike of all North American Indians, came to Philmont most frequently, although other tribes were also known to the area.

The Comanche, related linguistically to the Ute, had lived for many years in the Great Basin and Plateau region west of the Rocky Mountains. Because of pressure from other Indians, they slowly pushed eastward across the mountains and south through the Great Plains. By the early 1700s they had reached northern New Mexico. In company with the Ute they paid frequent visits to Taos Pueblo. In the decades that followed, they began to raid their weaker neighbors, especially the Jicarilla and Pueblo.

Essential to any understanding of the Plains Indians is the realization of how important the buffalo was. Clothing, shelter, food, tools, and even fuel came from these great shaggy beasts. Because agriculture was impossible, hunting became important and the Comanche, to keep moving in search of buffalo herds, lived in portable tepees instead of brush huts or adobe houses. In spite of romanticized tales about these people, life was hard. Successful pursuit of a buffalo by a man on foot required cunning, nerve, and above all, patience. Dogs provided a poor means of transporting goods from one place to another, obviously slowing down the Indians and limiting their travels.[6]

No single event except the coming of Europeans altered life on the Plains more than the procuring of horses. Buffalo hunting then became an enjoyable sport rather than a tedious necessity. The range for hunting increased manyfold. Stealing horses became the major occupation of many young braves, motivating most raids and counterraids among the various tribes.[7] This new mobility naturally altered Indian relations in northern New Mexico. Each tribe began to raid its neighbors, stealing horses, procuring slaves, and burning villages. Especially the Jicarilla and later the Ute constantly feared attack from the plains. Eventually, because they feared complete extinction, they turned to the Spanish for assistance in protecting themselves, but even skilled soldiers from Mexico were unable to overcome the Comanche. Not until late in the nineteenth century, after decades of battle, would the United States Army finally subdue these fierce warriors.

The Conquest of La Jicarilla

After more than 150 years in the Southwest, Spanish armies finally reached Philmont early in the 1700s.[8] Their coming resulted from many factors, but the beauty of the mountains and the wildness of the backcountry, which attract modern visitors, were not among them. The successful conquest of the Pueblo Indians made it possible to expand Spanish holdings northward and eastward from the Rio Grande Valley. Such expansion seemed even more prudent after rumors reached Santa Fe that the French were approaching the area from the Mississippi Valley. Unless the Spaniards took quick action, the riches thought to be north of New Mexico might be lost forever. Slightly less influential were the pleas of the Jicarilla Apache, who had allied themselves with the Spanish and now sought protection. Only by sending troops against the Ute and Comanche could their continuing raids from the plains be stopped and peace restored to the Sangre de Cristos. Finally, the Spaniards were concerned about a number of Pueblo Indians who had fled onto the plains. Until they could be returned, the final subjugation of the Rio Grande would be incomplete.

This last goal led directly to the first European penetration of Philmont. In the summer of 1706 the governor of New Mexico organized an expedition to locate and return some fugitives from Picuris Pueblo who had gone out onto the plains more than a decade earlier. Led by Juan de Ulibarri, forty mounted soldiers and a hundred Indian allies marched from Santa Fe north to Taos, then

The "Tooth of Time" juts skyward in the eastern foothills of the Sangre de Cristo range. (*Philmont Scout Ranch*)

A view eastward toward the "Tooth of Time." Beyond it lie the Great Plains and the Santa Fe Trail.

A prehistoric rock shelter in North Poñil Canyon, one of several in the Philmont country.

Buffalo roam again at Philmont. Great herds once darkened the land where plains and mountains met.

Antelope and other game are safe now in the primitive area and high, grassy valleys.

Carlos Beaubien, Mexican citizen and joint owner of the original Beaubien and Miranda Land Grant.

Guerito or "Man With Yellow Hair," a young Jicarilla
Apache leader in 1873. (*Smithsonian Institution*)

Christopher "Kit" Carson, famed frontier scout, once lived at Rayado in the Philmont country. (Museum of N.M.)

Lucien B. Maxwell, whose great ranch included the Beaubien and Miranda Grant. He began as a Mountain Man.

The village at Rayado, from an early sketch that exaggerated the size of some buildings.

The ghost mining camp of Elizabethtown, 1954. The mountains beyond are pitted with old mines.

The old log school at Elizabethtown was dismantled to provide timbers for new buildings at Eagle Nest.

Cimarron, N.M. in the 1870s, from an early photograph. Tallest structure was Maxwell's grain mill.

Lucien B. Maxwell's mansion, shown here after a fire, was open to all stage travellers who passed.

The old stone jail at Cimarron was a busy place during the violent days of the territory.

Still open in Cimarron is the Don Diego Tavern, built 1870-80 by Henry Lambert as the St. James Hotel.

Lucien Maxwell's mill at Cimarron processed flour for
Indians, troops, and settlers. It is now a museum.

turned east into the Sangre de Cristos. They named each of the rivers, valleys, lakes, and mountain ranges they crossed, but since few of these names are still in use, determining their exact route is very difficult. They apparently climbed the mountains east of Taos, dropped into the Moreno Valley along Philmont's western boundary, and skirted the south edge of the ranch across La Grulla Mesa. As they passed through the lush green meadows which today provide grazing for hundreds of cattle, they saw what would became Philmont. Far below was the rugged Rayado Canyon, beyond it the high mountains of the southern part of the ranch, and in the distance the Great Plains stretching out to the east. Descending to the flatlands along Moras Creek, they crossed Rayado Creek and spent the night of July 21 along Cimarroncito Creek near the present location of Philmont's ranch headquarters. The next day's travel carried them along the edge of the mountains, across the Cimarron and Ponil creeks near the future town of Cimarron, and out of Philmont along the edge of the Park Plateau.

In addition to being the first time Europeans set foot on Philmont, Ulibarri's expedition is important because it first encountered the Indians in the area. Several groups, apparently all Apache, led by a lame chief named Ysdalnisdael, approached the Spaniards. The meeting was friendly, and the Indians promised that on Ulibarri's return they would present him with raisins, "which they always reserved for the most worthy Spaniards." In his final report on the expedition, the commander added, "They were very good people. They had not stolen anything from anyone, but occupied themselves with their maize and cornfields which they harvest, because they are busy with the sewing [sic] of corn, frijoles [beans], and pumpkins."

Because their objective was a long way off, the Ulibarri party moved rapidly through New Mexico and into Colorado, where they finally located the Picuris Indians and secured their release. A month later, as they returned through the Apache country, the soldiers again met Chief Ysdalnisdael and several other Indians.

They "entertained us a great deal," reported Ulibarri. The natives had more important business, however, for two of their settlements had recently been raided by Ute and Comanche. The Jicarilla no doubt pleaded that the powerful Spanish army come to their aid. Such requests apparently fell on deaf ears, for the soldiers departed across the mountains to Taos and Santa Fe by the same route they had come, and the Apache were once again at the mercy of their enemies from the Plains.

Subsequently conditions worsened for the Jicarilla. Not only did the Ute and Comanche apparently continue to attack, but by 1715 the Faraon Apache who lived further out on the plains began to steal Jicarilla horses and mules. They also staged similar raids against several of the northeastern Pueblo groups. To stop such robberies, the lieutenant governor of Taos Pueblo proposed a joint expedition of Pueblo, Jicarilla (who pledged to spy as well as fight), and Spaniards. The New Mexico governor responded favorably. After several preliminary forays, he appointed General Juan Paez Hurtado to head a punitive expedition against the Faraon. Crossing the Sangre de Cristos south of Philmont, the Spaniards took along thirty Jicarilla auxiliaries. Hurtado's expedition failed to accomplish its stated purpose, however, and he returned to Santa Fe without having stopped the Faraon raids.

New threats in northeastern New Mexico soon necessitated still another major expedition into the area. After only a few years of relative quiet, the Comanche reinstituted their attacks against the Jicarilla and Pueblo. So desperate were the Jicarilla Indians that they went to a Taos priest, Father Juan de la Cruz, in 1719 to plead for protection. They also asked for the opportunity to be baptized. At almost the same time, rumors of renewed French interest in New Mexico reached Santa Fe. As a result, the viceroy in Mexico City ordered the New Mexico governor to send out a military force which could simultaneously pursue the Comanche and investigate stories of Frenchmen in the northeast.

The expedition which left Santa Fe in the summer of 1719 was one of the largest in many years. The governor, Don Antonio de Valverde, took command, accompanied by 100 Spaniards and twice as many Indians. Their route was much the same as Ulibarri's thirteen years before. Leaving Taos on September 20, they crossed the Moreno Valley and climbed onto the parklands south of Philmont. From Rimrock Lake they noted the "red hills with many outcroppings of ore, apparently mineralized." This probably referred to Crater Peak, a basalt outcropping directly across the Rayado gorge. Then they descended to the plains and spent the night along Rayado Creek, probably near the present Philmont camp of Rayado.

Nearby they found an Apache settlement including a small adobe house surrounded by cornfields. "As soon as these Apaches learned of the coming of the Spaniards," reported the official journal of the expedition, "they came to see the governor who received them very kindly and gave them tobacco and something to eat." Stories of Comanche raids were quickly related, as the Indians complained that their enemies from the Plains were persecuting and killing their people. The governor's explanation that he had come to punish these villains was very warmly received. "All the Apaches were very happy and appreciative of the benefit they were accorded of being safe in their lands. Thus they returned home with their wives."

Word of the governor's presence spread quickly along the edge of the mountains, and soon a large band of Apache arrived from a settlement the Spaniards called La Jicarilla. Their procession must have been impressive, for the chief carried a huge cross bearing an image of the Virgin Mary which he gave to the governor and his chaplain to kiss. Then the Indians sat down and began to tell the governor how they had been repeatedly attacked by the Ute and Comanche. So many of their women and children had been taken captive that the Apache "no longer knew where to go to live in safety." Of even greater concern to the Indians was the fact that three drops of blood had mysteriously appeared on their image of the Virgin. Perhaps this forecast even worse disasters in the future. The governor ingeniously turned the Indian's story to his own advantage, explaining that the blood was a warning that the Apache should "abandon their heathen and barbarous life" and accept Christianity. The Indians, so desperate that they probably would have done anything to secure peace, accepted the governor's advice and offered to be baptized. As the meeting broke up, Valverde distributed tobacco and chocolate to the Apache. More important, he assured them that if they needed anything, they should let him know and it would be provided.

On September 22, the Spaniards continued northward through Philmont to Cimarron Creek, where the Apache had planted corn, beans, and squash. Eager to avoid antagonizing them, Valverde ordered that "under no circumstances should anything be seized." While he and some Jicarilla ate, a chief named Carlana arrived from "Sierra Blanca," probably the Spanish Peaks. He reported that his people had been driven out of their homes by Ute and Comanche raiders. Perhaps the Jicarilla or Spaniards could help them. Once again the desperate Indians were overjoyed to hear that the Spaniards had at last come to their aid. "They went away greatly contented."

Next day the party again marched northward, this time stopping for the night along Vermejo Creek, just beyond the Philmont boundary. They found more Jicarilla at a settlement presided over by Chief Ysdalnisdael whom Ulibarri had met years before. The chief had gone to visit the Navajo, but two of his sons greeted the governor, who "with his accustomed kindness, entertained, fed them, and gave them tobacco." More tales of plundering from the plains were told. That very settlement had recently been attacked: sixty Indians died, sixty-four women and children were kidnapped, houses were burned, and food was stolen. "There were none of their possessions which had not been destroyed." Further upstream Valverde visited still another settlement; this one had canals and ditches to irrigate the fields. Some of the people lived in tepees. So eager were the Apache to secure peace that they offered to accompany the Spaniards on their campaign against the Comanche.

Valverde then left the Philmont area, moving north and east into Colorado and Kansas. They located many Comanche signs and several abandoned campsites, including one estimated to have housed 1000 warriors. Finally, the Spaniards met some Apache from a settlement called El Cuartelejo. One of the Indians reported that his people had been attacked by a band of Pawnee, Jumano, and Frenchmen. Only darkness had enabled the Apache to escape. Moreover, the French had reportedly built two large pueblos, "each as large as Taos." At last Valverde had confirmed the presence of the French on the Great Plains. He pledged to protect the Indians, rushed word of the Frenchmen to the viceroy in Mexico City, and rapidly retraced his steps to Santa Fe.

The frustrations encountered by Ulibarri, Hurtado, and Valverde convinced the viceroy in Mexico City that new techniques were required if the northeastern frontier was to be protected. It would be necessary, he concluded, to maintain a permanent Spanish contingent in the area. So the viceroy recommended the establishment of a fort or presidio with twenty to twenty-five soldiers and a few missionaries at El Cuartelejo settlement. Not only would this post block French expansion and keep a watch on the plains raiders, but it could also aid in converting the Apache to Christianity and persuading them to abandon their nomadic ways and become farmers.

When the governor received word of the viceroy's decision, he questioned the advisability of locating the proposed presido at El Cuartelejo. La Jicarilla, Valverde reasoned, was a highly preferable site. It was much nearer Santa Fe, thus facilitating its defense and supply. Moreover, it would be much easier to civilize the Jicarilla, who had long requested missionaries and were already farming, than the more primitive people of El Cuartelejo. A council called at Santa Fe to consider the relative merits of the two locations fully supported the governor's contention, emphasizing the availability of timber and water at La Jicarilla along with the friendliness of the Indians there. The viceroy then recommended that a presidio be located at La Jicarilla and dispatched the necessary orders to Valverde.

In the meantime the governor had organized yet another expedition to investigate further the situation in the northeast. Pedro de Villasur led forty soldiers and sixty Indian allies along the now familiar route of Ulibarri and Valverde north to Taos, across the mountains south of Philmont, and north along the edge of the Sangre de Cristos. He moved, rapidly east past El Cuartelejo and into western Nebraska and camped along the North Platte River, across from a village of Pawnee Indians. Without any warning, the Pawnee, possibly aided by French soldiers, attacked the expedition. Villasur, his chaplain, and most of his soldiers, died. The thirteen Spaniards who escaped fled to El Cuartelejo and eventually returned to Santa Fe.

The massacre of the Villasur expedition directly affected the proposal to establish a presidio at La Jicarilla. It demonstrated the presence of French troops in the area as well as their ability to ally with the Indians. Once more the need for troops in the northeast was clear. But the massacre also brought about the removal of Governor Valverde, the most ardent supporter of La Jicarilla, for having sent out a poorly equipped and ill-trained expedition under inexperienced leadership.

The new executive, Don Juan de Bustamante, immediately found himself thrust into the controversy over La Jicarilla. Chief Carlana and other Apache once more pleaded for help in defending their homes against the Comanche; they promised to settle in towns, accept Christianity, and obey every Spanish command in exchange for protection. To investigate the situation and select a site for the Apache settlements, Governor Bustamante himself set off for La Jicarilla late in the fall of 1724. He visited most of the settlements formerly recorded by Ulibarri and Valverde, including those of chiefs Ysdalnisdael and Carlana. Each pleaded for baptism and promised obedience if only Spanish troops were stationed among them. The governor, apparently convinced of the need for the much discussed presidio, responded by taking official possession of the area and thus assuming the responsibility for protecting its inhabitants. As an ensign waved the royal standard and soldiers fired a three-gun salute, the governor declared in a loud voice that he was "taking and took royal possession in the name of his majesty the King." Henceforth the Jicarilla were royal vassals whose safety was guaranteed by the monarch.

Returning to Santa Fe, the governor renewed the old request: after so many delays, a presidio must at last be established. Fifty soldiers would now be required. A large complex with "fortified towers, commanded by a gate" should be built; competent priests with the necessary ritual ornaments would also be needed, along "with provision for them for a period of one year until they harvest their crops, sets of tools, large hoes, plough shares for the cultivation of the land, and axes to cut wood to build their houses."

Unfortunately for the Jicarilla, securing real protection was not as simple as waving flags, making speeches, or writing letters. At first officials in Mexico City seemed to agree with Bustamante, and issued orders that the fifty men he had requested be sent to La Jicarilla. Just as establishment of the fort seemed imminent, new obstacles appeared. Principal among them was the arrival of a special inspector, Pedro Rivera, who was examining the entire northern frontier of New Spain. He believed that the Jicarilla were not really serious about becoming Christians and had only requested baptism to save themselves from the Comanche. The same ends could be accomplished at much less cost if the Indians relocated at Pecos or Taos. These recommendations were subsequently approved by economy-minded officials in Mexico City, ending forever the plans for setting up a military post on the land that became Philmont.

The lengthy efforts of the Jicarilla to secure protection against their enemies from the plains ended in failure. Bustamante visited the area once more in 1727 to inform the Apache of his government's decision. Most of them subsequently moved across the Sangre de Cristos to a spot north of Taos where the Spanish promised protection. Some apparently returned to their traditional homes in the Philmont area, reoccupying the old settlements along Rayado, Cimarron, Ponil, and Vermejo creeks. Life was extremely precarious, however, as raids by the Ute and Comanche continued. By the mid-1700s most Jicarilla had once more abandoned their settlements. Not until the United States government moved its Indian agency to Cimarron more than a century later would they return.

IV

EXPLORERS, TRADERS, AND TRAPPERS

During the first four decades of the nineteenth century, thousands of Americans trekked toward the Southwest. Soldiers exploring the newly acquired Louisiana Purchase marched across the Great Plains and into the foothills of the Rockies just a few miles from Philmont. Trappers, lured by the ease with which valuable beaver pelts could be secured, joined Mexicans and French Canadians along the streams of the Sangre de Cristos. Then came the merchants. Missouri entrepreneurs, certain that a warm reception and ready markets awaited them, piled goods into their wagons and left for New Mexico. As news of profits spread, trade increased until a multimillion-dollar business, supported by the American government and exploited by large mercantile corporations, linked St. Louis and Franklin, Missouri, with the Mexican towns of Taos, Santa Fe, and Chihuahua. Santa Fe traders frequently camped on what is now Philmont; by the 1840s a few had decided that it would be a good place to settle.

Yet the harsh Western frontier continually retarded exploration and settlement. A long, perilous journey separated Missouri from New Mexico. Fierce Indian tribes, especially the dreaded Comanche, attacked travelers. When springs and streams dried up or buffalo herds disappeared, dehydration and starvation stalked the traveler. On arrival in the Mexican provinces, hostile officials might impose exorbitant duties and jail trappers and traders or perhaps confiscate their goods.

Exploring the Great Southwest

Although a handful of American and French trappers already had reached Santa Fe, few non-Mexicans probed the Southwest before the United States acquired the Louisiana Territory in 1803. In 1800 when France, led by Napoleon Bonaparte, secured possession of Louisiana and threatened to close the Mississippi River to Americans, President Thomas Jefferson acted. James Monroe and Robert Livingston sailed to Paris ostensibly to purchase only the mouth of the Mississippi, but they were able to buy not only New Orleans but also the entire province of Louisiana which extended to the edge of the Rocky Mountains. In 1819 when Spain and the United States agreed on the Arkansas River as the southwestern border of the purchase, Philmont was less than a hundred miles from United States territory.

As soon as the purchase was completed, plans proceeded to explore the new territory. Meriwether Lewis and William Clark led the famous expedition up the Missouri and Yellowstone rivers and across the mountains to the Pacific. To determine the southern boundaries of Louisiana and learn the nature of the country he had acquired, Jefferson sent a series of expeditions into the Southwest.

The most important consisted of twenty-three men led by Lieutenant Zebulon M. Pike who rowed up the Osage River in the summer of 1806. Soon abandoning his boats, Pike continued west across the Kansas plains. Spain's opposition to the explorer's presence became evident as Pike learned that Spanish soldiers had orders to intercept his expedition. Pike avoided contact with the Spaniards, however, and continued to the Arkansas River. From there part of the group descended the river east of Philmont, while the remainder turned west to explore the "Mexican Mountains"—their name for the Sangre de Cristos—in search of the headwaters of the Red River.

Soon Pike began to encounter difficulties which plagued the remainder of the journey. His men suffered from the cold; food supplies ran low. In desperation the party struggled across the Sangre de Cristos into the San Luis Valley north of Taos where they erected a stockade and found some game. Then the Spaniards appeared, and the entire expedition was marched to Santa Fe and eventually south to Chihuahua City before finally being allowed to return to the United States.[1]

When Pike returned east, his published journals provided the first widely read descriptions of the Southwest. "The Santa Fe trade," Josiah Gregg wrote years later, "attracted little notice until the return of Captain Pike, whose exciting descriptions of the new El Dorado spread like wildfire throughout the western country."[2]

Although Pike's reports stimulated businessmen to think about the economic potential of New Mexico, a second military expedition, which approached much nearer to Philmont, was far less enthusiastic. More than a decade after Pike's return, Major Stephen H. Long reached the Rocky Mountains via the Platte River, continuing southward along the mountains until he reached the site of Pike's first stockade near present-day Pueblo, Colorado. Then part of the group headed down the Arkansas. The remainder veered southeastward, crossing the Purgatory River just north of Raton Pass, until they reached the Canadian River not far east of Philmont. Major Long followed it until his party eventually returned to Fort Smith, Arkansas.

Haphazardly organized and poorly directed, Long's party accomplished little in the way of exploring or mapping. Long collected a few botanical and geological specimens and climbed Pike's Peak for the first time. He is best remembered, however, for his description of the Great Plains. After wandering aimlessly across the grassy flatlands for months, he titled the region east of Philmont the "Great American Desert" and insisted that it was "wholly unfit for cultivation and of course uninhabitable by a people depending upon agriculture for their subsistence." The region's only value was as a "range for buffaloes, wild goats, and other wild game."[3]

Blazing the Santa Fe Trail

Although the unfortunate experiences of these and other Americans initially discouraged trading in the Southwest, conditions slowly improved during the years that followed. After a long and bloody revolution, Mexico won its independence from Spain. As a result, strict trade regulations were subsequently relaxed. Moreover, control of the northern provinces had become so weak that the New Mexico governor acted almost independently. Even American prisoners long held in Santa Fe jails received their release. By the early 1820s the time seemed ideal to begin commercial relations between the United States and New Mexico.

Captain William Becknell, often called "the founder of the Santa Fe trade and father of the Santa Fe trail," was one of a number of Americans who learned of the New Mexicans' eagerness to deal with American businessmen. A native of Kentucky and a long-time resident of the Missouri frontier, he advertised in the *Missouri Intelligencer* for men "to go westward for the purpose of trading for horses and mules and catching wild animals of every description." The expedition which left the United States in 1821 also carried some merchandise to sell or trade in New Mexico. Approaching the Rocky Mountains, Becknell met a party of Mexicans who agreed to accompany him to Santa Fe. There the Missourians easily disposed of their goods at high prices. The handsome profits they realized, together with the governor's announcement that he would welcome further commercial ventures, led to the blossoming of Santa Fe trade the following year.[4]

In response to news of Becknell's initial success, some seventy traders carried nearly $15,000 in goods to New Mexico during 1822.

Captain Benjamin Cooper left first in mid-May. Although it was rumored that he had been "robbed by Indians and left in a starving condition," Cooper traveled west without incident. Instead of tracing Becknell's earlier route to the edge of the Rockies before turning south over Raton Pass through the Philmont area, he apparently crossed the mountains to Taos on his way to Santa Fe.[5] No evidence indicates exactly where the party traveled, but it is entirely possible that they pulled their horses and mules through Cimarron Canyon or up Moras Canyon and south of Philmont on the old Spanish trail.

By 1832, a full decade after William Becknell first learned of the opportunities for trading in New Mexico, the "Commerce of the Prairies" had assumed a regular pattern. Annual caravans departing from Missouri followed reasonably well-established procedures and routes. The dangers and adventure remained. Indians seldom massacred an entire caravan, but they frequently stole livestock or killed a lone trader who roamed too far from his group. Shortages of food and water menaced many parties. Yet pioneering Americans willingly risked their lives by joining these westward treks, which constituted a colorful and significant episode in the development of the frontier. The presence of the Santa Fe trade at Philmont added another chapter to the ranch's long and picturesque history.

Despite the romance of the Santa Fe Trail, its use was essentially a business venture. "Missourians did not engage in this commerce through love of adventure, or to struggle with nature over hundreds of miles of plains and desert, to fight treacherous Indians, or wrangle with Mexican officials," one historian observed half a century ago. "The big profit, the economic fruits, these induced the bankers and merchant traders in Missouri to stand back of the trade."[6]

Across the American Desert

Tanned, buckskin-clad drivers inspected every inch of their equipment to ascertain that no spoke would crack, no strap break, no screw pull loose.[7] Certain that every possible item had been crammed into their great wagons, packers roped down their loads. Local merchants stood by to fill any empty space. Entrepreneurs in distinctive black attire whispered last-minute instructions to their representatives about how to avoid paying duties and how to make the best deals in Santa Fe. Mexicans who had herded mules, horses, or oxen from outlying pastures to join the Santa Fe caravan raced to harness their teams. Final farewells from tearful wives and excited children continued as the men moved to their places. Then from the front the call "Ready?" rang out up and down the line. A hundred voices soon answered "All's set!" With every wagon poised, the captain's cry "Stretch out!" blurred the noise of barking dogs and shouting families. The Santa Fe caravan headed west.

Normally the caravan left Missouri early in the spring, traded during the summer in New Mexico, and returned by late fall. Leaving before the snows had melted on the plains was impossible, but too late a departure could mean encountering winter weather before reaching the settlements on the return trip. In addition to the traders and their crews, a few tourists sometimes joined the party.

Actually there was no marked route across the plains, but each caravan found its own way along river bottoms or across grassy prairies. Detours were frequently necessitated by the need for pasturing livestock and the muddy ruts left by a previous caravan. Wagons usually traveled two or even four abreast, and a single caravan often covered a span as wide as fifty yards. "One need only compare the various records of travel to discover that the Santa Fe Trail was not a road nor even a trace," one recent historian has written, "but a series of tracks meandering over the plains in only the most general single course."[8]

For nearly every Missouri caravan, the first important stop was Council Grove, 150 miles or ten days west of Independence. A large clump of timber bordering a small stream, Council Grove received its name when a surveying party met there with the Osage Indians in 1825. At this stop much final work remained to be completed before a caravan entered the wilderness. Gathering in a meeting, the traders elected one of their members to lead them. A set of rules that amounted almost to a constitution prescribed rules for the journey. Because Council Grove was the last real source of timber, wagonmen gathered wood for repairing axles or spokes. They also cast lead bullets, cleaned rifles and pistols, and completed everything else necessary for the journey ahead.

West of Council Grove travelers entered the wilds. Only well-established campsites marked the route, for few landmarks broke the monotonous prairies which stretched for hundreds of miles in every direction. Boredom posed the greatest psychological problem, for man and beast alike tired of the dreary scenery and the restricted company. Nerves and tempers frequently frayed. But in the wilds also, the real adventure began. Indians might appear at any time. What looked like a tree against the horizon might be a native scout, an antelope, or a buffalo.

By the time the traders began their long trek along the Arkansas River, a routine had developed. The day began early, with cooks and teamsters arising before daylight to start buffalo-chip fires or hitch up the horses. By about six-thirty the captain's repeated calls of "Stretch out!" set the wagons on the move again. As long as the route remained flat and unimpeded by obstacles, the train proceeded steadily, but stream crossings posed considerable difficulty. First the guides rode up and down the creek to find a fording place, then banks had to be cut away so the wagons could be inched into the water. Sometimes teams had to be doubled, causing further delay. After a quick noonday meal, the march continued during the afternoon until the captain pulled the wagons into a night camp.

Soon every caravan had to decide which of two routes to follow. Crossing the Arkansas and heading directly southwest toward Santa Fe was shorter, but the Dry Cimarron route, pioneered years before by Captain Becknell, lacked water, grass, and wood; and the Comanche, Kiowa, and Pawnee in the area posed a constant menace. Moreover, finding the trail was so difficult that traders often wandered aimlessly for days in search of a landmark. The other choice—to follow the Arkansas River further west, beyond Charles Bent's trading post, before turning south over Raton Pass—was a longer, slower, but safer route. Bent's Fort provided an oasis of civilzation, a chance to rest and resupply, which appealed to many. In general the early traders favored the Bent's Fort route, but as the Indian threat lessened and the Dry Cimarron route became better marked, later caravans more frequently ventured on it.

Anyone who chose the Bent's Fort route, eventually passing through the Philmont region, faced the challenge of crossing the Raton Mountains, a range which protruded onto the plains and blocked travel along the edge of the Rockies. Years later, mountaineer Richens L. ("Uncle Dick") Wootton built a tollgate across the only pass; today the Santa Fe Railroad reaches its highest point when it surmounts this barrier. For early Santa Fe travelers, however, the steep, difficult ascent to the ridge and the equally precipitous descent onto the plains provided a major obstacle. Tourist Matt Field termed it "certainly the wildest and most romantic scenery" of the entire trip. Extra horses had to be attached to each wagon as it inched up the mountain; on the downhill side, ropes attached to the wagons were wrapped around trees so that they could be lowered gradually. It took as much as a week and sometimes longer to travel less than twenty miles.[9]

Soon after crossing Raton Pass, caravans passed through Philmont land. Nothing identified that tract as separate from the other hundreds of miles through which the wagons passed, but early travelers frequently recorded stops along Ponil, Cimarron, and Rayado creeks. The exact path they followed during those early days no one can ascertain, but several tracks still visible from the air indicate frequent use of the route fronting the Sangre de Cristo Mountains from Cimarron south through what is now Philmont's headquarters to Rayado, where the area's first permanent settlement was established.

For some, Philmont land marked the point of departure from the main Santa Fe Trail. While surveying the road in 1825, George Sibley noted a "gap" in the mountains through which a "trace" or primitive trail ran to Taos. Exactly what the surveyor referred to, no one knows, but it was evidently either Cimarron Canyon through the heart of Philmont or Moras Canyon just south of Rayado. Because Sibley reported that wagons could pass through the gap "with some labour,"[10] he probably did not mean the narrow and extremely rough Cimarron Canyon, which did not come into general use until after prospectors had discovered gold in the Moreno Valley. More likely, he was describing the Moras Canyon route, essentially the same one followed by Spanish explorers during the early 1700s. Trappers who used this route could reach Taos much more rapidly; traders might hurry over the mountains to reach Taos or Santa Fe in advance of those who continued along the eastern side of the Rockies.

Santa Fe travelers found no permanent settlements in the Philmont area before the mid-1840s, but there was one notable attempt to found a ranch in the area. In 1830, Samuel Chambers, a veteran Santa Fe trader and trapper, petitioned the Mexican government for permission to establish a colony on Ponil Creek on or near present-day Philmont. Examining his request and perhaps recalling the much earlier discussions about establishing a presidio at La Jicarilla, the New Mexico Departmental Assembly noted that Indians in the area were hostile and a threat to anyone who resided there. Until a sufficient military force could be secured, the assembly decreed that no ranches might be established along the northeastern frontier.[11]

Most traders chose not to tarry in the Philmont area and after another week's travel on the Dry Cimarron route approached Santa Fe. At Wagon Mound—a huge, shoe-shaped rock landmark—the Dry Cimarron and Bent's Fort branches of the Santa Fe Trail united. Just south was San Miguel del Vado, the first town through which the wagons passed. Turning westward, travelers then climbed a low mountain range via Glorieta Pass. Suddenly a feeling of excitement swept through the caravan. Men dirty from weeks of travel bathed, changed into clean shirts, put on Sunday suits, and glued their hair in place with bear grease. Wagoners piled as much as they could into each wagon to reduce import duties. With an enthusiasm unknown for months, the Santa Fe caravan rolled down the last hill and into the ancient capital of New Mexico.

An unusual bustle characterized the quiet Mexican town as the annual train arrived. Cries of "Los Americanos" and "los carros" rang through the narrow, crooked streets. Crowds of citizens flocked to stare at the gringos, most of whom stared at their strange surroundings with just as much curiosity. While their teamsters spied out the liveliest señoritas and the liveliest dance halls, merchants wrangled with customs officials, who appraised goods and exacted duties. At last the long trek was over.

Fur Trapping in the Southern Rockies

While merchants from Missouri marched westward over the Santa Fe Trail, an ever larger number of Americans explored the mountains and valleys of the Rocky Mountains in search of beaver. Like the traders, these mountain men played a significant role in opening and developing the Southwest.[12] Geographical exploration naturally resulted from their need for new hunting grounds. Trails they blazed across the wilderness eventually became roads to carry pioneers West. Many of the mountain men themselves served as guides for early government expeditions into the West.

The fur trade in the Southwest differed greatly from that to the north. Because of less severe winters, southern beaver produced poorer quality pelts which brought less on eastern markets. As a result, many trappers moved into New Mexico only after streams elsewhere had been depleted. Still more important, large corporations such as the Hudson's Bay Company and the Rocky Mountain Fur Company which dominated the trade in the northern Rockies never expanded into New Mexico. Most trapper parties consisted of a single man or a small group informally organized for one season.

Whereas the trappers connected with the great companies met for an annual rendezvous at some central location, the lone mountain man traded his furs and secured supplies for the next season in such towns as Taos or Santa Fe.

Beaver were probably trapped first along the eastern edge of the Rockies in the area that includes Philmont. Despite Spanish opposition and constant dangers from Indians, Frenchmen evidently sought furs periodically along the upper Canadian and Arkansas rivers throughout the eighteenth century. After the United States purchased Louisiana, Americans joined them in increasingly large numbers. Auguste P. Chouteau and Jules de Mun, arrested on the Arkansas in 1815, had trapped in the region for more than a year, while members of Joseph Philebert's party were reported to be trapping in northern New Mexico at the same time. Early Santa Fe traders were frequently interested in trapping as well as in selling dry goods. Becknell carried out traps and returned with pelts his men had obtained in New Mexico. Jacob Fowler was returning from a trip in search of beaver when he crossed through Philmont in 1821.[13]

By 1825 trapping parties were rapidly moving west out of the Philmont area. Taos remained the center of the southern fur trade, however, while at Bent's Fort on the Arkansas, trappers often brought their pelts to sell. Many men who later played significant roles in the development of the Philmont area came to New Mexico because of the fur trade; most lived in Taos. Besides the Bents and Ceran St. Vrain, Antoine Robidoux and several of his brothers, Bill Williams, Kit Carson, Dick Wootton, and many others trapped and hunted along the edge of the Sangre de Cristos.

By 1841 when the fur trader Charles Beaubien began his efforts to settle the Philmont area, the New Mexican frontier had been thoroughly explored. United States soldiers had investigated most of the Louisiana Purchase. Missouri traders and trappers had penetrated far into the Mexican hinterland. Commercial opportunities had been exploited. Dozens of foreigners had taken up residence in the area. During the decade that followed, American interests constantly increased until 1851 when New Mexico was organized as a United States territory. By then a permanent town had been established within the boundaries of Philmont.

V

THE BEAUBIEN AND MIRANDA
LAND GRANT

Early in 1841, Mexican Governor Manuel Armijo deeded a huge
tract of land including what is today Philmont to Charles Hypolite
Beaubien and Guadalupe Miranda.[1] During the following five years
while New Mexico remained under Mexican control, Beaubien
actively endeavored to populate the grant. Struggling against the
machinations of provincial politics, the bitter hatred of Taos priest
Antonio José Martínez, and the incursions of Indians who claimed
the region as their own, Beaubien was unable to establish a permanent settlement until the late 1840s. His role in proving the
fertility of the soil and the richness of the grasses, however, laid the
groundwork for the later establishment of a town on the Rayado
River and the development of the area by his son-in-law Lucien B.
Maxwell.

By 1841, Charles Beaubien was a prosperous and influential Taos
merchant. Born in Nicolet, Quebec, Canada, in October of 1800,
Beaubien studied classics at the seminary of Nicolet before he
journeyed to Quebec to prepare further for the priesthood. Soon,
however, Beaubien realized that he could never wholly devote himself to the work of the Church, and he fled Canada in 1821. In St.
Louis, he joined a party of trappers bound for the Indian Country.
There he was apparently employed by the Hudson's Bay Company,

47

for which he was trading when his party became lost and accidently entered New Mexico about 1823. The men, including Beaubien, were arrested, loaded into primitive carts by the local authorities, and hauled south to Mexico City. In the capital, government officials suddenly changed their tune and apologized for their unfriendly reception; they even consented to allow the foreigners to remain in New Mexico if they wished.

Beaubien chose to return to Taos, where he presented his American passport and opened a store to provide supplies for trappers and traders who frequented the upper Rio Grande. In 1827, "having seen at the end of the year the system and good government" of the Mexican Republic, Beaubien notified the *alcalde* of Taos that he intended to establish himself permanently in the province. That same year he fell in love with María Paula Lobato and soon applied to the Church for permission to marry her. Two years after the wedding, Beaubien became a Mexican citizen.

Meanwhile Beaubien's influence in northern New Mexico was rapidly increasing. His store did well, and he soon became one of the wealthiest citizens of Taos. In political matters he began to assume an important role as one of the leaders of the non-Mexican colony, gathering around him such men as Ceran St. Vrain, Charles and William Bent, John Rowland, Sylvester Pratte, and Stephen Louis Lee.

Beaubien often found himself in opposition to the political organization which Father Antonio José Martínez had built up since his arrival in 1826. A well-educated and thoughtful man, Martínez opened a school in Taos soon after he came there as parish priest and served as its principal-teacher for many years. Martínez was extremely suspicious of foreigners, directing much of his antipathy toward the American Charles Bent and the Canadian-born Charles Beaubien.

Government officials must have shared the clergyman's mistrust, for in 1840 all natural-born citizens of Mexico were exempted from paying taxes on their storehouses and shops in an obvious effort to place so heavy a taxation on foreigners and naturalized Mexicans as to drive them out of business. Informers were actively encouraged to report tax evaders and provincial officials even raided Beaubien, Bent, and other stores in search of contraband.

Obtaining a Grant of Land

Just when this antiforeign sentiment was rising, Charles Beaubien prepared to acquire a ranch on the eastern side of the Sangre de Cristo Mountains beside the Santa Fe Trail. There he could build himself a new empire, far from Father Martínez and the suspicious Mexican officials. A store along the trail would be profitable, he was sure, and the cattle and sheep raised would build a proper estate for his children. But Beaubien was certain also that Governor Manuel Armijo would never grant such a tract to anyone of foreign birth. To influence the powerful governor, Beaubien invited Guadalupe Miranda, the secretary of government in Santa Fe, to join him in the venture. As a distinguished Mexican who had once been superintendent of the Santa Fe public schools, Miranda could hopefully win the favor of the governor and help obtain the desired property.

Beaubien and Miranda submitted their petition to Armijo on January 8, 1841. They described the backward condition of the province: With the possible exception of California, they explained, New Mexico was the most retarded area in the country in brain power, industry, and manufacturing. Yet it had all the natural advantages of abundant water, useful timber, fertile soil, and rich mineral deposits. For want of enterprising men to exploit these resources, the land was not being used. They felt that only by granting undeveloped tracts to private individuals could the country be made productive. Moreover, they observed that the territory was full of idle people who were financially burdensome to the more industrious citizens. Put such unproductive hands to work, they urged, to improve the vacant land and develop New Mexico. Despite the unpromising situation they had just described, the two men believed that the future of the province was bright: "This is the age of progress and the march of intellect, and they are so rapid that we may expect, at a day not far distant, that they will reach even us."

Beaubien and Miranda then requested that they be granted a tract of land which they could improve by growing sugar beets or cotton and raising livestock of all kinds. The boundaries they suggested were typically vague. The ranch would commence at the junction of the Rayado and Colorado (Canadian) rivers, go north to Una de Gato Creek, continue east to the summit of the mountains, and return south to the place of beginning. As if some evidence were required to show need of the land, they added a postscript describing themselves as the heads of large families, and prayed to the governor to "take our joint petition under consideration, and be pleased to grant us the land we petition for, by which we shall receive grace and justice."

Beaubien's partnership with Miranda turned out to be a prudent one. Only three days after the petition was submitted, Governor Armijo scrawled his approval on the margin of the request for land, authorizing the grantees to "make the proper use of it which the law allows."

Not until February 12, 1843, did Beaubien and Miranda petition Taos Justice of the Peace Cornelio Vigil to put them in actual possession of their land. The official readily complied, and ten days later he accompanied them and five witnesses across the mountains to the boundary of the grant. There they erected a series of seven mounds to mark its outer boundaries and went through the ancient procedure by which possession was officially vested in the two men: "I took them by the hand," Vigil reported, "walked with them, caused them to throw earth, pull up weeds, and show other evidences of possession." After the ceremony, Vigil declared the pair in "perfect and personal possession" of their ranch, guaranteeing that the grantees, their children, and successors should retain possession of the land forever.

Returning to Taos, the partners quickly took further action to assure that they could use and develop the grant. To prevent Governor Armijo from hindering their plans, they apparently deeded him a one-fourth interest in the vast tract on March 2, 1843. From that day on, the governor always supported the owners against all attackers. More important, that same day, they negotiated an agreement with Charles Bent, the experienced American entrepreneur, whose Arkansas River post had been so successful. In exchange for superintending future colonization activities in the Philmont area, Bent was granted "the fourth part of the land which our possession includes . . . from which we separate our right." Although Beaubien would later deny that he ever made such an agreement, Bent, St. Vrain and Company did carry out settlement programs. And when, years later, Bent's heirs sued Lucien Maxwell for their one-fourth interest, the crafty Maxwell willingly paid some $18,000 to settle the claim.

As the landowners had probably anticipated, Father Martínez was furious when he heard what had happened. He immediately determined that the foreigners should be deprived of their property. Along with the chiefs of Taos Pueblo, Martínez protested that the grant included a part of the communal grazing and hunting land reserved to the Indians. Moreover, he insisted that everyone knew that Charles Bent had an interest in the property and that the government of the Republic of Mexico could not conceivably have wanted to give land to an unnaturalized foreigner. In Santa Fe, General Armijo had been temporarily removed from office and Miranda had lost his influence in political matters. The new executive, Don Mariano Chávez, blamed all foreigners for the killing of his brother by bandits the previous year and readily believed Martínez. Despite all the efforts of Bent, Miranda, and Beaubien, the grant was suspended on February 27, 1844.

Beaubien was quick to answer the charges made by Father Martínez. To statements that Charles Bent held a share in the grant, Beaubien answered, with what was evidently a lie, that Bent held no interest whatsoever. The priest had declared that the tract was enormous, yet its owner claimed that in reality it contained only fifteen to eighteen leagues. Martínez also alleged that the grant included the common grazing lands of some pueblos and that the Indians would perish when the buffalo they depended upon for food were exterminated. These statements were totally untrue, Beaubien asserted. As for himself, the landowner reported that he had a large number of families who were ready and willing to settle upon the grant. But not until Martínez's statements had been discredited and the decree of the governor rescinded could they venture out to develop an important sector of New Mexico's northeastern frontier.

Another new acting governor, Don Felipe Sena, who took office when Chávez resigned because of illness, received Beaubien's petition and forwarded it to the Departmental Assembly for review in mid-April of 1844. Meeting at Santa Fe on April 17, the legislators discussed the Taos priest's petition for revocation, but because a quorum was lacking, postponed action until the following day. After hearing all evidence from both sides and discussing the matter thoroughly, the representatives determined that the suspension had been "based upon a false statement" and ordered that full use of the land be returned to the claimants.

Philmont's First Settlers

Almost immediately Beaubien began plans to start colonies on his property along Ponil Creek and Cimarron River. A large number of persons had already been offered land, no doubt on a sharecrop basis, at the new settlement, and when the snows melted in the mountains they headed for the grant. One group under the direct leadership of Beaubien and Bent settled at a place called El Ponil, probably in the lower Ponil Canyon between Cimarron and the Philmont north-country. They built rude houses and planted corn or grain along the edge of the creek. A second colony was established along the Cimarron River, approximately where the village of Cimarron is now located. It was directed by Cornelio Vigil, the Taos justice who had put the grantees in possession of their land. Before long there were large fields of corn, beans, and pumpkins in the area, and several houses were built along the river.

Just as the settlements seemed to be flourishing, a new governor, apparently Mariano Martínez, assumed power in Santa Fe. Examining the laws, he discovered that foreigners were forbidden to settle along the frontier without express permission from the national government in Mexico City. Since Beaubien was foreign born, his colonization was to be immediately suspended. As soon as he received word of this suspension, Beaubien hastened to the capital and pleaded that the settlers at El Ponil be allowed to stay:

> Having put all good faith, application, and work, as well as considerable expense, to cultivating said land, we ask you to permit us to attend to the fields which we have made there, condescending to dispense to us your protection until we obtain the fruits of our labors. At the time of the harvest we promise to return to the place of our respective residences in compliance with the decree.

Realizing the injustice of his original order, the governor relented, allowing Beaubien and his friends to remain until their crops had been harvested, after which they apparently returned to Taos for the winter.

The following year, however, colonists were back on the Cimarron and the Ponil. The first two American settlers were probably Kit Carson, already famous for his service as guide to John C. Frémont's first Western expedition, and Richard Owens, who would soon make his own fame on the third Frémont trip. But at that time, the two men decided they had "rambled enough" and in the spring of 1845 settled along Cimarroncito Creek, probably near where Philmont's headquarters is now located. There they built a few small huts, put in at least fifteen acres of grain, and started cutting timber in order to make further improvements. In August, Carson and Owens left the area to join Frémont, but other settlers apparently remained in the Cimarron Valley and continued to cultivate its fertile soil. North of the Cimarron, Tom Boggs and John Hatcher built cabins on Ponil Creek in 1845 and were preparing to begin farming. The grizzly bear were so numerous that the men had to erect scaffolds in their fields from which to fight off the savage beasts that ruined their crops and killed their livestock. Finally, the pair decided that it was fruitless to raise corn and graze beef in such an inhospitable wilderness and abandoned their farm, returning to the relative security of Bent's Fort.

War and Massacre

All these difficulties seemed minor when war between the United States and Mexico threatened to break out early in 1846. Americans in New Mexico talked of a struggle which would link the territory politically with Eastern markets. Mexican natives predicted a fiasco which would bring more glory and honor to their republic.

Despite the increasing probability of armed conflict, Charles Bent continued to settle the Beaubien and Miranda Grant in 1846. In the spring he sent his brother George, with partner Ceran St. Vrain, across the mountains to begin large-scale cattle ranching. They selected a site for one ranch on the Cimarroncito and another on Vermejo Creek to the north. At Taos, Charles Bent was busy recruiting more colonists for the Ponil ranch and took them across the mountains on June 2.

Meanwhile Father Martínez was doing everything he could to retard settlement on the eastern frontier. When a party of Ute Indians raided ranches near Taos and stole 8000 sheep and 400 cattle, including some belonging to Martínez and his brother, the priest pointed an accusing finger at the colonizers. He charged Bent, St. Vrain and Company, and Beaubien with supplying ammunition to the natives from their Ponil and Vermejo ranches, and sent investigators across the mountains to seek out evidence. He was trying to "embaris [sic] the settling of our ranches," complained Bent.

The nationalistic program of Father Martínez received a mighty boost in early July when New Mexicans learned that an army of 3000 men under the command of General Stephen W. Kearny was marching toward Bent's Fort bound for New Mexico. Advance parties soon headed south to scout the enemy positions, and early in August the main army began to march east to the edge of the Sangre de Cristos and south over Raton Pass into New Mexico.

Word of the approaching troops sent the colonists on the Ponil Creek ranch fleeing. The soldiers took over the ranch and its cattle, together with the less developed colonies on the Cimarroncito and Vermejo. In the months that followed troops passing the area often used the abandoned settlements on present Philmont as campgrounds and grazing areas for their stock.

The American takeover of New Mexico caused great changes for the owners of the Beaubien and Miranda Grant. Both Beaubien and Bent, who had played key roles in the early settlement of the land, would now have to devote more of their time to new political duties (Bent had become governor). More important, two of their partners, Armijo and Miranda, had fled south before the invading Americans. Not only would they be unable to assist in the future development of the tract, but they would also want payment for their shares. Finally, new and complex legal problems confronted them. After six years of opposition from Father Martínez and Mexican officials, the claimants wondered how they would fare under American law.

These problems—together with the setbacks experienced by the settlers along the Cimarron, Vermejo, and Ponil—encouraged the grantees to consider selling their huge frontier ranch. By early December 1846, six men came forward to purchase the grant. Three had accompanied Kearny's army to the Southwest the previous summer; they were joined by Dunham Spaulding, New Mexico Chief Justice Joab Houghton, and Governor Charles Bent who apparently wished to retain some interest in the project. Retaining only 30,000

acres along the Rayado, where they probably planned future colonization, Beaubien, Miranda, Armijo, and Bent agreed to sell their
interest in the grant for $4000, to be divided equally among them.
For reasons beyond the control of anyone, however, final payment
was apparently never made.

The ease with which New Mexico was conquered soon proved to
be deceptive. During the fall of 1846, rumors of counterrevolution
circulated throughout the territory. Soldiers were kept busy patrol-
ling the streets, setting up heavy arms in preparation for trouble. At
Santa Fe a scheme to overthrow the government was uncovered late
in December; several plotters were arrested. But the real trouble spot
was Taos, where Martínez and his followers held sway. Bent felt
certain that he could quiet tempers in his hometown and decided
to pay it a personal visit. Disregarding pleas that he await the arrival
of an escort of soldiers, the governor and his party left the capital on
the morning of January 14, 1847. Included in the group was Beaubien's eldest son, Narciso, who had been away for five years at Cape
Girardeau College in Missouri, from which he had recently grad-
uated.

Bent and his party reached Taos after four days' travel and were
met by clamoring bands of Pueblo Indians, who demanded that some
of their friends be released from jail. Bent promised the Indians that
they would receive a fair hearing. They dispersed, and the travelers
scattered to their homes. That night was a busy one in Taos. Gun-
fire interrupted the cold silence as Indians roamed the streets. Bars
were crowded. Large groups of men gathered to hear anti-American
harangues. Then the various bands united into a single mob and
began to march through the village.

Sheriff Stephen L. Lee was dragged from his bed and hacked to
pieces. Cornelio Vigil, who tried to rescue Lee, was caught and similarly murdered. A leading attorney, J. W. Leal, was stripped naked,
marched through the streets, and scalped while still alive. Narciso Beaubien and a friend, Pablo Jaramillo, hid under a haystack,
but the rioters were directed to them by a woman who wanted to

"kill the young ones and they will never be men to trouble us." Discovering the pair, the attackers killed and scalped them. At the home of Charles Bent, everyone was awakened by the mob which crowded around the door, calling for the governor. As the women frantically dug through the back wall of the adobe building to open an avenue of escape, the governor tried to calm the rioters. He failed. Suddenly they rushed him, knocked him to the ground, murdered him, and cut away his scalp. The women and children fled to safety. All night long the plunder and murder continued at Taos and in other towns throughout northern New Mexico. Only the arrival of U.S. troops finally restored order to the area.

Fortunately for him, Beaubien was holding court at Tierra Amarilla at the time of the uprising, for, had he been in Taos, the judge would surely have shared the fate of all other foreigners there. As it was, he presided over the trials of those who participated in the revolt. But the future of Beaubien and the grant that he and Miranda had owned for just six years was immeasurably affected by the reign of terror which struck Taos that night. Beaubien's eldest son, who had come home to take over two grants; Charles Bent, who with St. Vrain had established ranches in the east; and Cornelio Vigil, who had recruited settlers and founded the Cimarron settlement, had all been murdered.

Beaubien, however, persisted in his plans to develop the property. In place of Bent and his son Narciso, he turned to his thirty-year-old son-in-law, Lucien B. Maxwell, whose name would become more indelibly associated with the Philmont area than his own. After spending his early life in Illinois and Missouri, where he was raised by his grandfather and two aunts, Maxwell joined John C. Frémont's first Western expedition as a hunter. There he met and became friends with Kit Carson. An uncle, Ceran St. Vrain, evidently took him to Taos, where he was introduced to Beaubien and his eldest daughter, Luz, who became his wife in June 1844. Subsequently, Maxwell worked for his father-in-law delivering messages and transporting goods from Bent's Fort to Taos.

The Founding of Rayado

Early in 1848, Beaubien decided to try once more to establish a lasting foothold on the eastern side of the Sangre de Cristos. He selected the fertile, well-watered valley of Rayado Creek, near the southern edge of Philmont and not far from the spot where the Taos trail left the main Santa Fe road. Few documents from the period have survived, and many of those are contradictory, but a survey of the available materials indicates the following probable sequence of events.

The first settlers—a small band of men including Tim Goodale, Manuel LeFavre, a carpenter named James White, and Maxwell— left Taos in February 1848 with a packtrain of mules carrying their initial supplies. Why they set out in mid-winter is difficult to understand. It may have been that Maxwell wished to sell horses and supplies to William Gilpin, who was camped on the Mora that winter. Whatever their reasons, the venture proved disastrous, for a snowstorm caught the men in the mountains, delaying them for several days and resulting in the loss of one mule. Eventually they struggled onto the plains and selected a location for their new settlement. No sooner had temporary log quarters been erected than most of the men began felling timber and sawing it into boards for more permanent buildings. By spring, when Calvin Jones, a Maxwell employee, arrived with a herd of cattle from Bent's Fort, enough lumber was on hand for three or four rooms.

Not everything needed to start a frontier settlement could be found locally, so at the first hint of spring Maxwell left with some of the men for Kansas to buy supplies. Quickly completing business affairs in the east, he left Council Grove late in May with Santa Fe merchant Preston Beck, mountaineer Tom Boggs, and others. A short stop was made at Bent's Fort before the group headed south into New Mexico. On June 12, while the party was in the Raton Mountains, a band of Jicarilla Apache attacked Maxwell's packtrain, driving off thirty mules and fifty horses; the loss, including 600 deer-skins, amounted to $7200, much of which must have been destined for Rayado.

Although the loss of these supplies was serious, the worst of Maxwell's difficulties had yet to occur. Regrouping along the Greenhorn River and later at Bent's Fort, the party decided to cross the mountains through Manco Burro Pass near the present New Mexico-Colorado boundary. Three days later they camped for the night and were eating dinner when a large group of Indians, apparently Ute, surrounded their camp and began to fire. Several men, including Maxwell, received serious wounds. Most eventually escaped into the woods and slowly made their way back to Taos.

Besides demonstrating how perilous life on the New Mexico frontier could be, the Manco Burro tragedy seriously jeopardized the existence of Rayado. Maxwell, whose leadership was vital to the settlement's success, had a bullet lodged deep in his neck. He traveled as fast as possible to the nearest physician in Santa Fe, where the bullet was cut out in an "extremely difficult and painful" operation. Not for many months would he recover sufficiently to take an active role at Rayado. Moreover, the supplies from the East could not be obtained for another year; the money to buy goods and employ laborers had been considerably reduced by the loss of the first train. Despite all these difficulties, Maxwell was able to sell enough hay to the army and supplies to travelers on the Santa Fe Trail to assure the continuation of the Rayado project. In January 1849, John C. Frémont wrote his wife from Taos that Maxwell was "at his father-in-law's doing a very prosperous business as a merchant and contractor for the troops."

Meanwhile in Taos, Carson had been debating his own future plans. On one hand Frémont suggested that he accompany him to California and eventually settle there. But Carson was reluctant, as Frémont put it, "to break off from Maxwell and family connections." During the early spring he decided to decline Frémont's offer and stay in New Mexico. "In April," Carson recorded in his autobiography,

> Maxwell and I concluded to make a settlement on the Rayado. We had been leading a roving life long enough and now was the time, if ever, to make a home for ourselves and children. We were getting old and could not expect to remain any length of time able to gain a livelihood as we had been for such a number of years.

At Maxwell's, Carson immediately began "building and making improvements." Soon, he recalled, "we were in a way of becoming prosperous."

Actually Carson was only one of many New Mexicans who moved across the mountains to the Philmont area in 1849. Most were Spanish-Americans, but a few were Indian slaves (mostly Navajo) and Anglo-Americans. By summer, forty or fifty men were busy pulling in timber from the nearby mountains and whipsawing it into lumber. Others were mowing the tall grass sold to the government as fodder. Increasing numbers of sheep, horses, mules, and cattle grazed on the surrounding pastures and meadows. Four farmers arrived that second spring to begin tilling the virgin soil and building ditches to carry water into their fields. Fifteen more families joined them the next season. Rather than sell land, Beaubien and Maxwell apparently arranged a system of shares whereby they and the farmers split whatever was produced.

The first description of Maxwell's settlement came when Charles E. Pancoast, a Pennsylvanian headed for the California goldfields, visited "Riadjo" in July 1849. Like many other Anglo-Americans, Pancoast was so overwhelmed by Carson that his whole report centered on the "famous mountaineer." He reported that the ranch was not at all "stylish." The central structure was a two-story log cabin; several smaller adobe huts adjoined it. High walls surrounding the entire complex protected it from Indian attack. Other adobe buildings outside the compound served as corrals, stables, and a slaughterhouse. More than a dozen Anglo-Americans and Mexicans and twenty Indian men and their squaws lived at the settlement.

At first Carson said little to his visitors, but as the evening wore on and the glow of the campfire deepened, he began to tell stories of his long career and his more recent difficulties in protecting the Rayado settlement from the Ute and Apache. Sometimes it was necessary to summon the army, but Carson led his listeners to believe that he had pursued the Indians "so severely that they found it their best policy to make their peace with him." Visiting Indians were always treated kindly and given food. Yet even Carson was not wholly convinced of the natives' friendliness, for he still guarded the livestock day and night. Pancoast and the others were so enthralled with Carson's stories and the battle wounds he displayed that it was eleven o'clock before they all retired for the night.

If Carson honestly believed that the Indians along the Philmont frontier could be so easily pacified, his optimism did not last long. In October 1849, only three months after Pancoast's visit, Apache attacked the J. M. White party along the Santa Fe Trail some eighty miles east of Rayado. Mr. White and five or six others died in the battle, while his wife and small daughter were apparently captured. Quickly, Captain (Brevet Major) William S. Grier with a company of dragoons set out from Taos to pursue the raiders. When the troops reached Rayado, Carson joined them.

For almost two weeks the soldiers followed Indian trails across the barren plains of northeastern New Mexico. At last they sighted the camp of what were presumed to be the guilty Apache. The troops halted to prepare for a parley, giving the Indians time to begin packing and preparing for battle. Suddenly a bullet hit Grier, miraculously embedding itself in his coat so that he suffered only surface injury. In the confusion, the natives rode away with the loss of only one warrior. In the rubble left behind, Carson and the others found the body of Mrs. White. Nearby lay a popular novel extolling the heroism of Carson, who this time had failed in his mission. No trace of White's daughter was ever found.

The Army at Philmont

The White massacre fully convinced United States officials of the need to station troops along the frontier. If Grier and his men had been nearer the scene of attack, they could have saved a great deal of time and perhaps rescued Mrs. White and the child. Rayado was the logical site for the army to stay. Probably encouraged by Beaubien, Maxwell, and Carson, the commanding officer agreed to station ten mounted dragoons under Sergeant William C. "Leigh" Holbrook at the frontier settlement. Their presence contributed much to the pacification of the area.

During the winter, cold and snow apparently restrained the Apache, but peace ended suddenly on April 5, 1850. Apache attacked a vulnerable outpost three miles from Rayado where horses and mules grazed, two of Maxwell's herders received severe wounds, and nearly all the riding stock in the area was driven off. No sooner had daylight come the next morning than Holbrook and his men, accompanied by Carson, galloped off in pursuit of the enemy. Twenty miles from Rayado they sighted the raiders. "We approached the Indians cautiously," Carson reported, "and when close, charged them." Five Apache were killed and one or two others wounded. The successful soldiers returned with all but four of the stolen animals. They carried five Indian scalps as gruesome trophies. "I regard the affair as a very handsome one," wrote Captain Grier, "and very creditable to the sergeant and his men."

The ability of the army in subduing the Apache and protecting the settlement at Rayado persuaded military officials to establish a permanent station on the Beaubien Grant. Necessary orders were issued on May 24, 1850, and Grier reached the new "Post at Rayado" with forty-three men from Companies G and I of the First Dragoons. Forty-five horses gave them needed mobility to pursue hostile Indians. The detachment had a six-pound cannon and a mountain howitzer, and each soldier carried a carbine. At first the troops lived in tents, apparently located along the Rayado east of the main complex. Maxwell soon agreed to quarter them in a building under construction as his residence. The officers had already moved in by early fall, and it was expected that the enlisted men would join them shortly.

In addition to providing protection, the military post also added appreciably to the revenue at Rayado. At first Maxwell contracted to rent quarters and stables for $2400 a year, but soon the price rose to $3400. Many supplies were also purchased locally. For example, the army bought an unspecified amount of hay in 1850 for $20 a ton; the following year, it had decided that Rayado was the best location to graze all the surplus government stock in the territory. As a result purchases totaled 600 tons with the price increased to $30 a ton. Wheat had been planted on most of the irrigated land, so the corn had to be purchased in Taos at a cost of $2 a bushel. The military also provided employment for five civilians, three as herders and two as teamsters. An inspector who visited the post a year after its founding suggested that although the location seemed wise from a military standpoint, it was "somewhat expensive" to maintain.

That such large expenditures were justifiable became increasingly evident during the summer and fall of 1850. Within a few weeks after the post was established, Indians variously described as Ute or Apache once again attacked. On June 26 they drove off a large herd of Maxwell's livestock grazing almost within sight of the main buildings. Six horses, four mules, and 175 head of cattle valued at more than $5000 were lost. In addition, an army bugler who had left camp unarmed was found dead, together with a civilian, probably the "brave and experienced" trapper William New. Such a daring raid convinced many New Mexicans that the small, ineffective forays against the Apache must end. A group of citizens including Maxwell, Beaubien, and Carson petitioned Governor John Munroe for a full-scale expedition to end the Indian menace forever.

The U.S. governor responded favorably to this request. By late July 1850, troops on one of the largest Indian campaigns carried out in northern New Mexico left Rayado. The entire party of more than

150 men headed north along the Sangre de Cristos to the Vermejo River, then moved westward into the mountains where they sighted an Apache trail. Late one night Lieutenant Adams attacked a small band of Indians, killing or wounding all of them and capturing their animals. An advance party of Spanish-Americans sighted and attacked another camp that same night. The next day the main body was at last spotted "on the edge of a mountain, in a thick and almost impenetrable growth of aspens." The surrounding area was so marshy and full of springs that an attack would have been difficult. Before the troops could be brought into position, the Apache sensed their presence, hurriedly abandoned camp, and fled higher into the mountains. Pursuit proved fruitless, although five or six Indian casualties were counted. One wounded soldier died the next day. Even though the Apache had not been dealt the blow many New Mexicans hoped for, the expedition did recover many horses, sheep, mules, and cattle stolen from Rayado and other settlements. Grier's superiors must have been satisfied with these results, for soon after the soldiers returned, Grier received orders to stay at Maxwell's Rayado ranch for a year.

In addition to pursuing Apache through the mountains, Grier had other more mundane but (at least by army standards) equally important concerns during late summer. An army inspector was to visit his command, and Grier's men devoted much time to cleaning guns, practicing maneuvers, and straightening up quarters for the arrival of Inspector General George A. McCall on September 16. McCall commented very favorably on what he found. Special praise went to Grier, who appeared "to have discharged his duties with zeal and ability." The post itself presented a pleasing appearance, especially in light of the short time since its establishment. But the troops looked bad. Since no new clothing had been issued for several months, many of their uniforms did "not conform to regulations." The soldiers had devoted insufficient time to their formal drill, and their marching techniques, the inspector reported, were "by no means perfect." In a classic understatement McCall described the men's appearance as "becoming hard service rather than parade duty." Grier must have taken such criticism seriously, for as soon as McCall left, the soldiers began devoting more of their time to drill.

The coming of winter only increased the difficulties along New Mexico's northeastern frontier. When the Eastern mail reached the area, for example, an escort from Rayado rode in two feet of snow to accompany it to Santa Fe. Similarly, soldiers were needed to guide the army paymaster and his wagon train across the Raton Mountains in January 1851. Heavy snows made it almost impossible for them to pull the loaded wagons over the pass, but after several days, the cold, tired troops reached the summit and sent the paymaster into Colorado. A private named James A. Bennett complained about conditions: "work hard all day in the snow; at night make a bed on a bank that would bury a man." The trip back almost ended in tragedy when the soldiers decided to try a new route to Rayado and became lost in a storm. By the time their guide found some trees in which to seek shelter, twenty men were so cold that they needed help to dismount. A week after returning to the warmth of their quarters, the men faced still another dangerous trip across the mountains to take an army surgeon to Taos.

Between escort duties, the soldiers also defended the settlements along the Sangre de Cristos. Winter drew large numbers of wolves out of the mountains to attack livestock. Frequently the troops pursued packs of 200. Nor did the cold weather totally eliminate the Indian menace. Late in November, a herder reported that 400 head of cattle had been driven off. Carson, who spent most of the winter at Rayado, led the soldiers seventy miles in pursuit. When they found the Indian camp and the stolen cows, pitch-covered baskets filled with milk hung in nearby trees. Bennett was convinced that the Apache were going "into the dairying business pretty largely." In the brief battle that followed, seven Indians were killed and one child taken captive. All the livestock was recovered and returned to its owner.

Two events during the spring forecast changes in the military posture in the area. Early in April, Grier, who had commanded at Rayado since the post was founded, relinquished command to Captain Richard Stoddard Ewell, who had been on detached service in Virginia. Ewell, who joined the Confederacy during the Civil War and became known as one of the South's most effective commanders, was much less willing to guard a minor frontier settlement than had been his predecessor. He may well have questioned the need for continuing the post. By early spring seven privates and two enlisted men had been imprisoned; two others had deserted. When a general court-martial convened at Rayado in April, five of the men were ordered discharged. Whatever the reason, such a high percentage of troublesome soldiers required some consideration.

Perhaps as a result of these events as well as the high cost of maintaining troops at Maxwell's and the inability of the military to win a decisive victory against the Indians, the army began to investigate the desirability of discontinuing the post. On March 12, 1851, Lieutenant John G. Parke was ordered to "make a particular examination" of the Rayado area to determine if it was the best site to station soldiers. He was to take into consideration the availability of wood and water as well as the capacity of the area for farming and grazing livestock. Most important, he was to evaluate the military advantage of the location, for his superiors wanted to be certain that soldiers there could operate "over the greatest area of country and on the essential points in the most prudent and effective manner."

Parke's report, submitted in mid-April 1851, dealt a blow to Post Rayado which hostile natives and inclement weather had failed to strike. Parke was particularly concerned that the post was located in an area between the mountains and the plains where mesas of varying elevations surrounded it on all sides. Trees and scrubby brush covering them provided excellent cover for approaching Indians. Moreover, the garrison had an "extremely limited view" of the surrounding countryside. Parke felt that it was militarily inadvisable to continue the post at its current location. Instead he recommended a site between Cimarron and Ponil creeks ten miles to the north.

Parke completed his report just as Colonel E. V. Sumner arrived in New Mexico to take command of the Ninth Military Department. Rather than spread his forces out among a number of small posts, he decided to consolidate men and reduce costs by locating one large fort on the Mora River thirty miles south of Rayado. In mid-May 1851, part of the Rayado detachment went to the new location to begin building Fort Union. Two months later, on July 25, Sumner ordered the post at Rayado broken up, and on August 31 it was abandoned.

Indian Attacks at Rayado

The increasingly secure status of the Rayado settlement was evidenced by the willingness of both Maxwell and Carson to leave the area for long periods. During much of the summer of 1851 the two men headed a party of eighteen trappers who went to Colorado and Wyoming. Two years later Carson purchased 6500 head of sheep which he drove to California. Maxwell followed with a second herd. After his return, Carson moved back to Taos, where the government employed him as agent to the Ute and Apache.

When the men were gone, the village along the Rayado was especially vulnerable to Indian attack. On one occasion a German boy sent to get water from the creek saw a large war party of Cheyenne. Mountaineer Tom Boggs, who was staying at the ranch at the time, recommended that instead of trying to fight off the Indians, the residents should feed them while one man rode to Fort Union for troops. Teresina Bent recalled what followed:

So we women all set to work cooking—coffee and meat and whatever else we had. I was twelve years old, and the chief of the war party saw me and wanted to buy me to make me his wife. He kept offering horses—ten, fifteen, twenty horses. Mr.

Boggs said for us to act friendly with the Indians and not make the chief angry. My, I was so frightened! And while I carried platters of food from the kitchen, the tears were running down my cheeks. That made the chief laugh. He was bound to buy me, and when they all got through eating he said that they would wait; if I was not delivered to him by the time the sun touched a hill there in the west he would take me by force.

The Cheyenne camped just outside the compound waiting for the sun to set. Within the adobe walls, the little girl Teresina helped the women prepare for battle. Just as the moment of attack neared, Carson and a company of soldiers rode dramatically up the road from Fort Union. The Indians fled.

Another story, perhaps legendary, involved Vidal Trujillo, who had married Beaubien's daughter Leonora and was also living at Rayado. One morning a small party of Apache appeared on a hill north of the settlement. Two men who went to see what they wanted were fired upon and fled to the safety of the compound. Suddenly 600 warriors topped the hill. Since most of the men had left and ammunition was scarce, Vidal Trujillo volunteered to ride to Fort Union for army help. The mount he chose was Rayado, a fine racehorse named for the ranch. The great gate flew open and out sped horse and rider.

Like a thunderbolt the big chestnut horse shot into the midst of the circling savages. Crouched low over his withers, Vidal, a professional jockey, guided him through the savages in the greatest race of his career. So unexpected the act, and so complete the surprise, the flying rider was through the line before the Indians knew what was happening. . . . Fate rode with Vidal Trujillo that day. Miraculously he escaped their missiles, and by virtue of the great horse under him, outran them.

Never daring to spare his animal, Trujillo pushed on as rapidly as possible. When he reached Fort Union, Rayado fell dead beneath him. The soldiers immediately departed for the north, but when they reached the settlement, the Indians had given up their siege and fled. Once more Rayado was secure.

In April 1854, many New Mexicans thought that the Indians had at last overpowered the residents of Rayado. A report reached Santa Fe that Apache had attacked the ranch and killed all its inhabitants. Eight women, ten men including Maxwell, and two or three children were reported dead. No such massacre actually occurred, but Carson, fearful that one might take place at any moment, appealed for troops. He reported that more than $100,000 in livestock was on the Rayado. Moving them to a more secure location was impossible because of a shortage of grass; many residents of the village would lose everything if they had to leave. He warned that trouble was likely unless government forces were sent soon.

Carson's appeal brought quick action from army officials. On July 16, 1854, Lieutenant J. W. Davidson established temporary camp at Rayado with sixty-one men from the First Dragoons. Apparently no major attack occurred, and the army was not convinced of the continuing need for troops in the area. By early September orders were issued to abandon the camp, and two weeks later the troops left.

Principally because of the continuing support of the army and the perserverance of the early settlers, Rayado had become well established by the mid-1850s. Maxwell had erected a large complex including living quarters, storage and work rooms, surrounded by a protective wall. Other buildings increased the value of his improvements to an estimated $15,000, some 200 acres of land had been put under cultivation, and 15,000 head of livestock grazed along the Sangre de Cristos. Occasionally Indians still raided the area, but no tribe could mount an offensive sufficient to drive out the settlers, and more of them were continually arriving.

Rayado's position as the major settlement on the Beaubien Grant subsequently diminished. In 1857 Maxwell decided to move his residence to the banks of the Cimarron River, where his ranch grew and prospered, especially after the government located the Ute and Apache Indian agency there in 1861. Today several of the buildings erected at Rayado during the early 1850s remain as part of Philmont's Individual Training Center, but fewer than a dozen people still call Rayado home.

VI

LUCIEN B. MAXWELL:
EMPIRE BUILDER

By 1857, Lucien B. Maxwell was ready to strike out on his own. For nearly a decade he had managed the Beaubien ranch on the Rayado and quietly watched as most of the profits went to his father-in-law. By now, however, the eastern frontier of New Mexico had been largely pacified. It was safe for others to establish ranches in the region.

Maxwell selected a spot along the Cimarron River about three miles below the mouth of its rugged canyon for his new settlement. Military reports indicated the defensive superiority of the location, and the valley around it provided sufficient water and rich soil for successful farming. Maxwell's site was also near the intersections of the Bent's Fort road and the Cimarron Canyon route to Taos, so a store would be even more profitable than the one at Rayado. Soon he moved to the Cimarron and put crews to work constructing his headquarters.

The buildings erected along the Cimarron indicated the expansive plans which Maxwell had for the ranch. The adobe house comprised a pair of large, two-story wings facing a central courtyard. As at the Rayado compound, massive walls excluded unwelcome visitors. Inside, the neatly plastered rooms were spacious but simply furnished. One visitor wrote:

The room we slept in was carpeted, but had not even a chair. However, in one corner, there was a pile of wool mattresses and bedding from which the servants made beds for us on the floor at night. So far as we saw, there was only one room in the house that had a bedstead and that was the one occupied by Maxwell and his wife.[1]

Following Mexican tradition, there were separate dining rooms for men and women. Because a large number of visitors and employees already had flocked to Cimarron, the men's eating area accommodated twenty persons.

From Maxwell's residence one could see great herds of cattle and flocks of sheep grazing on the ranch. Closer in, farmers cultivated extensive fields of grain and corn. A store, a blacksmith shop, barns, and countless smaller adobe huts encircled the ranch house. "The surroundings and whole atmosphere of the place," wrote an early chronicler, "reminded me of the descriptions that I had read of baronial estates in Europe in the middle ages."[2]

While Maxwell was building along the Cimarron, the owners of the land, Charles Beaubien and Guadalupe Miranda, took steps to have their grant confirmed by the United States government. In conformity with the requirements set down in the treaty of Guadalupe-Hidalgo which ended the Mexican War, they filed a petition for confirmation on February 23, 1857. Through their attorneys the men declared that they had cultivated and improved the land for more than a decade; the Americans ought to acknowledge their possession of it as the Mexicans had previously. A hearing was held in Santa Fe late in August. Three weeks later, New Mexico Surveyor General William Pelham approved the grant and forwarded the necessary documents to Washington for congressional action.[3] Many years passed before final confirmation was obtained.

Financial difficulties prevented Miranda from sharing in the development of the grant. Early in 1858 he wrote Beaubien expressing a desire to sell his interest: "Thrust out from my country, a portion of my property abandoned, and the rest for a year and months at the disposition of my enemies," he wrote, "my resources have been reduced to such a degree that today, in order to maintain my numerous family, I find myself obliged to dispose of that which remains to me. . . ."[4] Beaubien had no interest in acquiring Miranda's share, but his energetic son-in-law Lucien Maxwell was eager to take advantage of the offer. In April 1858, Miranda's son Pablo visited northern New Mexico to sell his father's interest to Maxwell for $2500. In addition, on September 14, 1858, Maxwell purchased Beaubien's share of a tract extending for two and one-quarter miles from his home for the nominal price of $500.[5]

Having acquired the land which surrounded his mansion, Maxwell immediately began another major construction project. An experienced stonemason, R. M. Blackmore, supervised the building of a three-story stone gristmill located several hundred yards west of the Maxwell home.[6] By the time it was completed, the demand for milled products had increased dramatically, for Cimarron had been selected as the site for an Indian agency. Naturally Maxwell expected to acquire the lucrative contracts for feeding the natives.

The Cimarron Indian Agency

For five years before it was moved to Cimarron, the agency for the Ute and Jicarilla Apache had been at Taos under Agent Kit Carson. In June 1861, when he resigned the Indian post to join the Union Army, government officials decided to move the 1500 Indians to a more remote section of New Mexico. Perhaps influenced by Maxwell, who knew from his experience at Rayado how profitable federal contracts could be, the officials selected Cimarron as the site.

The first Cimarron agent was William F. M. Arny, an ex-preacher and antislavery advocate who was dedicated to improving the condition of the Indians.[7] Shortly after his arrival, Arny proposed an elaborate program for the education and civilization of his charges. The sole hope for the improvement and elevation of the red man was the education of the children. If a "taste for civilized life" could be created among young Indians, it might be possible to erase the unsavory habits of their parents. Cimarron was the ideal location for an industrial and agricultural school for the Ute and Apache. Rich soil and adequate water could produce many varieties of vegetables and grains, and there were few Americans or Mexicans to corrupt the Indians.

Arny suggested that as a first step the government negotiate a new treaty with the Indians. Federal authorities should provide clothing and tools for farming; in exchange the Ute and Apache should agree to turn over all their children aged eight to sixteen to the agent, who would clothe, feed, and educate them. Reading and writing would be important parts of their schooling, but the young Indians would also devote three hours each day to laboring in the fields. In March 1862, Arny initiated his program by leasing 1280 acres in the Ponil Canyon north of Cimarron from Lucien Maxwell for $20 a year. The Cimarron rancher also supplied flour and beef to the agency at high prices.

Shortly, however, serious problems arose which threatened the existence of the Indian agency and the settlement at Cimarron. First, Confederate troops from Texas invaded New Mexico. After the surrender of Union soldiers in the southern part of New Mexico, the Confederates marched north through Albuquerque and Santa Fe, threatening to overrun all of New Mexico. Maxwell took advantage of the food shortage resulting from the invasion to increase the price of food sold to the government. Arny, who lacked sufficient funds to purchase corn and wheat for his charges, feared that they would either starve to death or provoke a war with the settlers by killing their livestock. To further complicate matters, a smallpox epidemic broke out among the Indians. Within a few days seventeen were dead. Arny vaccinated the remainder, but most of the Ute and Jicarilla rushed off into the mountains to keep from catching the dread disease.

Conditions improved after two Colorado generals, John P. Slough and John M. Chivington, marched their troops through Cimarron and past Fort Union to Glorieta Pass, where they destroyed the Confederate's supply lines and compelled the rebels to retreat. Food shortages were not so readily overcome. Maxwell refused to lower his prices; the Indians found little game in the mountains. They faced starvation unless they ventured out onto the plains to hunt buffalo, but there they were certain of tangling with their traditional enemies the Comanche and Kiowa. The Ute and Apache assured their agent that if only the government would feed them, they would do anything he asked.

The inevitable clash between the Cimarron tribes and the Plains Indians soon occurred. Arny heard rumors that 300 or more Comanche had crossed the Raton Mountains to fight the Ute. He warned the marauders that they would be met by armed citizens and troops. The Comanche did not heed Arny's warning, however, and continued on until they found ten Ute lodges. Cimarron residents who heard of the impending attack raced to the scene and pleaded with the intruders to leave the Ute alone, but their efforts were also fruitless. Soon a fight began, which continued until nine Indians were dead and one wounded; the two who remained unhurt dragged their injured chief and a dead brave into nearby brush. They continued to do battle until the Comanche at last grew tired and retreated. "Such an instance of bravery," reported Arny, "is scarcely to be found either in civilized or in savage history.

In the Ponil Valley, Arny began work which would enable the Indians to supply their own food and end their reliance on Maxwell's flour and beef. Agency buildings completed during the spring included offices, schoolrooms, a kitchen, a council room, and quarters for the agent and visiting troops. More important were the agent's plans for agricultural development:

> I erected at my own cost a corral for horses and cattle, and intended this fall to fence about five acres of ground adjoining the agency for cultivation as a vegetable garden for the use of the agency; also I have ploughed twenty acres more, which I intended to plant next spring in wheat, corn, and vegetables, and

divide into small patches, to be tended by such Indians as were willing to work, the product to belong to the Indian who cultivated the patch, and thus I hoped to be able to gradually induce the Indians of this agency to quit roaming over the country and cultivate industrial habits.

Many New Mexicans strongly criticized the location of the Indian agency at Cimarron. Samuel B. Watrous, an American rancher who grazed cattle along the eastern edge of the Rockies, complained of increased livestock losses and demanded that the Indians be moved back to the west side of the mountains. Arny's statements that whiskey was too easy to procure in Taos was a "transparent humbug," he insisted, arguing that there was far more liquor at Maxwell's than at Taos. An uprising at Cimarron was inevitable, according to Watrous, and when it occurred the responsibility rested on the shoulders of those who "fastened this scourge upon us, and sustained their action by the aid of forgery and lies."

Late in the summer of 1862, President Abraham Lincoln appointed Arny as secretary of New Mexico territory. In his place the government appointed Levi J. Keithly as Cimarron agent, who was described as "a plain, honest, straight-forward old farmer."[8] Keithly lacked the idealism and reforming spirit which had characterized his predecessor; he believed that Indians were "devoid of anything like generosity, honesty, or good faith." The only way to stop robberies was to confine Indians on a reservation policed by armed guards.

Keithly's attitudes were reflected in his methods of managing the agency. Arny's plans for an Indian school were quickly abandoned, for Keithly believed that even if provided with the best opportunities, Indians could not take advantage of them. The Apache he thought, were so addicted to whiskey that they would sell anything to obtain it. When they grew corn, it was only to turn it into a "kind of beer, which they drink day and night to excess, regardless of the wants of wife or child."

Despite the increasing profits which he reaped from the Indian agency, Maxwell also discovered that the presence of so many natives brought continued trouble. Late in August of 1863, some Arapaho and Cheyenne came to Cimarron to steal Ute horses. Eager for revenge, the Moache chased them. Although unsuccessful in recovering their stock, the natives killed one Cheyenne. A second visit by the Plainsmen cost Maxwell forty mares. The third time they surrounded the agency buildings and demanded to know where the Ute had camped. Someone warned the Ute and Apache of the pending attack, so they had time to mount an offensive and chase their enemies back to the plains. In the resulting skirmish an Arapaho died and a Ute was wounded.

The continued Indian trouble persuaded the government to move the Indians away from Cimarron. The man assigned as special agent to convince the Ute that they should move north to Colorado was Lucien Maxwell's brother Ferdinand. Agent Keithly was to take charge of moving the Jicarilla Apache to a reservation on the Pecos River several hundred miles southeast of Cimarron.

The half-hearted attempts of the two men to remove the Indians met with little success. The Jicarilla listened patiently to Keithly's explanations but responded that while Mexicans and Anglos might be delighted to have farms along the Pecos, the Indians preferred to follow the warpath and the chase. The unimaginative agent, convinced that the Apache would be content to "lead a vagabond life—begging, stealing, and otherwise depredating the flocks and herds of the citizens," soon abandoned his efforts. Ferdinand Maxwell, whose brother had profited from the presence of the agency at Cimarron, had just as little luck with the Ute.

Some indication of just how profitable the Indian agency had been for Lucien Maxwell became evident in 1864. Beaubien died early that year, dividing his interest in the property among his children. Immediately, Maxwell began buying up land from his brothers- and sisters-in-law. He purchased the interest of Frederick Muller, and his wife Theodora along with their one-square-mile ranch near the Cimarron River for $3500. The same amount obtained the shares of Joseph and Juana Clouthier and Paul Beaubien. Vidal Trujillo and his wife Leonora sold their rights for $3000.[9]

The Indian Crisis at Maxwell's

Meanwhile conditions at the Cimarron Indian agency further deteriorated. The national government, engaged in a Civil War which threatened to destroy the nation, devoted very little attention to Indian matters. Funds to buy goods and to feed the Indians were always short. Time after time Lucien Maxwell advanced corn, flour, or beef on the credit of the government, knowing, of course, that such action would assure him future contracts. The continued scarcity of game in the mountains forced the Indians to slaughter the cattle of local farmers. Indian officials in Washington reasoned that at least part of the responsibility rested with Keithly, and late in June 1865, they removed him from office.

A nation so recently at war still needed its best men in the army, and only the poorest could be spared for service in obscure Indian agencies. The man selected to replace Keithly was Lorenzo Labadie, a New Mexican with previous experience as a Navajo agent. Labadie was instructed to see that the Apache moved at once to the Pecos River reserve and that the Ute went to Colorado.

Labadie found the Ute and Jicarilla no more cooperative than had his predecessors. When he ordered them to new reservations, the Indians became very gloomy. They explained that the Great Spirit had created them in the Cimarron area, where they had lived for as long as anyone could remember. The bones of their forefathers had been buried there. The climate was pleasant and the water healthful. Moreover, they argued that the government had promised that they could remain forever. They also resented efforts to separate them into two tribes. By then the Ute and Jicarilla were "one family and one blood," united by ties which no federal official could cut.

When Labadie proved no more able to implement his proposals

than had his predecessors, Indian Bureau officials replaced him with Manuel S. Salazar, who spoke no English. One observer characterized him as totally lacking in either judgment or ability, and conditions continued to worsen. Ranchers east of Cimarron complained that Indians who said they were in the area to hunt buffalo had actually come to slaughter their cattle. Warnings that the tribes would have to pay for any damages produced no results.

To add to the belligerency of the Ute and Apache, several Americans who lived in Cimarron discovered the lucrative business of selling liquor to the natives. These dealings were carried on so clandestinely that it was almost impossible to discover the guilty parties. A government inspector threatened to confiscate all whiskey if the problem of drunkenness continued, and the situation improved while he was in Cimarron. But no sooner had he left than there were as many intoxicated Ute and Apache as ever.

Further agitating the Indians who returned to Cimarron in the early summer of 1866 was the diminishing number of buffalo on the Great Plains. By late June the Indians at Cimarron were in a pitiable state. Both the Apache and the Ute had spent eight weeks searching for buffalo but found none. Agent Salazar gave up in desperation in May, resigned his office, and left the agency without any supervision. In vain the naked, hungry Indians searched for anyone to help them. Even Lucien Maxwell, who had previously provided enough food to prevent their attacking his livestock, now refused to supply any more meat or flour without compensation. Finally the chief of Indian affairs in New Mexico, A. B. Norton, conferred with Territorial Governor Robert Mitchell and authorized Maxwell to issue up to $500 worth of beef and flour each month to prevent suffering. Norton then forwarded an account of his activities to Washington. Officials in the national capital, unaware of just how critical conditions had become, disapproved of Norton's emergency plan and ordered Maxwell to discontinue feeding the Indians. Maxwell predicted that with no agent to pacify them and no rations for food, hostilities would soon break out.

Within days the anticipated trouble began. Deprived of their usual rations, the Ute and Jicarilla started to requisition sheep and cattle from ranchers in the Cimarron area. Two Indians went to the ranch of Casimer Sais, where they killed three sheep. The rancher wished to avoid bloodshed and gave them an additional animal. An hour later another Ute, the son-in-law of a major chief, demanded food. Sais offered him a dead animal, but the man refused to accept it and signified his intention to kill a sheep. When the rancher refused, a fight ensued. After an arrow had been shot into his coat, Sais fired his pistol and killed the Indian. As soon as word of the murder reached the Indian camp near Cimarron, the whole tribe set out to avenge the death. Meanwhile Sais scurried south to Fort Union to seek protection from the army. Indians reaching the fort demanded that the "murderer" be turned over to them, but the District Commander General James H. Carleton refused to surrender his charge.

At this point Carleton decided to use his own authority to avoid war if possible. He asked the former Cimarron agent, W. F. M. Arny, to visit the Indians and explain the complexities of United States jurisprudence to them. At the same time Carleton hurried north to make a personal inspection of the agency. He reported:

I find that the Utes and Apaches who reside near this place are wholly destitute of food; their game is entirely gone, and they are forced to kill the stock of the people or starve. Their killing of the people's cattle and sheep herds leads to collisions; already blood has been spilled and [there is] much hostile and bitter feeling on the part of the Indians. . . . In this matter the Indians cannot be blamed. The Indian department does not feed them and there is really left but one alternative for the Indians, that is to kill stock, let the consequences be what they may, or perish. We cannot make war upon people driven to such extremities. We have taken possession of their country. Their game is all gone, and now to kill them for committing depredations solely to save life cannot be justified. . . . This is not only a true story, but the whole story.[10]

To alleviate the critical situation, Carleton ordered Lieutenant George I. Campbell, who commanded a cavalry unit temporarily stationed at Cimarron, to buy enough wheat and beef from Maxwell to supply each Indian with half a pound of meal and meat daily. It was clearly explained to the chiefs that the arrangement was temporary. In the meantime, if any stock was stolen or ranches attacked, food distribution would cease immediately.

Just as the Indians seemed to have quieted down, residents of the frontier town of Trinidad, Colorado, north of the Raton Mountains, called for protection against the Ute. Lieutenant Colonel A. J. Alexander rushed his troops north from Cimarron and arrived at Trinidad early the next morning. He found that the Indians were once again destroying crops, killing cattle, and generally abusing the residents of the area. Their chief defiantly insisted that the land was his and that whenever he and his people needed food they would gather and eat it. His language was so menacing that Alexander thought it prudent to gather the local residents in preparation for battle.

As he investigated the situation, Alexander learned that much of the responsibility for the sudden deterioration of Indian-white relations rested with Lieutenant Campbell, who was still commanding the troops at Cimarron. Campbell had become intoxicated, drawn a pistol on a Ute chief, and threatened to kill him. Fortunately, Maxwell prevented the officer from carrying out his threat. As a result of this affair, the Indians hated all whites, civilian and military. It was too late for Alexander to restore friendly relations, however, and on October 3 his forces fought a pitched battle with the Ute. Initial reports indicated that twelve Indians and one soldier were killed, but later figures were greatly reduced.

The outbreak of war in Trinidad focused the attention of many New Mexicans on Cimarron. Governor Robert B. Mitchell rushed north from Santa Fe to investigate the situation. When Indian Superintendent Norton reached Cimarron, Maxwell proposed that the government purchase the entire Beaubien and Miranda Grant as an Indian reservation. For only $250,000, Maxwell offered to sell the 40-by-60-mile tract of land, his flour mill worth over $50,000, a sawmill, storehouse, barns, corrals, and dwellings. But neither Norton nor his superiors in Washington were interested.

The first six years of the Ute and Apache agency at Cimarron certainly were no credit to the United States government. During most of the period, the Civil War consumed the interests and money of the nation; only inferior officials and surplus funds were available to the Indian Bureau. As a result, inept agents with insufficient supplies plagued the Cimarron agency and hundreds of others like it throughout the West. Furthermore, because no national Indian policy had ever been promulgated, each agent followed his own whims in directing his agency. Some showed initiative and imagination, but most did not.

The Indians suffered from this sort of poor administration. Never certain of exactly what they were expected to do; or when they would receive annuities, presents, and rations; or which of a large number of bureaucrats should be obeyed, the Ute and Jicarilla groped their way blindly through a maze of conflicting policies. When there was no money for food or clothing, the Indians were hungry and cold. When they grew exasperated and tried to rebel, unsympathetic soldiers punished them.

Only Lucien Maxwell seemed to profit from the presence of Indians at his ranch. He prospered because his fields and herds were seldom damaged by Indians. Soldiers frequently camped at Cimarron, providing the security which attracted settlers to the property. Primarily, however, Maxwell profited from the new markets opened by the Indian agency. He controlled sales of beef and flour and thus provided them to the government without the inconvenience of competitive bidding. Then, too, the Maxwell Ranch was being advertised because of the presence of the Indians. Every time there was an outbreak of the Indians, a distinguished visitor arrived or a new agent was appointed, and Santa Fe newspapers printed a full report. By this means many New Mexicans became aware of Maxwell's growing settlement and of the potential for economic development in northeastern New Mexico. Soon the discovery of precious minerals provided additional wealth and publicity. It also led to dramatic changes in the history of the area and further worsened conditions for the Indians.

VII

BONANZA
ON BALDY MOUNTAIN

In the mountains near Philmont, many shale-covered peaks tower above the dark pine and spruce forests. The highest of these is 12,441-foot Baldy Mountain. Every spring its white snowcap produces countless streams that rush downward, carving deep gullies where they flow. To the west, Humbug, Grouse, and Nigger gulches, and Willow Canyon mark historic paths into broad, flat Moreno Valley which separates the Cimarron Range from the main Rocky Mountain chain. Ute, South Ponil, and Black Horse canyons provide southern and eastern paths to the plains.

Once Baldy Mountain overlooked a prosperous mining community, but the men and women who lived and labored on its slopes long ago departed. Visitors to the area still find many remnants of the past. Deep shafts honeycomb the mountain and the ridges that radiate from it. Unnaturally heaped stones clutter the sites of long-abandoned placer operations. Decayed buildings stand vacant. More than $7 million in gold was taken out of the Baldy district during the last century. Now it is totally abandoned.

Gold Rush on Maxwell's Ranch

The initial discovery of gold at Cimarron resulted from the dissatisfaction of the Ute and Jicarilla Apache with their meager govern-

84

ment dole. From their camps along the Cimarron River, they roamed the slopes of Baldy and other mountains in search of game. When a party of their hunters found a hillside covered with lumps of colorful copper float, they gathered chunks of the "pretty rock" and took it back to Cimarron. The soldiers who had come from Fort Union to investigate Indian attacks on livestock probably heard of the discovery and saw this ore. With the Civil War over, the army men would shortly be mustered out of the service. A copper mine could make them rich.

William H. Moore and others from the fort paid the Indians for the rock and sent one man off with an Indian to locate the source of the copper. The pair had climbed nearly to the top of Baldy before they found a slope thickly blanketed with ore. The delegate from the fort laid out a claim, known afterward as the "Copper Mine" or "Mystic Lode," jotted down its location, and raced back to tell Moore and the others of the discovery.[1]

The reports which reached Fort Union, together with the samples of ore brought to the post, further excited the soldiers. Moore, William Kroenig, and several others became the leaders of the copper mining interests. They ordered Larry Bronson, Pete Kinsinger, and a man named Kelley back to Baldy in October of 1866 to do necessary assessment work and to start uncovering ore for shipment. The three traveled to Cimarron, continued west through the narrow Cimarron Canyon, and turned into Moreno Valley. From there they climbed up Willow Creek, the southernmost stream flowing off the western side of Baldy.

It was late afternoon when they arrived near the top. Rather than start work so late in the day, the men decided to set up camp and spend the night. Bronson and Kinsinger cooked supper, while Kelley took a gold pan from his pack and washed some creek gravel in it. Before long he ran to the cooks, showing them the gold flakes he had found in the pan. Supper was abandoned. The trio picked up tools and began to work the stream bed. Thoughts of a copper bonanza were forgotten the next few days as the three explored their private gold field, digging exploratory trenches, working gravel beds, and chipping away at likely looking rocks. Each swore to say nothing of the discovery until spring when they would return to a carefully marked tree under which they had camped, lay out claims, and make themselves rich.[2]

The three discoverers, seething with excitement over their find, could never have kept their secret. Within weeks after their return to Fort Union, everyone had heard of their story. Some especially anxious men may even have left the post and spent the winter prospecting and mining on the still snow-covered mountain. Hundreds more saw the coarse gold flakes taken from Baldy; each told a few "close" friends, and soon the southern Rockies echoed with news of the gold strike on the Maxwell Ranch. Many crowded around Maxwell's mansion even before the last snow. With the first warm rays of the spring sun, prospectors flooded the new El Dorado, taking up claims and washing out gold. Surely, one miner declared, northern New Mexico would be "another California."[3]

Developing the Moreno Valley

The initial discoverers themselves returned to Willow Creek in the spring of 1867 to find many other prospectors already at work. Larry Bronson brought three partners with him. Calling themselves "Arthur and Company," the men laid out five 200-foot claims from "Discovery Tree," where they had camped the previous fall. The company took out fourteen ounces of gold during the summer, then decided to go ahead with bigger plans and contracted to secure water from nearby Bear and Willow canyons. Matthew Lynch and Tim Foley, who would play important roles in the camp, arrived early in the spring, staked out claims, and set to work. Reports circulated that one group had found "dirt" yielding thirty-five cents to the pan, but a disheartened gold seeker reported that the "best prospect" he had seen was worth "no more than fifteen cents to the pan." Dissatisfied with such secondhand information, the owner of a hotel in Denver paid a personal visit to the mines. After examining the entire length of Willow Canyon, he declared the new diggings near Cimarron to be "as rich as any yet 'struck' on the North American continent."[4]

News like this drew even more miners into the district. Before long seventeen companies had staked claims along Willow Creek, and prospectors overflowed into nearby gullies on the western slopes of Baldy Mountain. A second Fort Union group, the Michigan Company, found gold in the flats of the Moreno Valley. Pete Kinsinger, one of the original discoverers, joined Tom Lowthian and Colonel Edward J. Bergmann, a Union commander in New Mexico during the Civil War, on Spanish Bar at the mouth of Grouse Gulch. They may have been the first to use hydraulicking, where water was sprayed on the mountain from powerful hoses. Other miners laid out claims in Nigger, Mills, California, and Mexican gulches which ran off the western slopes of the high bald mountain and into the Moreno Valley.[5]

The miners in the valley soon realized that some form of government was absolutely necessary to provide for the lawful, orderly location and working of their claims. They met on May 13, 1867, under the leadership of the Michigan Company. John Codlin from Fort Union served as chairman of the meeting which proceeded to organize the district. A committee drew up the constitution which laid down sizes for lode and placer mines and requirements as to how much work was necessary to keep a claim active. To assure that accurate records were kept, the miners elected William O'Neill as recorder. He was to serve for two years, filing mining notices, water and timber rights, bills of sale, and deeds. The prospectors made certain that there would be no underhanded activities by demanding that his books be open to examination by any miner.[6]

During the summer of 1867, local people grew increasingly confident that the area would have enduring importance and commenced more permanent development of it. Mines demanded better routes through the narrow Cimarron Canyon separating Maxwell's ranch from their mining valley. Plans were laid that summer to improve the road at a cost of $3000 to $4000. Thereafter it replaced the traditional Mora Canyon trail as the major route to Taos. Of more immediate importance to placer miners was the development of an adequate supply of water, for large quantities were necessary to remove gold from the rich gravels of the area. By early June one company had anticipated the impending water shortages and had already begun to construct a ten-mile ditch. It was planned to collect water from high mountain streams and carry it via wooden flumes and ditches to the mining operations on the slopes of Baldy. A second project, six miles long and built to carry 2000 miner's inches of water, was scheduled to be completed by the middle of August. A consolidated company, reportedly made up of "the most enterprising men . . . reputed for their honesty and integrity," started a third ditch to carry water from the upper reaches of Moreno and Mills creeks to placer operators lower down in the Moreno Valley.[7]

Such large-scale construction of flumes, sluice boxes, and living quarters increased the demand for lumber throughout the district. A man named Bough erected the first sawmill, got up a "full head of steam" to power his saws, and set about "ripping out" 3000 feet of lumber a day. By fall William Kroenig and Lucien B. Maxwell also had sawmills operating in the district.[8]

Much of the lumber went into the construction of a little town overlooking the Moreno Valley. During the first summer John Moore, George Buck, and other pioneer miners asked T. G. Rowe to survey a town site, laying out blocks of lots in checkerboard fashion with wide avenues. The local citizens paid tribute to Moore, who had been instrumental in organizing the village, by naming it "Elizabethtown" after his daughter. Before long there were five small mercantile businesses—described by one visitor as together equal to "half a country store"—selling supplies to the prospectors. Soon twenty buildings had been completed, and many more were under construction.[9]

New activity in the camp diminished during the winter when freezing weather and shortages of water ended sluicing operations. Although some miners left for bigger or warmer towns to await spring, many remained. Especially popular were places like the May Flower Saloon where cold miners warmed "the inner as well as the outer man." "That house across the street" with its "two smiling faces" was particularly inviting to many who missed feminine companionship. "You will be richer in pocket, better in health, and wiser [in] mind," warned an oldster, "if you stay away from there."[10] Most miners paid little attention to such advice. They were too young and too excited about the prospects of becoming rich to worry about moral questions.

By the end of the season an air of enthusiasm hung over the new mining district in northeastern New Mexico. Most miners who stayed during the first winter were optimistic. Their wait would pay off when the snow melted in the spring and the streams once again carried water down the mountain. They had scarcely scratched the hardrock interior of Baldy Mountain from which the rich gravel in the gulches and valleys had originally washed. They needed time, capital, and heavy equipment to explore and develop these lodes. Mining companies had only temporarily solved the persistent problem of securing sufficient water to initiate large-scale placer and hydraulicking operations. Yet, while less than $100,000 in gold left the Moreno Valley during the first hard summer, the season constituted a good foundation for later developments. News of the discoveries had spread, attracting new miners to the valley almost every day. Prospectors had explored the placer grounds and found rich new deposits; they had laid out a town and opened stores to supply an increasing population. Most important, investors had heard of the district and slowly come to show some interest in it. All these factors would merge during 1868 to make the Baldy district a real El Dorado in New Mexico.

Prosperity and Growth in 1868

Most of the early miners on Baldy Mountain had given little thought
to the fact that they were on Lucien B. Maxwell's land, if, indeed,
they were even aware of the fact. Certainly Maxwell had done nothing to draw their attention to the fact. He was friendly to prospectors
who passed through Cimarron, and more than once had offered
them lodging in his great adobe mansion or a grubstake to get started
on. There were, however, limits to his hospitality. When one prospecting company tried to cross the mountains and locate a ditch and
claim sites along Ute Creek, now part of Philmont, Maxwell ran
them out. The intruders were unimpressed by their eviction, claimed
"miner's rights," quoted sections of United States law, and vowed
to return.[11] These were the first of a long series of settlers and miners
who defied Maxwell and later claimants of the Beaubien and Miranda Grant.

During the winter of 1867-68 the Cimarron land baron determined to profit from the discovery of gold on his holdings and sent
Colonel J. D. Henderson to lease claims to the miners. Maxwell's
supporters insisted that his desire to encourage the settlement of the
country was demonstrated by his "usual liberality" in negotiating
agreements. For periods of one to ten years a miner could lease a plot
500 feet square for one dollar a month. Most gold seekers were quite
willing to deal with Henderson, and by February he and his assistants
had leased 1280 claims.[12]

Late in 1867, Maxwell also set about on another but less profitable
scheme. He united with some of the most prominent men in New
Mexico to promote the development of a second town in the Moreno
Valley, to be called "Virginia City" after Maxwell's daughter. The
men selected a site in the lower Moreno Valley, near where it intersected the Cimarron Canyon. After having 400 lots surveyed, the
promoters announced a public auction starting on January 6, 1868.
Ignoring the existence of Elizabethtown, they assured prospective

Saddlemen still ride the working cattle ranges in the Philmont country. (*Philmont Scout Ranch*)

The little St. Louis, Rocky Mountain & Pacific Railroad had an ambitious name and a short but busy life.

Loggers at work in the early days of timbering activity in Poñil Canyon. (*Seton Museum*)

The mining camp of Baldy Town in the 1930s, revived for another attempt at mineral riches. (*J. W. Leitzell*)

Another view of Baldy Town, showing the tramway that ran down from the higher mines.

Baldy Town street scene in the 1930s. The town now is within Philmont Scout Ranch boundaries. (*Matt Gorman*)

Ruins of the old general store at Baldy Town, once stocked with cartridges and miners' candles. (*Philmont Scout Ranch*)

Mill of the Four Creeks Mining Company on Black Horse Mountain, southeast of Baldy.

French Henry's millsite, showing the old tramway beyond, north of Baldy Town. (*W. Edmonds Claussen*)

Hardrock miners in the famous Aztec Mine during its revival in the 1930s. (Seton Museum)

Boy Scouts and Explorer Scouts today pan for gold in the mountain streams of the Philmont country.

Prehistoric petroglyphs dot canyon walls around Philmont
and are still a mystery. (*Philmont Scout Ranch*)

Waite Phillips (left) and Scout official Ray H. Bryan in front of Phillips's mansion on the ranch.

The trophy room in Phillips's mansion reflects early Mexican styles and is now a Philmont Scout Ranch showplace.

Indian tepees have pointed skyward again in the Philmont country, serving as Scout lodges.

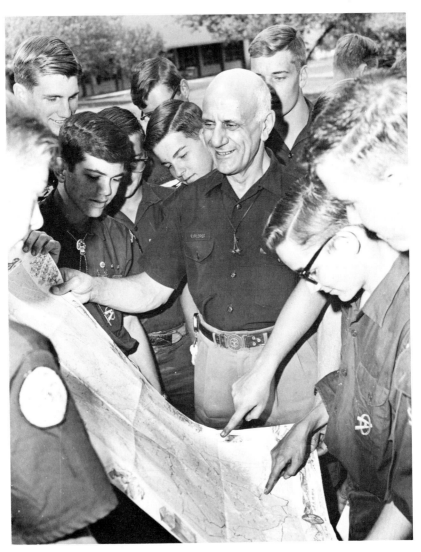

Joe Davis, former Philmont Scout Ranch director of camping,
shows a map of the great Maxwell ranch to new arrivals.

buyers that Maxwell's holdings were "so extensive as to preclude the idea of a rival town." By New Year's Day, hopes were high. Many miners asked about lots, and some even purchased lumber to start construction immediately after sales opened. Fully a hundred houses and 2000 inhabitants were expected by spring.

The whole project was a dismal failure. Shortly after the auction got under way, the promoters boasted of "room enough to build a town as large as any other Virginia City in any other mining district," a reference to the boom towns in Nevada and Montana. Yet their tract contained only one tent—the sales office. Forty houses were expected by mid-March, but only fifteen, half roofless, had been started. A sarcastic visitor reported that there was "one store here, but no hotel, stable, restaurant, or barbershop to greet the weary traveler." A long search was needed to find some corner to sleep in, but one's horse would still have to stand "in two foot snow, with no hay and only a quart or two of bad corn." By mid-summer the town had completely "played out." "Virginia City moved up here yesterday," reported a citizen of Elizabethtown, "came up on a burro; says it is too lonesome down there and can't stand it; had to go three miles just to speak to anyone."[13]

The mail service improved greatly when a stage line inaugurated triweekly runs between the Maxwell Ranch and Elizabethtown early in 1868. The owner of the company, V. S. Shelby of Santa Fe, promised "utmost attention . . . to the comfort of passengers." Some miners thought less about the comforts provided than of the rich investors who might now travel to the district; others imagined that the stage line would bring some women into the district. "With a Concord Coach for a conveyance," one man declared, "we will expect them." The line was so successful during the spring of 1868 that daily service started July 1. Thereafter anyone who could stand the wet, bumpy road along the Cimarron River was able to visit the mines for $8. Many did. The coaches pulled in one day loaded with passengers and departed the next loaded with "many an ounce of gold dust." Shelby's success stimulated additional stages, and soon a second line from Taos to Elizabethtown provided a more direct route to and from Santa Fe.[14]

It was primarily due to Maxwell that plans were developed to provide a year-round water supply to the mines. Captain Nicholas S. Davis, who had come to New Mexico with General Carleton and stayed on as a civil engineer, studied the water problem during the fall of 1867 and proposed as a solution the construction of an extensive system of flumes and canals to transport water to the eastern side of the Moreno Valley. It would start at Red River (today a feeder of the Rio Grande and popular as a tourist center), carry it through the mountains between the Moreno and Red River valleys, and deposit it in the gold-rich gulches of Baldy Mountain. Together with Davis and others, Maxwell organized the Moreno Water and Mining Company. Actual construction began on May 12, 1868.[15]

Expectations rose as work progressed; it was commonly predicted that the "Big Ditch" would provide enough water to employ "thousands of men for a generation." Many miners joined the construction crews working on the ditch; soon 400 men were building "à la Union Pacific." Davis hoped for completion by September, but the need for huge wooden flumes to carry water over gulches and valleys slowed the work considerably. When the longest aboveground stretch, 2800 feet of flume trestled 79 feet above the ground, was completed in November, only nine miles remained to be built. But work had to be suspended for the winter, and it was not until July 8, 1869, that the first water reached Humbug Gulch just above Elizabethtown.

An engineering feat of the first magnitude, the system was supposed to transport water from the watershed of the Rio Grande to that of the Mississippi. It was more than forty-one miles long and had three miles of aqueducts and sidehill flumes traversing incredibly steep mountain country. Total costs exceeded $200,000. Unfortunately, although the system was designed to carry 700 inches of water, numerous leaks and breaks in the line let only 100 inches trickle out of the huge wooden flume.[16] While visitors gawked in awe at the ditch, disappointed miners wondered if their hopes for wealth would ever be realized.

The Aztec Strike

Although overshadowed by the readily profitable placer mining, some miners had explored the possibility of extracting gold from the hard rock of Baldy during the early years. Although at first sidetracked by their placer discoveries, Kelley and his friends later did some work at the Mystic Lode. They formed a company which sank a preliminary shaft and drove a 300-foot tunnel 150 feet below the original outcropping. In addition to the anticipated vein of rich copper, the miners found a ten-foot-wide lead of quartz impregnated with gold.[17] Prospectors made several other minor lode discoveries throughout the district, but no extensive work was done on their finds.

The first step toward discovery of a very rich vein of ore was taken when Tim Foley and Matthew Lynch, Willow Creek prospectors, together with Robert Doherty sneaked past Maxwell and prospected Ute Creek in May of 1867. They found rich deposits of gold in the creek bed, but apparently gave up their work without extensive development or any attempt to trace the gold to its source.

They returned a year later, however, determined to explore the hillsides along the creek and locate the source of the nuggets they had found. Gold pans dipped into the icy stream; deft fingers sloshed water and gravel until only flakes remained in their pans. The adventurers were certain that those tiny yellow pieces had washed from some exposed gold vein by the melting snow—if only they could find that spot. Slowly, carefully, they prospected upstream. Then the gold flakes disappeared. Excitedly they scoured the hills above. There, on a spur separating Ute Creek from South Ponil Creek was the source of the gold. After thoroughly exploring the mountainside, they found a 30-foot depression full of rotted quartz that shimmered with gold. Further investigation revealed three well-defined veins, each three feet wide and a foot apart. Maxwell soon learned of the discovery and, together with Lynch, V. S. Shelby, and Colonel Edward Bergmann, filed location papers on the claim. They called their mine the Aztec.[18]

Before long, mining experts throughout the West had heard of the Aztec. One man who saw a chunk of the ore exclaimed that "if all is like it, one or two tons of this rock would be a fortune for anyone." When Maxwell sent a sample of ore to O. D. Munson, assayer at the United States branch mint in Denver, a skeptical Santa Fe editor printed the cold, scholarly report without significant comment. Decomposed quartz from the Aztec lode yielded $19,455.37 a ton in gold and $189.08 in silver, in all a "very handsome sum" indeed. The editor of Santa Fe's other newspaper, the New Mexican, proclaimed excitedly that the "Ute Creek Lode" was undoubtedly the richest gold quartz mine ever discovered; none anywhere could equal its value. Stories spread quickly. One editor took three weeks, worked over his figures, and computed Maxwell's wealth. Assuming the presence of only 100 tons of ore, Maxwell and his partners would make the "princely sum" of $2 million. If by chance it turned out to be very large, the rancher in Cimarron might soon be "the richest gold producer in the world."[19]

Maxwell immediately began to develop the mine. He sent an engineer to Chicago to buy a fifteen-stamp mill to process the ore after it had been removed from the mine. Each 435-pound stamp would crash down on an iron base thirty-three times a minute, breaking the rock into fine powder. The entire apparatus cost $8000 delivered. Installed in a building near the present Philmont camp at Baldy Town, the machinery went through its initial testing and became operative on October 29, 1868. Once the ore had been ground into fine powder, it was put into a sluice box through which ran a rapid stream of water. Most of the gold, being heavier than other minerals, settled on the bottom. What did not was caught by a layer of mercury in the bottom of a second sluice.

Colonel Edward Bergmann superintended the five men who operated the mill. Even Maxwell marveled at his success. In the first six days, the machinery extracted 120 ounces of gold valued at $2640. Mining men estimated that the Aztec would bring in a yearly profit of over $100,000 if run at the same rate for only 300 days a year. In the mine, eighteen men kept busy supplying the mill; four drills ran during the day and two at night. The Aztec continued to run at that rate for nearly a year. Between October 1868 and July 1869, about 1810 tons of ore produced gold valued at slightly over $100,000. Surely, Maxwell had found his bonanza at last.[20]

Maxwell's success at the Aztec Mine stimulated additional prospecting. A man called Big Jack discovered another rich lode southeast of the Aztec. Maxwell himself owned most of the claim, appropriately named the Montezuma. A mill pounding away on its ore was netting $1000 a day by the middle of November. Inexpensive procedures, coupled with the ease of removing gold from partially decomposed rock, kept the cost of milling down from $10 to $20 a ton. Initial profits from the Montezuma prompted New Mexico Chief Justice John S. Watts to declare it "the best lode in America."[21]

Prospectors also explored the north side of Aztec Ridge along the banks of South Ponil Creek. A group of Frenchmen led by Henry Buruel opened the French Henry Mine in 1869. Buruel obtained a deed to the lode from Maxwell, only to discover that he had no way to mill his rock. Maxwell's equipment was too busy stamping ore from the Montezuma and the Aztec to bother with outside "custom" work. Moreover the cost of shipping it to a smelter in Denver, Colorado Springs, or El Paso was prohibitively high. Unable to defeat Maxwell's milling monopoly, Buruel could accomplish little, and he soon shut the mine down. It would reopen in later years, and today a Philmont camp nearby recognizes the pioneering efforts of Buruel and his men.[22]

Maxwell's almost absolute control on the slopes of Baldy extended to placer operations. Along Ute Creek, near where Miranda and

Baldy Town camps are now located, spots of exceedingly rich gravel could be profitably worked with a minimum of equipment. In July of 1869, for example, a lucky miner found a nugget worth $40 in the creek bed. Maxwell heard of this discovery and immediately set to work developing placer mines along the stream. He built a house for himself and started a full-scale hydraulicking operation. Under his personal supervision, employees worked gravel from the surface down to bedrock—a distance varying from ten to thirty feet. Thirty miners, supplied with two powerful hoses, kept busy through the summer of 1869. In one very productive week they extracted $700 worth of gold; six weeks' effort produced $1700 for Maxwell's coffers. Less extensive placer operations were carried out on South Ponil Creek along the current trail from Pueblano camp into the Baldy area, but little of value was located there.[23]

Continuing Moreno Valley Boom

While Maxwell reaped profits from the Aztec and the Montezuma mines and his Ute Creek placers, small operators took advantage of the limited quantities of water supplied by the big ditch and made a good living in the Moreno Valley placer mines. Hydraulicking became increasingly common. One of the most productive operations in Willow Creek belonged to Arthur and Company. Supplied with forty inches of water and six-inch hoses, they sprayed water under high pressure at their rich beds of gravel. Two hundred feet of sluice boxes caught the mud, rock, and gold as it raced downhill. Log riffles in the bottoms of the boxes collected most of the gold, but the miners also distributed six pounds of quicksilver in the last two boxes to catch any flakes which did not naturally drop out of the muddy torrent. As long as water lasted, work proceeded well.

Elizabethtown, where many of the miners lived, was very much "on the boom" in 1868. Despite its newness, the town still pretended to have a certain "class." On June 1, 1868, for example, the town demonstrated its social abilities with the opening of the Moreno

Hotel in a flurry of glamor. To celebrate the event, eighty-three guests enjoyed a "splendid repast" served on the finest china in the territory. A few glasses of Mumm's Dry Imperial Champagne brought forth toasts of all descriptions, many to the prosperity of the district. The first hotel's flourishing business attracted other ventures. Henry Lambert, a colorful Frenchman who claimed to have cooked for General U. S. Grant during the battle of Vicksburg and for President Abraham Lincoln in the White House, threw together a building of "logs and lumber" which he named the "E-town Hotel." Soon Lambert was making a small fortune feeding miners.[24] The ditch company opened a store under the management of V. S. Shelby. Prosperity and growth were fast making Elizabeth-town—by now universally known as "E-town"—the most important city in the northern part of the territory. Its citizens demanded political recognition.

Territorial officials recognized the maturity of Elizabethtown early in 1869. On January 25 the legislature heeded the demands of the leading citizens of the gold camp and established a new county named after Vice-President-elect Schuyler Colfax. The seat of Colfax County was temporarily located at Elizabethtown, although a permanent site for the courthouse was to be chosen at the first general election. Early in March residents of the area went to the polls. Besides reaffirming the selection of E-town as county seat, they elected Maxwell probate judge by a large plurality. Not surprisingly he received virtually unanimous support from the citizens of Cimarron and Ute Creek, both of which he owned. A year later, in February 1870, the New Mexico lawmakers incorporated E-town.[25]

Other evidence of the area's maturity was the arrival of a minister and the establishment of newspapers in the valley. A Methodist elder, the Reverend J. L. Dyer, reached the district during the late 1860s. Soon newspapers reported "quite a revival of religion" at the Baldy mining camp.[26] The first newspaper in the region, the *Moreno Lantern*, began in the summer of 1869, but lasted only a short time. By early October, Will D. Dawson had established a new paper which he called the *Elizabethtown Telegraph*. Beset with trouble from the first, the weekly once appeared as a half-sheet when its supplies of paper failed to arrive by press time. Despite such problems, the paper survived, although Dawson sold out to a stock company after a year. By January 1871, he resumed his own publication. The *New Mexican* praised the "handsomely printed" weekly and noted that it was "a great improvement over the previous paper." Ash Upson started a competing paper in the spring of 1871, the *Elizabethtown Argus*, edited by Major R. E. Sprigman.[27]

Many columns in these papers were devoted to reporting the activities of "high society" in E-town. In December 1870, for example, Colonel Edward H. Bergmann, the retired soldier who had superintended mill operations at the Aztec, married Augusta Schwenck. Their wedding and reception preceded a "splendid ball" held in Garrick Hall. It was an event "longly and kindly remembered by all participants." An equally lively event occurred July 4, 1871, when the citizens of the Baldy district celebrated the nation's birth in a "due and ancient fashion." Shots rang out over the gold-laden hills as a parade of 500 people marched to a nearby grove of trees for the festivities. There, Major Sprigman, editor of the *Argus*, read the Declaration of Independence, after which M. W. Mills, a prosperous mine owner, lawyer, and politician, delivered a "spread-eagle" oration, "much above the average addresses upon such 4th of July-ing." As was customary, a great ball closed the day.[28] Unfortunately the ball marked the final act in the boom on Baldy. The town would wait a long time for another such celebration.

Decline of the Baldy District

Many factors led to a decline in mining activities on the slopes of Baldy Mountain near Cimarron. Some miners fled the district because of difficulties with the English company which had by that time purchased the Beaubien and Miranda Grant. In addition, the richest ore bodies were gone by 1870, and inexpensive transportation was necessary if profitable operations were to be continued with lower quality ore. Despite much talk of railroad construction, the decline in gold production and population, together with difficulties with the Maxwell company, ended building plans. Placer miners did not need the railroad desperately, but they did require a permanent solution to their water problems. With water too expensive and too scant for profitable mining except in a few especially rich areas, most men soon left the district.

As the population of Elizabethtown dwindled, many of its businessmen also left. Henry Lambert was one of the first to go. Successfully forecasting the trends, he moved his hostelry to Cimarron, where he opened the St. James Hotel, still a landmark in the town. That same year the territorial legislature moved the county seat down the canyon to Maxwell's old headquarters. Although a few residents remained, Elizabethtown and the Baldy Mountain district were virtually deserted by 1875. Six years later, C. M. Chase, an eastern newspaper editor, described the old county seat:

> It makes one lonesome to walk the streets of Elizabethtown. Although not an old place, it is deserted and, instead of the crowded streets and knock-downs of a few years ago, a sort of tumble down appearance is everywhere observed. There is one store, part of another hotel, the tail end of a Catholic church, a barn, a good deal of glass and other fragments of former prosperity left, but the pith, the vitality of village life has departed no more to return, unless more water is brought from Red River, or some large companies are formed to begin pounding up the quartz rocks by steam.[29]

VIII
REDSKINS AND BRITISHERS

The discovery of gold in Willow Canyon in 1866 transformed the tranquil agricultural area along the Cimarron River into a bustling community of industrious miners and businessmen. Almost overnight Lucien Maxwell became extremely wealthy, began to assume airs of superiority, and started to demand absolute obedience of everyone. New settlements such as Elizabethtown and Baldy quickly outshone older villages like Rayado; new men assumed importance alongside such pioneers as Jesús Abreu and Maxwell. The influx of outsiders further worsened the situation of the Ute and Jicarilla Apache.

The individual most dramatically affected by the discovery of gold was Maxwell. In addition to profitable contracts for feeding the Indians and for sale of cattle, sheep, and grain to local settlers, he now earned additional income from his Aztec and Montezuma mines, from leases of placer claims, and from sales of supplies to goldseekers. By 1868 Maxwell's annual income amounted to nearly $50,000, and he was one of the wealthiest men in New Mexico.[1]

As Maxwell's name became known throughout the Southwest, stories of his personal eccentricities spread far and wide. One report circulated that despite the large quantities of cash which he frequently had at his Cimarron mansion, Maxwell steadfastly refused to obtain a safe. Instead, his money—frequently amounting to $30,-

ooo in gold, silver, greenbacks, and negotiable government drafts—
was kept in the bottom drawer of an old bureau, "the most anti-
quated concern of common pine imaginable." When a friend suggested that it would be wise to purchase a more secure vault, the
Cimarron landowner merely smiled and, while a "strange resolute
look flashed from his dark eyes," answered: "God help the man who
attempted to rob me and I knew him."[2]

Maxwell's reply typified the unbending, autocratic character he
assumed after the discovery of gold on his ranch. A friend described
him as "a man that nothing in the world would prevent from ac-
complishing what he undertook to do," adding that he knew of no
one who ever dared stand in Maxwell's way. Employees found him
an absolute tyrant, behaving "just as if he owned the whole outfit."
Calvin Jones, who worked for Maxwell from 1848 through the 1860s,
described his boss's treatment of workers who displeased him:

> If a Mexican servant didn't suit him or did anything against
> his orders, he took a board or plank or anything he could get
> hold of, and whipped him with it. I knew him to tie up one
> man, a Mexican, and shave off the side of his head close to the
> skin with a butcher knife, then he struck him fifteen or twenty
> lashes with a cowhide, and told him if he ever caught him on
> the place again, he would kill him. Some twelve or fifteen years
> later, he came back with a bunch of stolen horses, and Maxwell
> did kill him.

On another occasion, two men broke into Maxwell's Cimarron
store, stole $200 worth of goods and a horse, and fled south. A
posse sent after the robbers discovered one of them at Rayado trying
to peddle the loot and returned him to Cimarron. Maxwell fastened
a forty-pound chain around the prisoner's neck and locked him in his
cellar. After nearly two days without food or water, the accused was
again brought before Maxwell, who ordered him stripped and tied
to a post. Then he handed a cowhide whip to one of his men and
ordered him to give the robber twenty-five lashes. After the punish-

ment had been administered, Maxwell released the prisoner and had the whipper himself stripped and tied. "I will show you how to whip a thief," said Maxwell, and he struck the man fourteen or fifteen times until he fainted. "Now when I put you to whip a man," he admonished after the man had revived, "I want you to do it as I whipped you."[3]

On a more favorable side, Maxwell hosted almost everyone who visited his Cimarron home. Miners on their way to Elizabethtown, Taos, or Baldy; military officers coming or going from New Mexico assignments; stagecoach passengers whose trip had been delayed by broken-down equipment or high water—all were welcome to stay for as long as they wished. Maxwell did not expect payment for his services and seems to have been insulted by any offer. One morning as the stage passengers prepared to resume their journey after a night at his ranch, a well-dressed New Yorker asked the driver to point out the landlord. Directed to Maxwell, the man asked how much his breakfast cost. The wealthy landowner replied that he expected nothing, but the man insisted that he wanted no favors and would pay for what he ate. Maxwell became furious and answered, "Well then, it is $20, G—— d——— it!" The visitor looked at Maxwell in astonishment for a minute before handing him a twenty-dollar bill. Without a word, Maxwell stepped to the fireplace and threw the greenback into the blaze.[4]

Maxwell's eccentricity also manifested itself in his gambling. Nearly every night he played seven-up, poker, or some other popular card game with whoever happened to be staying at the house. If he won, Maxwell demanded payment of every last cent. But often the next morning he gave or loaned his unsuccessful opponents funds to tide them over. He also enjoyed horse racing, and in the spring of 1865 employed Squire T. Hart especially to train and care for his stable. For the next six years Hart lived at Cimarron and trained horses whenever there was the prospect of a race. At least once a week and sometimes more often, Maxwell's fleet animals were matched against the finest mounts in the territory.[5]

Trouble at the Cimarron Agency

While Lucien Maxwell grew wealthy and famous, others in the Cimarron area suffered because of the discovery of gold. Hardest hit were the very people who had generated the rush, the Ute and Jicarilla headquartered at the Maxwell Ranch.[6] In addition to the inept and disinterested management which had so long plagued their agency, an increasing population in the area brought on new problems. Military men and then church representatives took over the administration in the years that followed, but none was successful. Friction between Anglos and Indians grew. By the time Maxwell accepted an offer to buy his ranch and transferred it to an English corporation in 1870, the Indian situation had deteriorated to the point that a full-scale war seemed unavoidable. Attempts to remove the natives from fast-growing Cimarron were constantly frustrated. Until the Indians finally left, conditions remained critical.

The Indians foresaw trouble as soon as swarms of miners began to arrive in the Baldy area during the spring of 1867. The mountains of the district had long been their homes—the place where they had been born, where they sought refuge from their traditional enemies, and where their ancestors were buried. They grew uneasy seeing the mountains invaded by prospectors. The Ute were also dissatisfied because their chief Ka-ni-atche had signed a treaty agreeing to move to a new reservation in Colorado. When the headman returned to Cimarron after signing the document, his act was repudiated by the tribe, and he was dismissed from office. Thus the tribe hoped to nullify their obligation to obey the treaty. The American government refused to write off the document and told the Ute that they could collect their annuities only at the new Colorado agency. The Indians just as steadfastly refused to leave Cimarron.

In the midst of this difficult situation, lawmakers in Washington realized that a major reorganization in the Indian Bureau was necessary. Congress voted to place military officers on detached service at the head of each Indian agency. At Cimarron the change was especially timely, since the government was continuing its efforts to remove the Ute and Apache to Colorado. Many felt certain that only the army could persuade them to go. The man selected to take charge of the agency at Maxwell's was Captain Alexander S. B. Keyes.

No sooner had Keyes reached his post than he realized the enormity of the task facing him. Neglected by their agent during the height of the gold-rush, the Indians lacked clothing and blankets necessary to face the cold New Mexico winter ahead. Unless they were supplied, he was certain that it would be impossible even to consider removal to Colorado. The required goods failed to come, however, and when the 1500 Indians appeared for their annual issue late in October, Keyes had only thirty-nine blankets on hand. Officials in Washington demanded that the Indians be held to the provisions of the 1868 treaty and forbade Keyes to issue any goods until the agency moved to Colorado.

Lucien Maxwell, who had lived with the Ute and Jicarilla for nearly a quarter of a century, expected trouble and pleaded with General William Grier, the old commander at Post Rayado, for assistance. "There is now imminent danger of a general uprising against the settlements," Maxwell warned, and "unless prompt measures be taken to anticipate and prevent the outbreak, it will be sure and terrible." If a company of cavalry were sent to Cimarron, Maxwell thought that peace might be preserved and bloodshed avoided. Otherwise, an attack was certain. "I trust for the sake of humanity," he wrote, "that this warning and entreaty shall be heeded and acted upon immediately." In a rare moment of unanimity among the inhabitants of Cimarron, Keyes added his full support to Maxwell's petition.

For once the appeals from Cimarron fell on responsive ears, and Department Commander General George W. Getty ordered 100 soldiers to Maxwell's ranch. The arrival of the troops on December 16 and the acquisition of 450 more blankets quieted the Indians at least temporarily and prevented the continuation of depredations on the livestock of local residents.

Survey and Sale of the Beaubien Grant

Throughout 1869 other negotiations were being carried on which would result in the sale of the area and in the process further anger the Ute and Apache. Early in the year Jerome B. Chaffee, George M. Chilcott, and Charles F. Holly, all Colorado mining men, approached Maxwell about the purchase of his interest in the Beaubien and Miranda Grant. No doubt Maxwell realized by this time that the growing population of the region required more careful and expert management than he was capable or desirous of giving. Moreover, questions as to the validity of his title and the exact quantity of land in the grant were already being raised. They would grow louder as the area's full value was realized. If Maxwell could negotiate a cash sale while interest was high and turn over future development of the grant to others, he would be certain of lifelong financial security without managerial responsibility. Therefore, on May 26, 1869, Maxwell and his wife gave the three Coloradans an option to buy the entire grant, excluding for themselves the 1000-acre home ranch and its buildings.[7]

Maxwell meanwhile began to employ experts to aid in the sale of the property. A Santa Fe lawyer, Stephen B. Elkins, managed legal affairs. Another politician, John S. Watts, began to arrange for mapping the ranch. Maxwell deposited $5000 to pay for a survey, and on June 5, Surveyor General T. Rush Spencer contracted with William W. Griffin to do the work. When the agreement was submitted to Washington officials, however, it was disapproved on the suspicion that the proposed survey would include more than the maximum of eleven square leagues that Mexican law allowed. Thus began a dispute over the boundaries of the Beaubien and Miranda Grant which lasted for over twenty-five years and was eventually settled by the Supreme Court of the United States.[8]

As soon as he heard of the rejection, Maxwell conferred with the would-be purchasers, their attorneys, and his, and drafted a long, legalistic reply supporting his claim to full rights to the land. On the recommendation of the surveyor general, they argued, Congress had confirmed the Beaubien and Miranda Grant on June 21, 1860. Never had Maxwell suspected that the United States government, "which had pledged its faith to that of Mexico and had by solemn legislative act 'quit claimed and relinquished' all its right," would question his ownership.

As to the boundaries of the grant proposed in the survey application, they might be considered vague by Eastern bureaucrats, but considering the nature of the terrain involved, were as complete and well defined as possible. "It is absolutely impossible," Maxwell insisted, "to describe this tract with more or greater certainty except by actual survey."

Upon receipt of Maxwell's letter and other evidence as to the extent and validity of the grant, Secretary of the Interior Jacob D. Cox concluded that the boundaries describing natural features gave "no clue whatever" as to the extent of the land claimed. Therefore, the only evidence Congress could have relied upon when it confirmed the claim in 1860 was Beaubien's personal statement that he claimed only fifteen to eighteen leagues. Now, however, it appeared that Maxwell was claiming upwards of 450 leagues or over 2 million acres. To settle this and all similar matters, Cox ruled:

> that where a Mexican colonization grant is confirmed without measurement of boundaries or of district specification or quantity confirmed, in statute or in the report upon which confirmation was made, no greater quantity than eleven leagues to each claimant shall be surveyed in tracts of eleven square leagues each, the general position of such tracts to be selected by the grantee and the tract to be then surveyed as compactly as practicable.

If Maxwell wished to select twenty-two leagues (eleven each for Beaubien and Miranda) for surveying, the department would be happy to undertake the work. If not, the deposit was to be returned and the survey contract voided.

Although Secretary Cox may not have been aware of it at the time of his pronouncement, the survey which he forbade had started more than six months earlier. The work was completed late in the year, and the notes were deposited with the General Land Office in Santa Fe just as though the survey were official. When the land commissioner learned of Maxwell's apparent defiance, he ordered his subordinates henceforth to regard the entire grant as public land open to settlement under the laws of the United States.

Meanwhile, as if title to the property were clear, Chilcott, Chaffee, and Holly busily sought out purchasers for the grant. Chaffee prepared and had printed an elaborate report which described all aspects of the estate in glowing terms and assured prospective buyers that the title was "complete and perfect." The property as he described it was truly a paradise on earth: "It is accessible, it has a hospitable climate, it is in the immediate vicinity of large agricultural resources, immense beds of coal, and surrounded with never-ending quantities of timber." He assured readers that after several weeks of personal investigation in the region, he was more certain than ever of the tremendous potential of the area. With the steady development of the "Great West," the value of the grant would inevitably increase manyfold.[9]

The sales campaign thus instigated by the Colorado men paid quick dividends as a group of investors led by John Collinson of London showed an interest in the grant. Maxwell and the three promoters crossed the continent to New York to complete final arrangements for the transfer of the estate. On January 28, 1870, the Colorado trio negotiated a new option to buy the grant within six months for $1,350,000. The same day they assigned their option to the newly organized Maxwell Land Grant and Railway Company, which completed purchase of the entire grant, except for the home ranch, Maxwell's interest in the Aztec and Montezuma mines, and other property retained by Maxwell or previously sold to others.[10]

Agents and Indians: Continuing Trouble for All

While Maxwell was busy dickering over the sale of his ranch, affairs at the Cimarron agency deteriorated further. The presence of troops kept the Ute and Apache quiet, but a determined campaign was now being waged in Colorado to force the Indians to move to that territory so businessmen there could share the lucrative contracts long monopolized by Maxwell and other New Mexicans. A Denver newspaper claimed to describe the "real" situation in Cimarron:

> The rumors of war were started by Maxwell and he succeeded in getting a troop of cavalry stationed on his ground, for nothing in God's name but to sell them grain and forage. I also saw Capt. Keyes who claims to be agent for what are known as "Maxwell's Utes and a few bands of Apaches." He has goods and makes issues to them. He is young and sweet on Maxwell's daughter. The milk in the cocoa nut is satisfactorily accounted for.

Keyes did not take such a personal attack quietly and wrote the paper to demand the name of the letter writer so that he could challenge him to a duel. Complaining that he had been "shoved around enough," he also petitioned to return to the regular army where he could escape "being lied about and left to the mercy of such kind of men who grow here."

The reports published in Colorado may not have been as spurious as Keyes wanted people to believe, however, for his romance with Virginia Maxwell soon proved to be true. She had been reared according to the Mexican tradition of feminine isolation and sent to a St. Louis convent for formal education. Returning to Cimarron, she met and fell in love with the handsome, young, Protestant Indian agent. After only a short courtship they decided to marry. Virginia approached Reverend Thomas Harwood, a Methodist circuit rider and asked him to perform the ceremony. When Harwood reached Cimarron, Virginia had made all the arrangements:

No army general could have planned for a battle more wisely than she had planned for this marriage. She had made a confident of Mrs. Rinehardt, a good Methodist and the miller's wife. It was Indian ration days. There would be hundreds of Apaches at the mill to draw rations of meat and flour. "Mr. Keyes is their agent," said Miss Maxwell, "and will be there to issue rations to the Indians. Mrs. Rinehardt and I will go down to the mill at 4 p.m. You must go down a little before that and go up into the third story of the mill.

Everything went exactly as anticipated. When the clergyman reached the third story of Maxwell's mill, he found the room swept and carpeted with various kinds of robes in anticipation of the ceremony to be performed there. When the young couple appeared, Harwood married them with only Rinehardt and his wife present as witnesses.

Keyes and his bride dared not reveal their secret for fear of Maxwell's anger on hearing that his daughter had married without even consulting him. All through April the couple anxiously awaited word of the captain's requested transfer. Official orders relieving him of the Indian post and transferring him to Fort Sill, Indian Territory, were issued April 2, but delays in the arrival of his successor at the agency kept Keyes in New Mexico until May. When Keyes and his wife were safely on the stage bound east, he handed the driver a copy of their wedding certificate to be delivered to Lucien Maxwell at Cimarron.[11]

Despite recommendations that a churchman would have more success at Cimarron than a soldier, another military officer, Captain W. P. Wilson, succeeded Keyes at the agency. During his first four months in New Mexico, Wilson found his charges to be quiet. Things were so dull that he moved to Fort Union, where he could enjoy the company of other soldiers. Only when the Indians were to receive supplies did he appear in Cimarron.

By September word reached the Ute that Maxwell had sold the ranch and would soon leave. Suddenly they grew extremely restive.

The Indians argued that they had allowed their friend Maxwell to live on their land, but rather than let a British company take possession, they would "clean out the country." Maxwell Land Grant Company officials, who were already arriving at Cimarron to take charge as soon as Maxwell left, did their best to conciliate the Ute and Apache, but to little avail. Agent Wilson recommended that a company of soldiers be stationed at Cimarron during the transition period.

Rumors circulated throughout New Mexico that the Indians would provoke a war if the land were sold; there were even stories of threats on Maxwell's life. Ex-agent W. F. M. Arny heard of the trouble and rushed to Cimarron. Arny learned from the Indians that several days earlier a party of drunken Apache tried to break into Maxwell's store. One, who had indeed threatened Maxwell, accidentally shot himself. The next issue day Arny called together the Indian chiefs for a council. They not only complained to him about the sale of the grant, but also protested that their new agent lived at Fort Union instead of with them. They petitioned that Wilson be suspended and replaced by Lucien Maxwell.

Wilson had had enough of working with Indians and before he could be removed requested retirement or reassignment to active service. Maxwell had moved to his new home at Fort Sumner. When rumors circulated in Cimarron that E. B. Denison, who had held the post previously, was to be reappointed, officials of the land grant company protested. Denison drank so heavily, they complained, that he was mentally and physically unfit for duty. "For the well-being and peace" of the territory, someone else ought to be appointed. Before this protest could reach its destination, Denison received the appointment. His tenure was extremely short, however, for only five days later President U. S. Grant ordered him removed. Charles F. Roedel, a nominee of the Presbyterian church, was to take charge. Typically, countless delays prevented the new agent from arriving until mid-December.

Deterioration of the Cimarron Agency

When Agent Roedel arrived in New Mexico, he found the condition of the Indians shocking. Many had only worn-out cotton shirts and poor Mexican-style blankets to shield them from the harsh winter air. The contract for provisions to feed them was scheduled to expire on the first of the year, and nothing had yet been done by the government to renew it. Snow covered the ground by late February. Roedel ran out of shirts and pants of his own to distribute. Still his pleas for help went unheeded.

The anticipated trouble came in March when San Francisco, an Apache who was considered the tribe's lawyer, was shot to death near the Maxwell company store at Cimarron. As soon as Roedel learned of the incident, he rode three-quarters of a mile until he found the spot where the Indian had died. By the time Roedel returned to town, word of the shooting had spread through the Apache camps. A party of angry young Indians waited to see him. They threatened vengeance on the clerk who had shot their friend and demanded that the store be opened and the murderer surrendered. "We put on a bold, determined front," Roedel reported, "flatly refused their every demand & told them that whenever their chiefs arrived, we would talk with them."

While the leaders of the tribe gathered, Roedel took steps to prevent an outbreak. He telegraphed to Fort Union for troops and begged Lucien Maxwell to come up from Rayado, where he was visiting the Abreu family, to meet with the chiefs. Maxwell had not yet arrived when the chiefs reached Cimarron the following afternoon, but since they seemed willing to arrange a peaceful settlement without him, the meeting went on. Company officials agreed to give the Indians two ponies, $70 worth of goods, and $30 in cash. The Indians accepted the offer and returned to their mountain camps peacefully.

Roedel next proposed several changes in agency policy which he hoped would prevent a recurrence of the incident. A new jail would soon be completed in Cimarron. Any Indians found drunk or roaming around town after dark would be imprisoned. In addition, he realized that many of the food complaints resulted from mixing bran with the wheat distributed to the Ute and Apache. They removed the bran before using it, thus losing about a third of their rations. Roedel suggested that the bran simply be omitted. The seriousness of this seemingly minor problem was demonstrated only a few days later when the Indians refused to accept the meal offered them. Too little was left, they claimed, after the bran had been sifted out. Only when the English company that owned the former Maxwell land agreed to exchange the objectionable meal for a poor quality of flour called shorts did the Indians take the food and leave.

Removal of the Cimarron Agency

The temporary pacification of the Cimarron Indians failed to solve the long-range problems of the area. The growing population of Colfax County made it imperative that definite steps be taken to remove the natives from the land claimed by the Maxwell Land Grant Company. Just as in Taos a decade earlier, liquor was so readily available that every time food was issued dozens of "fearfully intoxicated" Indians roamed through Cimarron. Little game could be found in the nearby mountains, and many braves spent their entire time hanging around the agent's house "picking up rapidly the vices and carefully shunning the virtues of the settlers." The only real solution to these problems was the removal of the agency to a less settled country; yet it seemed impossible to persuade the Indians to make such a move. Part of the reason for the government's inability to develop a constructive program for the peaceful removal of the Indians from the Philmont area resulted from the rapid turnover of Indian agents. In less than a year five men held the position.

More important than any action taken at Cimarron by this series of agents were events that took place in Colorado and in Washington that summer. Early in August, Agent Thomas Dolan left Cimarron with the major Ute chiefs and traveled into the San Juan River country of southwestern Colorado. There a meeting of several Ute bands with special commissioners from Washington was held and a treaty negotiated which provided for the settlement of the Indians in Colorado. They seemed pleased with the treaty, especially after their principal chiefs accompanied Dolan on a trip to visit the President and other United States officials in Washington, D.C.

But just as these positive reports accumulated, everything seemed to collapse. First the United States Congress refused to ratify the treaty, apparently because they thought that precious minerals might be located on the land set aside for Indian reservations. Second, Agent Dolan, who had done a superior job with the Indians, visited Santa Fe to provide testimony against men in Cimarron who had sold liquor to his charges. In the capital he "became intoxicated, indulged in gambling," and bartered away several government certificates which belonged to the Indians. Dolan resigned and apparently departed the territory by the first available stage.

The agency quickly returned to its typically perilous condition. William White took temporary charge but was soon replaced by Dr. Robert Longwill, now titled "Farmer in Charge," a somewhat ironic term because the Ute and Apache owned no land on which they could farm. Sales of liquor grew so common that drunken tribesmen constantly roamed the streets of Cimarron. A grand jury indicted Maurice Traner, who had charge of the agency for a time, for illegal sale of alcohol, only to have him acquitted by a local jury. The superintendent agreed to appoint a private detective, but apparently little could be done to alleviate the problem.

The growing antagonism between the Indians, government agents, and citizens of the area now part of Philmont finally flared into violence in 1875. Longwill's successor, the conscientious Alexander G. Irvine, was distributing the weekly dole of food to the Indians when a band of drunken Apache started a fray. The immediate cause was their refusal to accept meat they said was spoiled.

Shots suddenly rang out. All the agency employees plus several onlookers retreated inside the old Maxwell mill. About a dozen Apache began firing at them through the windows of the mill; Irvine, who had been shot in the hand, returned their fire, injuring several.

As soon as the angry natives departed for the mountains, Irvine rushed to the telegraph office and wired Fort Union for help. Lieutenant J. Lafferty of the Eighth Cavalry arrived the next day with fifteen men. In the Indian camp he found the Apache "all armed & ready for the war path." They agreed to a conference the next day and gathered on the Cimarron town plaza to meet Irvine. He demanded that three guilty Apache—Juan Julian, Juan Barilla, and Chico—be turned over to him for trial. Until they were, no further rations would be issued. The Indians refused, although Barilla was soon arrested and lodged in the Cimarron jail.

Hopes that the crisis had ended were dashed by events on November 23. When a jailer entered Barilla's cell that morning, he was threatened by Barilla with a rock and knife. Soldiers summoned to disarm the prisoner cautiously entered the cell. Suddenly Barilla burst forward grabbing for their carbines; and in the scuffle that followed, during which several shots were fired, the Indian fell dead. The tribe demanded retribution for the death of their comrade. Irvine warned his superiors that hostilities could be expected at any time.

Since the Indian Bureau obviously had lost control of the situation at Cimarron, Irvine asked for immediate release from his responsibilities and requested the army to take over the agency. The plan was adopted. More soldiers rapidly moved into the area from Fort Union. The army also sent General Nelson A. Miles, one of the best known Indian fighters in the West. He hurried from Kansas via train and stage to Cimarron in hope of averting a serious war.

Miles's report, drafted after lengthy conferences with both Indians and whites, was extremely sympathetic to the Ute and Apache. The government had frequently failed to provide them the annuity goods promised in treaties. The food issued had been "inadequate in quantity and quality to sustain human life." Contractors expected them to live on the meat of "old, worn-out oxen" used for carrying goods across the plains. The bran they got was practically inedible. No people could be expected to accept starvation quietly, Miles argued, suggesting that only desperation brought on hostilities. Miles appointed an army officer to run the agency and went away satisfied that the Indians would remain at peace. "It was gratifying to avoid an Indian war by acts of justice and humanity rather than to end it by the use of force," the general concluded.[12]

The wounding of Agent Irvine and the death of Juan Barilla had the positive result of speeding up the closing of the Cimarron Indian agency. After almost a decade of inactivity, the government finally initiated plans to find new homes for the Ute and Jicarilla tribes. The Ute moved to a reservation along the Rio de los Piños in southern Colorado, where they still live. At first the Jicarilla resided with the Mescalero Apache near Fort Stanton in south central New Mexico. Years later the government established a new Jicarilla reserve adjoining that of the Ute in the northwestern part of the territory. There they remain today, raising livestock and carrying on extensive lumbering. Officially the Cimarron agency closed in September 1876, although a few Indians may have remained in the area for several years.[13]

No aspect of the history of the Philmont county is more dismal than the United States's handling of the Ute and Apache. Pushed out of their traditional homeland by farmers, ranchers, and miners, the Indians were unable to feed themselves. The government seldom provided adequate food or supplies. Well-meaning but inept agents, as well as corrupt and self-seeking agents, did little to alleviate the suffering. Frequently the army prevented Indians from stealing or killing, but soldiers did little to solve long-term problems. Only the final removal of the tribesmen brought peace and opened the area to more development. No sooner had the Indian troubles ended, however, than new battles were under way between the settlers and the foreign owners of the Maxwell Land Grant.

IX

THE COLFAX COUNTY WAR

Violence, a common characteristic of the American frontier, haunted the mountains and plains which today comprise Philmont. First, one tribe of Indians attacked another to steal, to plunder, to kill. Then Spaniards and Americans sent troops into the area, continuing the bloodshed for several centuries. But the worst fighting, the most gruesome killings, occurred during the last third of the nineteenth century in the notorious Colfax County War. For fifteen years after 1875, settlers on the old Beaubien and Miranda Grant fought the English and Dutch companies which claimed to own a vast section of northeastern New Mexico. Only a decision by the Supreme Court of the United States stopped the shooting.

The essential questions revolved around how much land the Mexican government had granted to Beaubien and Miranda in 1841. Confusing evidence, contradictory government decisions, and evidence of graft clouded the controversy, making it virtually impossible for anyone to determine the real facts of the case. Passions gained supremacy over reason, enlarging the controversy beyond courts and lawyers. The mysterious death of a Cimarron clergyman initiated a series of murders and lynchings which put Colfax County on the front pages of newspapers all over the nation. No one in the area dared be impartial, and few were so foolhardy as to travel unarmed. Today, almost a century later, the hate and distrust generated by more than a decade of bitter feuding still linger in the quiet towns and remote ranches of the region around Philmont.

The Death of Parson Tolby

Even though Secretary of the Interior Jacob Cox had limited the Beaubien and Miranda Land Grant to twenty-two square leagues, or less than 100,000 acres, the English company which bought the land from Maxwell continued to claim a much larger tract. The area surveyed by William W. Griffin in 1870 stretched from south of Philmont north beyond the Colorado boundary. It included a broad swath from just east of Taos far out onto the plains. The exact quantity was unknown, but observers estimated that it exceeded 2 million acres. Anyone who wished to settle in the area had to negotiate with the land grant company. Trouble seemed inevitable when the government's General Land Office extended its public land surveys over much of the same territory, declared it open for settlement, and began to issue deeds to homesteaders and ranchers.[1]

Many residents of the area complained about the arbitrary and apparently illegal acts of the company. Among the first were the miners. They heard of the property's transfer early in September 1870, and called a meeting for the third of the month. There the residents of the Baldy district "coolly and dispassionately" decided what to do. They claimed that their rights to the land where they had established themselves were greater than those of either the company or the Indians. Only if the new owners could show a valid United States government patent to the land and a survey specifically delineating the boundaries (which of course they could not) would they even agree to negotiate.

Peaceful meetings rapidly gave way to violence. On the night of October 27, 1870, a riot broke out in Elizabethtown when the miners became infuriated over the company's attempts to throw them off their claims. After the home of Justice of the Peace McBride burned, Stephen B. Elkins joined with McBride in appealing for help from

Santa Fe. Governor William A. Pile was out of the territory, but word of the trouble reached the district military headquarters, and troops were ordered to the Moreno Valley. Immediately a lieutenant and twenty-one men hurried up the Cimarron Canyon to take care of matters. Meanwhile Henry Wetter, the acting governor, issued a proclamation "authorizing and requiring" the civil officials of the county to organize posses, arrest lawbreakers, "maintain peace, and protect the lives and property of citizens."

These efforts were only temporarily successful, for new riots broke out in the spring. This time they were along Ute Creek in the area now part of Philmont. At a meeting called on January 2 the miners refused to recognize the company's right to collect rent on their placer claims. When a band of Maxwell company employees marched into the placers and began to work them in mid-April, the miners organized to expel them. "Unlawfully and violently combined together," the men disarmed the invaders and held them as hostages. This time Governor William A. Pile himself rushed north from Santa Fe and immediately ordered the miners to dissolve their organization, free the prisoners, and abstain from future violence. Anyone who was dissatisfied, Pile insisted, should submit his claims to the courts. To make sure that these admonitions were obeyed, Pile saw to it that Major D. H. Clendenin and soldiers from Fort Union were stationed in the area. The troops were authorized to aid the civil authorities in "sustaining the laws," although Clendenin was warned to avoid direct support for either of the disputing parties.

Farmers and ranchers on the eastern side of the mountains were also organizing their forces. In Cimarron their principal vehicle was a "squatters club" organized early in 1871. At a meeting on March 31 the group decided to employ an attorney and begin a law suit to test the validity of the Maxwell company's claim. A week later the club staged a mass meeting in front of the county courthouse to collect funds and demonstrate their strength.[2]

Antigrant agitation apparently quieted down until 1875 when a series of events combined and brought tensions to the exploding point. The central figure this time was the Reverend F. J. Tolby, a Methodist minister, who had apparently denounced the Maxwell Land Grant and Railway Company from the pulpit and otherwise made it known that he had no use for the English proprietors.

In September 1875, Tolby left Cimarron for Elizabethtown, where he also served as pastor. On the return trip, someone attacked and murdered him while he was riding through the Cimarron Canyon west of present Philmont. Robbery could not have been the motive, for his horse and personal effects had not been stolen. Why, then, had Tolby been killed? Reverend Thomas Harwood, the head of Methodist missions in New Mexico, suspected that the murder resulted from Tolby's having recently witnessed a shooting in Cimarron. As the only witness, his testimony in court might well have convicted the culprit.[3] Others who learned of the death concluded that perhaps the English company had hired someone to silence one of their most vocal and influential critics.

No sooner had Tolby's body been found than another Cimarron minister, Reverend Oscar P. McMains, began a personal crusade to track down his friend's murderer. Quickly convinced that the land grant company was at fault, McMains devoted the next two decades to opposing the foreign corporation's claim to the vast tract of land. His speeches and writings inflamed the passions of partisans on both sides; frequent trips to Washington and letter-writing campaigns to politicians convinced the United States government of the need to investigate and challenge the rights of the company. Frequently McMains led the settlers in direct defiance of land grant officials. He was, as one historian has put it, "champion of a lost cause."[4]

McMains was certain that the one man who could identify Tolby's murderer was Cruz Vega, a Spanish-American who had carried the mail from Elizabethtown to Cimarron the day of the murder. In a carefully arranged plot, a farmer living along Ponil Creek hired Vega to watch his corn; that way he would be available for the interrogation. One Saturday evening, while Vega dozed beside a fire, five men including McMains rode up. One took a rope from his saddle and threw it around Vega's neck. What followed was in the worst tradition of the Ku-Klux Klan. They dragged the frightened victim to a nearby telegraph pole, threw the rope over a wire, and began to pull him off the ground. Several times they let him down to ask more questions about the death of Tolby, only to raise him further the next time. Evidence on the body indicated that other even more extreme methods of torture had also been used. When the men finally had the information they wanted, they went away, leaving the body hanging several feet off the ground.

The brutality had not ended, for in the process of torturing Vega, McMains and his men had obtained evidence that a man named Cárdenas was responsible for Tolby's death. He was arrested in Cimarron and taken before the justice of the peace. During the hearing he confessed to the murder. But no trial was ever held, for while he was being transferred from the hearing room to the jail, a number of armed men attacked and killed him.

Not even the death of Cárdenas ended the furor over Tolby's murder, for soon McMains and the antigranters began to accuse almost anyone who supported the land grant company of complicity in the crime. Among those against whom charges were hurled were Dr. R. H. Longwill, the sometime Indian agent who now served as probate judge, and M. W. Mills, an E-town lawyer. Courts in Cimarron, Taos, or Santa Fe eventually cleared all these men of the crime, but they fled the area in fear for their lives.

By late in November, Tolby's death and the resulting bloodshed had created a "complete state of anarchy" in Cimarron. When Judge Longwill arrived at Santa Fe, he immediately contacted the civil and military officials of the territory and persuaded them to send twenty soldiers to Cimarron. "It is hoped that the deplorable spirit of lawlessness so rampant in Colfax County for the past few days will now quiet down," editorialized the Santa Fe New Mexican, adding that "lynch law never was good law."[5]

Apparently such admonitions had little effect for lawlessness returned to Cimarron early in 1876. This time the immediate cause of violence was control of the only newspaper in the area. Soon after the English company purchased the Maxwell Grant, it established a weekly paper, *The Cimarron News*, primarily for the purpose of promoting land sales and advertising the wealth on its property. Two men edited the weekly: Frank Springer, a young Iowa lawyer who subsequently played a major role in the history of the grant, and William R. Morley, a railroad engineer appointed as executive officer of the British-owned corporation. Increasing demands on their time persuaded Springer and Morley to approach Will Dawson, editor of the Elizabethtown *Railway, Press, and Telegraph* and propose a merger. A one-year contract signed late in 1874 provided for the creation of the *Cimarron News and Press*. Dawson would handle the printing end of the business, while Morley and Springer managed the editorial department. Dawson could contribute articles provided they "should not conflict with the general tenor of the paper." On land grant questions the paper would be "strictly neutral, publishing facts on either side but not advocating either side in editorials."

Soon a bitter conflict raged in the paper's editorial offices. Morley naturally supported the company and condemned the squatters' violence and disorder. Meanwhile, McMains hired Springer as his lawyer, so despite his association with the grant company, the young Iowan may have been at least moderately sympathetic to the preacher and his supporters. Dawson probably took a stand which became increasingly sympathetic toward the antigrant forces. As the initial contract neared expiration, the question naturally arose as to the future of the paper. The answer seemed clear when the first issue in 1876 announced an editorial change. Because of disagreements "political and otherwise," Morley and Springer would retire; henceforth Dawson would have full control. He promised to be "independent in politics and religion, looking to the best and permanent interests of the whole people, regardless of rings, cliques, sects, companies, or parties."

Apparently not everyone agreed with the new editor's "independent" principles. One night late in January 1876, a mob entered the office of the *Cimarron News and Press* and destroyed its equipment. According to legend, the press and the type were thrown into the Cimarron River where a local boy discovered them many years later. Exactly who was responsible for the attack is unknown. Several months passed before the paper reappeared. Dawson, who by then had lost two newspaper offices to mobs, departed for a more friendly environment; and Frank Springer, who was still defending McMains in court, resumed the editorial chair.[6]

Meanwhile other steps were being taken to assure that those responsible for violence would be brought to justice. Territorial officials doubted that a fair trial could be held in Cimarron, so they introduced a bill into the legislature which combined Colfax and Taos counties for judicial purposes. Thus criminals could be indicted and tried amid cooler conditions. Despite the protests of many area residents, the bill passed and was signed by the governor. One of the first cases involved Parson McMains, whom a Taos grand jury indicted for the murder of Cruz Vega. Because of numerous delays, however, it was 1877 before the case finally came to trial in Mora, the sleepy little Spanish-American town south of present Philmont. Witnesses described in detail the "interrogation" of Vega, but no one could pin the killing directly on McMains. A jury, after having heard the evidence, found him guilty in the "fifth degree" and assessed a fine of $300. The judge set aside even this decision on a technicality, however; and although a retrial should have been scheduled, none ever occurred.[7] To this day the murders of Tolby, Vega, and Cárdenas are legally unsolved.

Indecision in Washington: The Land Office and the Maxwell Grant Case

Even though McMains and his supporters met with little success in their attempts to expel the English company from the area, government officials in Washington generally supported their antigrant contentions—at least for a time. In 1871 attorneys for the Englishmen requested Secretary of the Interior C. Delano to order an official government survey of the Beaubien and Miranda Grant. The only basis for it would be the geographical descriptions contained in the original Mexican documents. Perhaps Delano was more astute than expected, for he researched the files in the land office and found the earlier ruling by Secretary Cox which limited the grant to twenty-two square leagues. He absolutely refused to reconsider the case. "If I can review and reverse any action, my successor, if he should differ with me and agree with my predecessor, could review and reverse my action," he wrote. Theoretically such reversals could continue indefinitely, "and there would be no end to controversy."[8] Thus it seemed that the case was closed permanently.

The controversy was not solved so easily, however, for during its October 1876 term, the Supreme Court heard the case of *John Tameling versus the United States Freehold and Immigration Company*, which in many ways paralleled the Maxwell Grant situation. It involved the Sangre de Cristo or Trinchera Grant originally given by Governor Manuel Armijo to Beaubien's son Narciso and Sheriff Stephen L. Lee of Taos. Tameling claimed ownership of a 160-acre homestead on what the freehold company said was a part of their land grant. Like McMains, Tameling argued that according to Mexican law a land grant was limited to eleven square leagues per grantee. Acreage in excess of that was open to settlement as public domain. The court disagreed and decided in favor of the land company. A Mexican grant which had been confirmed by Congress, they ruled, was not limited to any particular size but ought to be surveyed and patented according to the geographical descriptions in the Mexican documents.

Apparently after conferring with Land Commissioner J. A. Williamson and other Washington officials, the Maxwell Grant Company reinitiated its plea that the government survey their land and issue them a patent. Within a few weeks the New Mexico surveyor general contracted with William W. Griffin (who had previously undertaken a private survey of the region) and C. Fitch to complete the work and forwarded the agreement to Washington for approval. Williamson disapproved the contract, but for reasons entirely different from those of his predecessors. Since there were major variations between the boundary descriptions in Beaubien and Miranda's original request and the document by which Cornelio Vigil gave them possession of the grant, Williamson ruled that only the original request was to be considered. He also thought that Griffin and Fitch might not be wholly objective and ordered the surveyor general to find a surveyor who "had no connection or business transaction" with the owners of the grant to assure that he would be "free from any bias or undue influence in the lawful execution of the survey." No mention was made either of the twenty-two league limitation previously placed on the grant or of the earlier decision by Secretary Cox.

More peculiar in light of Williamson's concern with impartiality were Marmon and Elkins, whom he allowed to do the surveying. John Marmon, for example, had very little experience with transit and line; and John Elkins was the brother of Stephen B. Elkins, long associated with the land grant owners. Williamson apparently ignored these facts and approved the contract. In just over three weeks the two surveyors completed their work and filed their notes with the surveyor general's office in Santa Fe. The government issued a patent giving the foreigners full title to the 1,714,764.94-acre Beaubien and Miranda Grant.[9]

Other activities in New Mexico further diminished the hopes of the antigrant people. Poor management, inadequate capitalization, and local antagonism had seriously jeopardized the financial standing of the Maxwell Land Grant and Railway Company ever since its founding. As a result by the mid-1870s it faced bankruptcy, unable to pay either its outstanding debts or local taxes. Its employees went unpaid. A local Cimarron court ordered the property sold for back taxes, and an auction took place on the steps of the Cimarron courthouse late in 1877. A series of extremely complicated legal and financial transactions eventually resulted in the reorganization of the company by a group of Dutch who owned most of the old English corporation's outstanding bonds. By the early 1880s, a new Maxwell Land Grant Company chartered in Holland gained control of the land. They immediately began to evict squatters and initiated a program for the economic development of the region.[10]

The Supreme Court Decision

McMains, who was no more intimidated by the Dutch than by the English claimants, continued his fight against the new company. The election of President Garfield and the resulting change in officials at the Department of the Interior and General Land Office persuaded McMains to try once more to have the Beaubien and Miranda Grant declared invalid and its patent revoked. Early in 1881 he petitioned Secretary of the Interior S. J. Kirkwood to investigate the case. An examination of the documents convinced the secretary that the patent had been incorrectly issued and a large tract of public land deeded to the company. He therefore requested the attorney general of the United States to initiate a court suit for its cancellation. Because of the precedent-setting Tameling decision, he no longer argued that the tract be limited to twenty-two leagues. Instead Kirkwood's major objection was that the survey completed by Marmon and Elkins included a great deal more territory than had been described in Beaubien and Miranda's original petition or shown on the accompanying map. No one doubted the proper inclusion of the southern part of the grant (the section of which Philmont is a part), but they questioned whether Beaubien and Miranda had received any land whatever in Colorado. As a result the government filed its principal suit in the Eighth Circuit Court of that state in August 1882.

No clear-out conclusions can be reached from the voluminous, but frequently contradictory, evidence. The preponderance of factual data seem to suggest that the size of the land grant had been expanded considerably from the time Armijo granted it to Beaubien and Miranda until its sale to the English company. The original descriptions were too vague and unclear to establish any definite boundary line, but historically Maxwell and Beaubien had emphasized the southern portion of their claim. The first settlers lived along the Vermejo, Cimarron, Ponil, and Rayado creeks, and paid no major attention to the area further north. Moreover, Maxwell had neglected the Moreno Valley until the discovery of gold there, which suggests that it might not initially have been included. Probably the "main mountains" which formed the western boundary were originally the peaks along the western edge of Philmont, not the higher range centered at Wheeler Peak further west.

The government had not, however, proved its original charges that Marmon and Elkins knowingly surveyed a fraudulent boundary; convincing a court to rescind the patent would therefore be exceedingly difficult.[11] The trial held before the circuit judge in Denver was inconclusive, and the Supreme Court agreed to hear the United States Versus the Maxwell Land Grant Company on March 8-11, 1887. The decision which the court issued on April 18, 1887, fully confirmed the rights of the Maxwell Land Grant Company to its huge tract of land in northeastern New Mexico and southeastern Colorado. The decision dealt specifically with three questions: first, did the colonization laws of Mexico limiting grants to eleven leagues apply to this grant despite its confirmation by Congress? The court simply reaffirmed the Tameling decision: congressional action was final and could not be reversed or even considered by the court. Second, was there sufficient evidence of inaccuracy in the Marmon and Elkins survey to justify canceling the patent? Again the answer was no, pointing out that the General Land Office and not the Supreme Court was charged with carrying out surveys. Since the commissioner had approved the work, his correctness on matters of detail and technique should be assumed. Third, was there adequate proof of fraud either in the survey or in the land office to invalidate the patent? Again it was reasoned that despite accusations by the squatters and the government, no one had presented conclusive evidence of corruption. In response to a subsequent request for rehearing, the decision concluded: "We are entirely satisfied that the grant, as confirmed by Congress, is a valid grant; [and] that the survey and patent issued upon it are entirely free from any fraud on the part of the grantees or those claiming under them."[12] Thus the Dutch company received title to nearly two million acres, even though what is now Philmont probably includes the vast bulk of land originally granted Beaubien and Miranda by the Mexican government.

Final Efforts of Parson McMains

Disheartening though the Supreme Court decision must have been to the squatters in northeastern New Mexico, it did not suddenly end the Colfax County War or wholly dampen the spirits of anti-grant leaders. As a result, Parson McMains continued to call meetings and issue statements.[13] Ignoring the decision of the nation's highest court, he denounced the Maxwell company and pledged to continue defying its demands that the settlers sell or leave. "Only contemptible cowards would tamely submit to be kicked off from public land as trespassers by an official gang of public land thieves," he exhorted in a typical harangue. More and more frequently he suggested that if legal means failed to secure the settlers' lands, it might be necessary to use violence against the foreign company. Once more, rumors circulated throughout the area that a civil war was in the offing.

The final hope of the settlers lay with the President of the United States. Many had heard that the new chief executive, Grover Cleveland, a Democrat, sympathized more with the common man than had his Republican predecessors. Perhaps he would intervene. But before McMains could appeal to the President, M. P. Pels, who headed the Maxwell Land Grant Company, wrote to Cleveland, described the violence which threatened to engulf the region, and asked him to notify the "ignorant and ill-advised" settlers that the Supreme Court decision was final. McMains was shocked when

Cleveland did exactly as requested. "The judgement of the supreme court of the United States on the subjects involved therein is au-thorat[at]ive and conclusive," he wrote. "Its judgement must be respected and obeyed." At first McMains argued that the letter was a forgery, but as evidence of its authenticity accumulated, he and his people had to admit defeat.

Many of the squatters soon began to abandon their strong anti-grant stand. Especially in the southern, uncontested, portion of the grant, near present-day Philmont, most setters either negotiated with the Dutch to buy their property or sold their improvements and left. The company tried to deal fairly where possible, but if a settler proved stubborn, it was ready to use the full force of the law to evict him. Sometimes these actions were successful; often they brought an equally determined reaction from the squatters. Several company officials received orders to leave the territory or take the conse-quences. Threatening mobs followed other grant company sup-porters, and unknown assailants shot at a few Dutch sympathizers. The most violent incidents occurred in the Stonewall area of ex-treme southern Colorado, where several men on both sides were killed or wounded. Further south, settlers living in the Vermejo Creek region put up a determined fight before finally giving in to the Dutch.

In an attempt to force the settlers who lived along Ponil Creek to negotiate the purchase of their farms or leave, the Maxwell Grant Company employed Deputy Sheriff George W. Cook to serve court injunctions on the residents of the area. He had completed most of the work and was returning down the North Ponil Canyon near where Philmont's Old Camp is today. Suddenly he saw a flash and felt the pain of a bullet entering his hip. More shots rang out before he was able to spur his horse out of what is now Cook Canyon and escape.

The man suspected of the attack was Julio Martínez, a Navajo, who apparently operated a small ranch along the North Ponil. Cook had arrested him a few days earlier for possession of stolen beef. This, he reasoned, was an attempt at revenge. Several days after the shooting, Cook had recovered enough to accompany Zebulon V. Russell, another deputy, to the area to arrest Martínez. Exactly what happened is unclear. According to the deputies, they were forced to shoot when the Indian ran to his cabin for a gun. Others insisted the lawmen massacred Martínez from behind an adobe oven.

Slowly, almost imperceptibly, open opposition to the Maxwell Land Grant Company declined. Parson McMains, unsuccessful in his efforts at Stonewall, moved to Colorado, where he lived in obscurity. His death was noted only by the recollection that he had been a pioneer clergyman in New Mexico. Other protestors began to accept the inevitability of Dutch control and bought their land. As violence diminished, men stopped carrying guns, and wives worried less about their husbands' returning home. As peace returned, it was possible to continue economic development. Soon great herds of cattle were growing fat on the rich grasses, huge trees were being cut into lumber or railroad ties, and once again the rich gravel and rock of the Baldy area produced gold and made men wealthy.

In addition to the organized violence of the Colfax County War, the region had its share of outlaws, but local myths have so exaggerated their deeds that it is difficult to separate fact from fiction. Charlie Kennedy supposedly invited visitors to his Moreno Valley cabin, robbed and murdered them, burying the bodies in his cellar; strangely, no contemporary newspaper reported the story. Clay Allison, a local cowboy, shot up bars and reportedly helped dump the newspaper's printing press into the Cimarron River. Long after most other bad men were dead, "Black Jack" Ketchum was still robbing trains in northern New Mexico. After a chase up Turkey Creek Canyon, he and some of his gang were supposedly captured near what is now called Black Jack's Hideout. Colorful though these men and others may be, they contributed little to the history of the area and are thus of much less significance than the cattle-raisers, railroad builders, or miners of the region.

X

COWBOYS AND CATTLEMEN

Even before squabbles over ownership of the Maxwell Land Grant ended, the grassy plains and high mountain meadows which would someday become Philmont supported an important livestock industry. Hundreds of thousands of cattle fattened on the rich grass of a dozen or more major ranches. Cowboys by the hundred rounded up stock each year for branding, cared for them during droughts and blizzards, and mended the many miles of fence. Several of the larger operators became wealthy. "The profits of stock raising in this western country are so great," a visiting journalist wrote from Cimarron in 1881, "that should I tell the exact truth, it might be taken as an exaggeration." Fifteen years later a Santa Fe newspaper labeled Colfax County as "the banner grazing country in the big Southwest."[1] Many early ranches still survive, some of them raising cattle much as they did almost a century ago.

Despite individual differences, most Colfax County ranches had certain similarities. Each cattleman, for example, wanted some of his property to be located along the edge of the Sangre de Cristos where stock could be grazed during the cold winter months. Here, too, usually beside a stream, were the headquarter buildings, often surrounded by orchards and gardens. It was also desirable to own mountain land, for the lush, green meadows and valleys of the backcountry provided the best summer pasture. Once each spring and again in the fall, drives were held to move the cattle from one area to the other. Scattered throughout each ranch were camps where cowboys lived while watching the herds. Today many of these, especially in the high mountains, are the sites of Philmont camps.

Ranchers also shared certain common enemies, among the worst of which were the wolves which frequently attacked their herds. As early as the 1850s soldiers from Post Rayado pursued packs of 200 or more. Forty years later they were still such a threat that cattlemen organized hunts to scour the foothills around Philmont.[2]

Weather conditions were as potentially dangerous to a herd of cattle as wolves. Sometimes, as in 1880, light winter snows combined with poor spring rains to retard the growth of grass in the mountains. Ranchers who had nothing in reserve to feed their stock faced the alternatives of selling off at a loss or watching their animals starve. At other times, winter blizzards isolated cattle and kept them from reaching food. When several feet of snow covered the Moreno Valley and the area along the edge of the mountains in 1891, for example, ranchers reported "famished animals standing, huddled together, hemmed in by mountains of snow." Unless warm weather came soon, hundreds would die. During most years, however, conditions were good. "The grass on the range is in excellent condition," a Santa Fe reporter wrote from Colfax County in 1896; the cattle looked "round and sleek."[3]

Even ideal weather conditions failed to lessen the threat that range criminals frequently posed to pioneer cattlemen. Unfenced pastures made rustling especially common. News in 1882 that "cattle thieves are operating in Colfax County" probably surprised no one. Apprehending the guilty parties was difficult, but as a man named Marion Hillsworth discovered in 1897, not everyone escaped. He stole a number of Maxwell Land Grant cattle and drove them to North Ponil Canyon where their brands could be changed. The work was still incomplete when two deputy sheriffs arrived, identified the true owners of the animals, and arrested Hillsworth. Fence cutting, another crime common to stock-raising areas, also occurred. In 1885, soon after fencing became common, someone cut a ninety-mile stretch of wire running east from the Ponil country. Many ranchers were furious. M. M. Chase threatened to put armed men out to protect his fences "at all hazzards, even if good red blood must flow."[4]

Several major ranches and a number of smaller ones operated in the area now comprising Philmont. Oldest was the Rayado, owned and run for many years by the Abreu family. The central portion of Philmont was once the Urraca Ranch, while to the north M. M. Chase and H. M. Porter controlled large spreads. A brief history of each will demonstrate more fully the similarities and differences among large New Mexico ranches.

The Abreus of Rayado

The departure of Lucien Maxwell from the Rayado did not mean the total abandonment of Philmont's pioneer settlement. At first the ranch was apparently operated by the Spaniard José Pley, a friend of Beaubien. When Pley divorced his wife, sold his property, and returned to Europe, his interest in the Rayado Ranch was transferred to Jesús G. Abreu, a son-in-law of Beaubien, who spent the rest of his life in the area.

Although smaller than Maxwell's, Abreu's ranch impressed visitors such as Mrs. Eveline Alexander who saw it in 1866. The settlement beside the Rayado reminded her of the days when European lords controlled huge estates with hundreds of serfs. Maxwell's original adobe home with its high protective walls broken by a single entrance still dominated the scene, but by then grass and trees grew inside the courtyard. Many smaller huts for ranch employees surrounded the main compound. So many women and children scurried about that Mrs. Alexander's husband thought a thousand Mexicans might live at Rayado. His estimate was of course extremely exaggerated, but there were a growing number of families working for Abreu on shares. He provided the livestock and equipment as well as the land; the farmers contributed their labor in exchange for half the produce.[5] Rayado had become a prosperous, stable community, contrasting boldly with its tenuous status a decade and a half earlier.

Abreu's enterprises at the ranch included a store just south of the main house which provided groceries and other supplies to the local farmers and travelers and which also became a restaurant for passengers along the stage route to Santa Fe. Jesús's son Narciso recalled that when a coach topped the last hill and dropped down into the Rayado Valley, the driver signaled with a bugle to indicate the number of meals required. Everyone then rushed to set tables and warm food so that an appetizing meal could be ready when the passengers arrived. One visitor, who reached Rayado before the stage was due, complained that he could get nothing to eat until it finally pulled in many hours later.[6] Sheep and cattle also grazed the ranch in large numbers, although livestock raising was less important at Rayado than on other ranches in the area.

As the years passed Abreu took advantage of plentiful supplies of water to expand the amount of land under irrigation. By 1860 hay and alfalfa were being produced on 150 acres. Twenty years later Jesús employed a "first class market gardener" and planned to put in apple and cherry orchards, vineyards, gardens, and greenhouse.

The Abreus discovered that the scenic beauty and excellent fishing of the Rayado Creek appealed to many local residents. By the early 1890s, weekend visits to the area were common. One Springer group returned home describing "the splendid time" they had and the many trout they caught. Their experience was typical. As one editor asked, "Who ever went fishing on the Rayado that didn't catch a 'heap' of fish?" Two of the Abreu sons—Charles and Jesús, Jr.,—decided to develop the stream's recreational potential. An agreement with the Maxwell Land Grant Company gave them control of the river all the way to its headwaters far back into the mountains of what is now Philmont. The pair planned to stock 100,000 trout, build ponds, and clear out underbrush along the river to further encourage angling.

The death of Jesús Abreu early in July 1900 marked the passing of one of the best-known early settlers in northeastern New Mexico. It also initiated a series of changes at Rayado. The old adobe fortress which had served as the family residence for over forty years badly needed modernization. Soon a peaked, American-style roof topped by new red brick chimneys replaced the old, flat adobe covering. The wall which had long protected Maxwells and Abreus from Indian attack fell into disrepair and was eventually torn down. One room of the compound had traditionally served as the family chapel, but soon after her husband's death, Mrs. Abreu decided to erect a new church across the Santa Fe road from her home. Aided by her daughters Sofia and Victoriana, she completed the building and deeded it to the archbishop in Santa Fe in trust for the Catholic Church. Today services for visiting Scouts are still held every Sunday during the summer. In 1914 friends and family members gathered at the chapel to pay their last respects to Petra Beaubien Abreu. Her remains were interred next to her husband's just a few hundred yards from the home where they had spent most of their married life.

After the death of Jesús, management of the ranch passed into the hands of his sons. At first they ran the Rayado much as their father had, raising livestock and growing fruit and vegetables. Irrigation was becoming increasingly popular in northern New Mexico, and the Abreu brothers decided to alter their methods accordingly. In 1907, they organized the Rayado Land and Irrigation Company. They outlined elaborate plans for the construction of dams and ditches to expand the acreages under cultivation. It soon became evident, however, that the Abreu brothers could not properly develop their property. Inexperience, inadequate capitalization, and brotherly squabbling for the next four years persuaded them to dispose of the ranch. Sale of the 33,000-acre tract to a group of Colorado businessmen calling themselves the Rayado Colonization Company in April 1911 ended the Abreu family's control over its historic home and opened a new era at Rayado.[7]

The Urraca Ranch

Just north of the Abreu home and almost as historic was the Urraca Ranch. On the east it bordered the old Santa Fe road running from Rayado to Cimarron, on the west lay the "main mountains," on the south the Maxwell-Pley-Abreu lands, and on the north the ridge separating waters flowing into the Urraca and Cimarroncito creeks. Here, directly below the Tooth of Time, a long series of men ran cattle, sheep, and horses in the exact spot where the Boy Scouts eventually established the headquarters for Philmont.

The origins of the Urraca spread can be traced back to Peter Joseph, a Portuguese (or West Indian) immigrant who had trapped and traded with both Maxwell and Carson. In March 1861, Maxwell and Beaubien sold the Urraca property to Joseph for the bargain price of $660. Little is known of Joseph's activities on the ranch, but by the time of his death less than a year later, one ten-acre plot, probably along the Urraca Creek, had been surrounded by a board fence so that it could be farmed. Another stone and log barrier, portions of which still survive, had been erected across the divide separating Joseph's property from that of José Pley on the Rayado. Today that area is known as Stonewall Pass. Joseph's will transferred ownership of the ranch to his children, but through an exchange agreed to in 1866, his son Antonio, who was still a schoolboy, gained full control of it. Other activities left Joseph little time for ranching, and the property apparently was little used.

By 1880, when Joseph at last disposed of the Urraca Ranch, he turned to Frank R. Sherwin, a Massachusetts-born speculator, who had been active in the New York and London stock markets before purchasing large blocks of Maxwell Land Grant and Railway Company stocks and bonds in the 1870s. Sherwin apparently wished to acquire property in the Cimarron area, for in September 1880, he paid Joseph $8500 for the Urraca tract. The next year he almost doubled his holdings by leasing from the grant company (in the name of his minor son) a tract stretching northward almost to the Cimarron River and east to its confluence with the Cimarroncito. Because Sherwin himself was president of that company and was thus leasing land to himself, the annual rent was a nominal $200.

Unlike many of his neighbors, Sherwin was not a rancher and had no real interest in producing quality livestock for the market or even in making a profit. Instead he ran the Urraca as a hobby, providing entertainment for himself, his family, and friends. No sooner had the new owner taken over, for example, than local newspapers announced the arrival on the Urraca of a number of thoroughbred horses from England. Grooms accompanied the animals from England and made certain that they were unloaded from the train at Springer and moved to Cimarron. Sherwin had already begun construction of elaborate facilities to house his stock. A 4000-acre pasture along the Cimarroncito, apparently near where Waite Phillips later kept his polo ponies, contained knee-deep gramma grass. The nearby foothills provided excellent shelter.[8] The exact location of Sherwin's horse barns is unknown, but they may well have provided the nucleus for the huge complex today known as Ranch Headquarters out of which the support and supply services are provided for Philmont campers.

While Sherwin was establishing his horse farm along the Cimarroncito, his family and friends found other recreational opportunities in the area. One man, for example, enjoyed shooting wild pigeons along the Urraca. Like many other young men since, Sherwin's son, Frank, Jr., yearned to conquer the mountains which formed the ranch's western boundary. Together with a friend, E. L. Sheldon, whose father was governor of New Mexico Territory, he set off one day in the spring of 1881 to climb what he called El Capitan, because of its resemblance to the famed Yosemite landmark. Today it is known as the Tooth of Time. Once on top, the boys planted a flag to commemorate their feat, ate lunch, and then lay back to admire the view around them. Far to the south, mesas stretched almost to Santa Fe, or so it seemed; the Spanish Peaks in

Colorado were clearly visible in the north, while to the east it seemed that the plains stretched out forever. Against the golden background below them the two hikers marveled at the "shadows of hundreds of dark clouds of fantastic shapes as clearly defined by contrast as though engraved upon a white surface." Surely this was a site to thrill the imagination of the finest painters.[9]

By 1885, after enjoying the Urraca property for only four years, Sherwin decided to sell. He and his family found little time to spend at Cimarron, especially in light of the increasing complexities of Maxwell Grant business. Moreover, the high cost of maintaining a property which produced little or no income may have encouraged him to dispose of it. Fortunately, Sherwin discovered a local cattleman, Francis Clutton, who was interested in acquiring just such a property. An Englishman by birth, Clutton had come to New Mexico early in the 1880s, locating on a few sections of government land in eastern Colfax County. By 1885 a Las Vegas newspaper termed Clutton "one of the rising young big magnates of the county." The loss of long lengths of fence to cutters, however, convinced Clutton of the need to obtain better quality land nearer the mountains. As a result, on March 4, 1885, he purchased the Urraca ranch for $12,000 and assumed the Maxwell Land Grant Company lease.[10]

As soon as he took possession of the property, Clutton began to introduce modern livestock techniques to the area. Emphasis was placed on the quality of beef produced, necessitating the purchase of several Hereford bulls. Using the irrigated fields along the Cimarroncito and Urraca, Clutton also grew large amounts of alfalfa which he used to feed his range stock during the winter months. Sale prices were excellent. Clutton was so financially successful that by 1887 he expressed an interest in purchasing the land formerly leased from the grant company. He took another big step toward prosperity by his marriage in December 1887 to the daughter of Maxwell company manager M. P. Pels.[11]

Clutton also initiated a new way of making money from ranching.

Previously only full-grown cattle—bulls, steers, cows, or heifers—had been marketed in northern New Mexico. In the late summer of 1894, however, Clutton began shipping calves via train to eastern cities. The demand increased rapidly, and between August and October 1000 animals averaging 250 pounds each were sold. Prices averaged over $7.50 a head, for a total of more than $8300.[12] More than half a century later, the sale of calves is still a major part of the livestock business in Colfax County, where Philmont, among many ranches, markets several hundred every fall.

As the Urraca herd gained recognition for its high quality, Clutton also discovered a growing interest in his bulls. One of the major purchasers was Captain William French, who owned a large ranch near Socorro in southwestern New Mexico and who soon bought a huge tract between Springer and Cimarron.

Anxious to raise the quality of his own herd, he arranged for a visit to the Urraca. He found the ranch impressive and the bulls "far above the average for that time." The men agreed on a price of $75 each for 100 animals.

Despite the appearance of prosperity Clutton gave French and several reporters he talked to, his financial status became increasingly perilous. Early in 1889, apparently to pay for improving his herd and facilities, Clutton and the Maxwell company secretary Harry Whigham obtained a $30,000 loan using the Urraca Ranch and Sherwin lease as collateral. Payments of $1500 were due every six months starting in 1894. As the first date neared, conditions in the cattle industry worsened and Clutton found himself unable to make the payment. Several other outstanding loans were also coming due, and high costs in maintaining the ranch also continued. As a result, Clutton offered to lease the entire 80,000-acre property to French for five cents an acre a year, thus providing him with the $1500-biannual mortgage payments plus $1000 annually to live on. French agreed, and as soon as the papers were signed, Clutton and his wife and two children moved to Denver in hope of improving their financial status.[13]

The new environment failed to change Clutton's luck. Further business reverses followed, and soon mortgage foreclosures and tax sales cost him much New Mexico property. Among them was the Urraca Ranch, first leased and later sold to Stanley McCormick, son of the Chicago industrialist. The death of his eight-year-old son further depressed Clutton. Increasingly desperate for funds, he finally sought work escorting shipments of cattle to Chicago for their owners, but despite daily trips to the local stockyards, no employment could be had. At last on November 30, 1901, Clutton entered a bar, bought a glass of beer and a cigar, and went outside to perch on a corral fence. Suddenly a shot broke the quiet. Those who rushed toward the sound found Francis Clutton's body, a gaping wound in the forehead, a smoking pistol in his hand.[14] One of Philmont's pioneer cattlemen, a man who had introduced many innovations to the area, was dead. An era of ranching history had ended.

Ponil Pastures: Ranching in Philmont's North-Country

Geographical considerations prevented ranching from becoming as important in the northern part of Philmont as it did in the southern part. The broad plains and high mountain parks which provided pastures for the Urraca Ranch, as an example, did not extend north of the Cimarron River. Narrow, steep-walled canyons provided grass for relatively few animals. Much of the area remained in the control of the Maxwell Land Grant Company well into the twentieth century; some was not sold until the arrival of Waite Phillips. But several important ranches with special characteristics did exist.

The most important ranch along Ponil Creek belonged to M. M. Chase, whose homeplace was southeast of the Philmont boundary between Cimarron and Ponil camp. Chase had come to the Southwest soon after the Civil War and gone into partnership with J. M. Dawson. In 1871 Chase obtained through trade and purchase 1000 acres along the lower Ponil Canyon, including the site where Indian Agent W. F. M. Army had attempted to establish the Ute and

Apache agency a decade earlier. Soon a two-story adobe home, as well as barns, corrals, and a bunkhouse marked the Chase headquarters. Most of these buildings still stand, evidence of the high quality of their construction.

Chase believed that the rich soil and plentiful water on his property should be used, and he instituted a major development program. About 320 acres were put under cultivation, half in alfalfa and half in gardens and orchards. In 1872 he purchased apple seedlings in Ohio and laid out one of the largest orchards in the territory. The trees flourished, producing great quantities of high-quality fruit. Within a few years, Chase's apples were known as some of the best in the Southwest.

In addition to its own production, the Chase ranch provided headquarters for a livestock operation which extended throughout much of the territory. In 1881, a relative of Chase's who was also a newspaperman visited Cimarron and reported that only 300 head of cattle and a few horses were at the homeplace; most of the horses were for pleasure riding or belonged to the Chase children. Fifteen miles north, along the Vermejo River, Chase, Taylor Maulding, and S. M. Folson owned a 50,000-acre tract where they kept 2500 head of cattle. In addition, Chase owned part of a sheep ranch in eastern New Mexico.[15] One of Chase's daughters, Mary, married cattleman Charles Springer and purchased a large tract of land along the Ponil Canyon. It also seems likely that Chase grazed livestock either for himself or one of the companies in which he was interested in the Ponil country.

During the 1880s, Chase expanded his operations by establishing a series of cattle companies which controlled a good share of the livestock industry in northeastern New Mexico. Chase needed financing, most of which came from H. M. Porter, an enterprising businessman who had first come to New Mexico to open a store at Elizabethtown. Charles Springer, whose brother Frank was legal counsel for the Maxwell Land Grant Company during its many court battles, also participated in these cattle ventures. Together with other, less influential investors, they organized the Cimarron Cattle Company, Red River Cattle Company, and Gila Cattle Company, all huge operations controlling vast tracts of land not only in the Philmont area but also extending into southern New Mexico, Texas, and Oklahoma. The management of these properties usually fell to Chase, who in 1886 was said to be running "more cattle than any one in New Mexico."[16]

H. M. Porter, the wealthiest of Chase's partners, also owned several ranches in the Philmont area. The largest, known as the Urraca or Cimarroncito pasture, was located just east of the Clutton ranch. An initial tract bought in 1872 was supplemented by leases and purchases until by 1900 Porter owned about 25,000 acres. Another similarly sized ranch further south adjoined the eastern edge of the Abreu place. Most of the land was fenced, and adequate provision was always made to supplement the available food supplies during droughts or blizzards. Like other progressive ranchers, Porter invested in pure-bred Hereford bulls, so that the quality of his herd continually increased. An average of 1300 to 1700 head of cattle on the property earned him an average annual profit of over $25,000.

Two of the men who managed Porter's cattle operation and aided considerably in producing such high earnings have been honored by having parts of Philmont's north-country named after them. The first was Robert Dean, who worked for Porter from 1883 until 1892. Apparently he had come to New Mexico during the 1870s and established by lease or purchase a ranch in the canyon just southwest of the Ponil. The ruins of his cabin can still be seen there. Dean's sudden death in 1892 ended their relationship. To replace Dean, Porter turned to H. H. Chandler, another pioneer cattle raiser. For many years an employee on Clutton's Urraca spread, Chandler took over as Porter's foreman in 1895, retaining the position until the land was sold in 1917.[17] Chandler also owned a ranch of his own on the north side of the Cimarron River, including the lower portion of Turkey Creek Canyon. Eventually Waite Phillips added it to Philmont.

The Heck and Nash Ranches

Not all ranchers in northeastern New Mexico owned thousands of cattle or harvested hundreds of bushels of fruit. Some were family operations comprising as few as a thousand acres. These people made no great fortunes, but many did earn a good living over a number of years. Two rather typical small ranches, both now part of Philmont, belonged to Mathias Heck along the Cimarroncito and J. H. Nash near the Cimarron River.

Heck was a German who came to the United States in 1844. He spent several years peddling jewelry in the South before joining the throngs who headed for California during the gold rush. The outbreak of the Civil War led him to join the California Column which marched to New Mexico. Like other New Mexico veterans, Heck spent some time at the Baldy mines after his discharge, but soon he opened a stage station and store at the Sweetwater crossing of the Santa Fe Trail south of Rayado. The rapid growth of the cattle industry attracted Heck, and in 1876 he purchased a large tract along the Cimarroncito adjoining the Urraca Ranch.

Improvements slowly transformed the Heck Ranch into an established agricultural unit. A large adobe house, portions of which are still in use, was surrounded by the usual barns, corrals, and other outbuildings. Two orchards produced a variety of fruit; hay and alfalfa were regularly cut on nearby irrigated fields. A small but highly respected cattle herd, bearing a brand said to be the oldest in New Mexico, grazed along the Cimarroncito during the winter. Leased land in the Moreno Valley usually provided summer pasture. As Mathias Heck grew older, management of the ranch fell more and more to his son, Mat, Jr. The property continued in the family until Waite Phillips purchased it during the 1920s.[18] Today the Heck family is still among the most respected around Cimarron; one Heck still works at Philmont.

Few ranches lasted as long or were as generally successful as the

Heck's. A good example is the shorter history of a lesser known stockman, J. H. Nash, and his attempts to build a cattle ranch on what would later become Philmont.

A native of Mississippi, Nash spent most of his life in the cattle business. In 1895 he came to the Philmont area and at first ran cattle on land leased from the Maxwell Land Grant Company, later purchasing a small tract on the Ponil. Reinvestment of profits enabled him to slowly increase his holdings. Next he acquired a large piece of land near the mouth of the Cimarron Canyon and extending southwest along what is now called Nash Gulch toward the Cimarroncito. Ten carloads of cattle arrived from Arizona to stock the land.

As the extent of his holdings increased, so did Nash's social and economic standing. Local citizens expressed their confidence by selecting him as county commissioner. His name frequently appeared beside the names of Chase, Porter, and Springer who were shipping livestock to Kansas City packing plants. After a short trip to Arkansas, Nash returned home with a pretty young wife, but unfortunately the couple's happiness lasted only a short time.

One afternoon in the summer of 1901, Nash and a boy who worked for him were saddling their horses for the afternoon's work. While the youth went inside the house on an errand, Nash stood on the rope of the boy's horse while continuing to saddle his own. Something frightened the boy's mount, causing it to rear up and run. The rope wrapped tightly around Nash's leg, and before anything could be done, the horse dragged him several hundred yards to a terrible death. "One of the most genial, upright, thorough business men" in Cimarron was dead just as his ranch was starting to prosper. The death of Nash ended the short history of his ranch. His widow, who moved to Denver and eventually remarried, sold the cattle but retained the property until 1913, when Mat Heck bought it and incorporated it into his holdings.[19] Much of the ranch is now used to graze Philmont's famed buffalo herd.

Cowboys at Early Philmont

Thus far in describing the cattle industry in northeastern New Mexico, attention has focused on the ranch owners. Men like Abreu, Clutton, Chase, and Porter were businessmen, who managed their vast spreads much as present-day corporate officials operate factories. Other men, seldom publicized in the newspapers, actually tended the cattle. These cowboys, some of the most colorful figures in Philmont's history, were described by a city dweller who spent several days with them in 1888. The scene was somewhat north of present-day Philmont, but the description applies just as well.

The visitor rode out of Cimarron for several hours before reaching a cow camp high in the Sangre de Cristos. His guide was Marion Littrell, one of the best-known cattlemen in the area and a distant relative of Philmont's current ranch manager. Soon the cowboys arrived on horseback. Shortly a simple but filling meal was ready: boiled potatoes and bacon or ham were the usual fare, but that night the accidental killing of a calf added beef to the supper. The men then climbed into their bedrolls for the night. The greenhorn spent an uneasy night on the hard ground.

The next day was especially busy, since several nearby ranches were joining together to round up cattle. By four o'clock in the morning, camp noises—"the lowing of cattle, the barking of dogs, the neighing of horses, and the shouting of cowboys"—awakened the tenderfoot. Some of the men gathered up the horses; everyone else grabbed a quick breakfast, remarkably similar in content to the previous evening's meal. The first event was the roundup itself, during which mounted cowboys scattered through the high mountain parks and valleys to locate every animal and drive it to the central collecting area. During winter, cold winds sometimes scattered cattle for twenty or thirty miles from their home range, so that a great deal of riding was necessary. Next each rancher had his employees cut out their stock according to brand.

Many of the newborn calves had yet to be branded. A huge fire was built so the irons could be heated until they were red hot. The men rode up to each calf, lassoed it around the neck or leg, and dragged it toward the fire. Quickly grabbing the frightened, bawling animal, one cowboy threw it to the ground while another applied the iron to its flank. Sometimes a third man simultaneously notched its ear. Only a few seconds had passed, but an important part of the calf's "growing up" process was over.

That night as the city man sat around a campfire, he learned that many of his notions about cowboys were erroneous. When a whiskey bottle passed from man to man, he expected that everyone would get drunk. Many took nothing, and no one drank very much. He later learned that this ranch, like many others, had strict regulations prohibiting the consumption of alcohol during roundups. Moreover, few cowboys carried handguns; in fact, all of the local cattlemen had agreed not to employ men with revolvers. In general he found that the cowboys were "very good-natured fellows." Never once had he "heard an unpleasant word, nor was there any quarreling."

Each of the "outfits" on the ranch followed a fairly regular schedule throughout the year. The summer was spent "herding the cattle, rounding them up, branding the cattle, and breaking in their saddle horses." Winter brought less work, as the men made permanent camp, usually in a log cabin. It was their job to watch the stock, bringing in weak or sick animals which might not be able to survive the bitter cold. On more progressive ranches, hay and alfalfa were available to feed hungry cattle, although a few owners still let their herds fend for themselves.[20]

Today ranching is still the major industry in northeastern New Mexico. The Abreu, Urraca, Cimarroncito, and Ponil ranches are now part of Philmont. Cattle still graze the fertile grasslands along the Sangre de Cristos, although in smaller numbers than during the nineteenth century. Cowboys lead lives not very different from their pioneer predecessors, although modern techniques and equipment ease their work somewhat. Surrounding Philmont are other ranches ranging in size from one-family operations like the old Heck or Nash places to vast corporate properties covering hundreds of thousands of acres. Wherever you go there is much evidence of the rich heritage of the cattle industry, an important aspect of Philmont's colorful past.

XI

REVIVAL
OF BALDY MINING

Between 1893 and 1895 the Baldy mining district awakened after twenty years of inactivity. Word-of-mouth stories of spectacular discoveries did not induce the excitement this time. Rather the Maxwell Land Grant Company under the leadership of Frank Springer achieved the new boom through carefully planned advertisement of the district's potential. The sad status of the area was demonstrated by the United States Census returns for 1890. In that year only $15,451 worth of gold was taken from the rich placers of the Moreno, Ute, and South Ponil creeks. Only half that amount came from the once famous lode mines. Springer was well aware of the difficulties and proceeded with a well-calculated program to attract miners and capital to the district. The day of the small operator with a sluice box was gone. Bigger companies with more money to develop lode mines and secure ore-crushing equipment would be the only key to renewed vigor and profit in the area around Philmont.

The Maxwell Land Grant Company also attempted to attract small investors and prospectors into the area to complement and assist the big capitalists. The mining regulations laid down many years before by the miners of the Cimarron district were long forgotten. Now that the company had won the long legal battle over control of the grant, it had the right to regulate the development of mines. The Maxwell Land Grant Company therefore established a new mining code. Written and approved in the spring of 1894, the new rules were entitled "Regulations for Mineral Prospectors and Intending Locators upon the Maxwell Land Grant" and advertised as "more liberal" than those of the United States government.

The Maxwell company regulations provided that any man could lay claim to a plot of ground 1500 feet long by 300 to 600 feet wide simply by posting an information notice on the site and laying out boundary markers. Within sixty days after the initial discovery, he was required to sink a 10-foot exploratory shaft and file a "certificate or notice of location" in the offices of the company, paying a $12 fee. The Maxwell company reserved for itself extensions on either end of the claim, which prevented long chains of claims and assured the company part ownership in every rich lode. The miner would then enjoy rights of "possession" for two years. By the end of that time, if he decided that the lode was rich enough to merit the work and money required, the prospector had to have a 30-foot exploratory shaft completed. The company would then survey the claim, and, if no adverse claimants came forward, the miner could finally buy his claim outright for $10 an acre. The company's proposals appealed to many Eastern and Midwestern workingmen and to numerous recently arrived foreign immigrants. All climbed aboard the Santa Fe and headed west to New Mexico.

Lode Mining Along Ute Creek

Most of the outside capital and labor was funneled into Ute Creek, now part of Philmont, where scores of lodes were discovered, investigated, and worked in the last years of the nineteenth century. Most of the new operations were relatively small. An investor with limited funds, or a group of men who contributed capital and labor, organized as a company, would find a rich vein, locate it according to the regulations prescribed by the Dutch corporation, and proceed with limited operations. If the ore proved to be rich and plentiful, they built a small mill to process it; if not, they carried their rock to a nearby stamp mill or shipped it to smelters outside the district. Most of the miners barely eked out a living for themselves and their families. No great fortunes were made. But like twentieth-century slot-machine players, miners kept on working, hoping, and praying, but not expecting, that the next day would bring a strike equal to that of the Aztec.

There were fewer mines on Ute Creek, where the steep slopes of Baldy left less room for laying out claims, than on the Moreno Valley side of the mountain. Up and down both Ute Creek and the South Ponil Creek, north and south of the Aztec, companies struck rich ore. Many were able to follow their leads for long distances and make considerable profit. The more numerous mines looking down onto the Moreno Valley were less prosperous. Too many geologic faults and too much erosion combined to make operations there more precarious, more difficult. The Moreno Valley had made its reputation for placers; Ute Creek would be famous for lode mining.

The Aztec was the largest and most productive mine on the slopes of Baldy Mountain. It opened for a time during the 1880s under the ownership of a group of Santa Fe capitalists, but had closed down in 1889. After pouring an immense amount of money into the effort, the Santa Fe men were anxious to sell their interest and dispose of a lease they had from the Maxwell Land Grant Company. They interested a London syndicate under Clinton Butterfield in their mine. When the Englishmen sent an "expert" to visit the site, a resident manager took him to "every good place" in the mine and showed him the best possible prospects. The Londoners actually visited the premises and found the mine and mill in operation, but little did they realize that everything had been activated especially to impress them with the profit-making potential of the district. The purchase was soon completed, although the Maxwell company insisted on retaining its majority control.[1]

The foreigners incorporated the Aztec Gold Mining and Milling Company in June 1893. The new corporation took over control of the Aztec when it purchased minority control from the Santa Fe men plus the lease on the grant company's seven-twelfths interest. A year later Butterfield bought an additional 320-acre plot around the lode for a mill and town site and hired Sherman G. Sackett to superintend the work. He put the mine in first-class condition and installed modern equipment with the money poured into the venture by the Englishmen. Sackett's men put in a 30-stamp mill and a tramway to connect the mill and mine, and renovated residences and constructed business buildings to reincarnate the town of Baldy.

Despite the available capital, Sackett had nothing but trouble at the mine. Four men tried to jump a part of the Aztec claim. They timbered two old tunnels, built a cabin to live in, and proceeded to haul out the Englishmen's richest ore. Sackett seemed powerless to stop them. "French Henry" Buruel, asserting rights to an old claim, declared his ownership of the Aztec mill site and the water flowing past it. These problems must have been satisfactorily solved, for work proceeded until the fall of 1895 when Sackett suddenly announced that there was no more ore to feed the mill and closed down operations. Soon the company's creditors foreclosed and the Maxwell company reassumed control of its famous, but often unproductive, mine.[2]

The Black Horse Mine, located on a tributary of Ute Creek, was typical of lode operations on the east side of Baldy Mountain. The claim was discovered in 1871, but went unworked until Thomas W. Knott and Charles L. Mills relocated it in 1880. The new owners lacked vigor and capital, so they, too, accomplished little until "Baron" Phillip H. VanZuylen joined their enterprise in 1891. VanZuylen, a Dutchman who claimed to come from a wealthy, titled family, moved his equipment to Black Horse Canyon where he enlarged it and added concentrator tables to remove a larger percentage of the gold. For the next fifteen years the Dutchman was associated with the Black Horse in one capacity or another. He bought and sold interests in the mine and mill, supervised operations, and provided manual labor.[3] The Black Horse is frequently visited today by Scouts hiking from Baldy Town to Miranda Camp.

In addition to newly worked mines like the Black Horse, many of the older producers on the east side of Baldy were reactivated. The Mystic, where copper float had attracted the attention of Indians and soldiers thirty years before, stayed in the news because of the frequency with which it changed owners. During a two-year period, it was bought, sold, or leased five times. Apparently the difficult milling process necessary to remove the silver, gold, and copper combinations reduced profits and retarded development.

On Ponil Creek, the French Henry also came to life. In 1894 operations there began under the Claude Mining and Milling Company which installed a stamp mill and a 2700-foot bucket tramway. J. B. Wheeler of Colorado Springs next bought the mill and mine and overhauled them enough to extract ore for several years. Today many of the buildings and pieces of equipment seen when visiting the French Henry millsite on the way from Pueblano to Copper Park date from this period. Scores of other mines had similar histories. None were spectacular successes, but many provided good incomes to their owners and operators and added to the production records of the Baldy district.

Boom in the Moreno Valley

While activities got under way on Ute and South Ponil creeks, other mining enterprises also started on the western slopes of Baldy Mountain. The men who bored into the mountain in search of glittering minerals were usually less successful than their friends along Ute Creek. The geological irregularity of the Moreno area made it more difficult to follow a vein for any distance; faults, slides, and intrusions seemed to break off rich veins which could not then be found again. The gentler western slopes of the mountains had washed more, too; the same process which produced rich placers in

Willow Canyon and in Grouse and Humbug gulches sapped the mountain of much internal wealth.

The Legal Tender Mine, located on a ridge between Willow Canyon and Grouse Gulch, was one of the oldest on the eastern slope of Baldy. Six or eight men already had 600 feet of development work completed in 1894. Even though the men extracted gold ore worth $20 to $200 a ton, they were still using a primitive arrastra in which to mill it. Manager C. W. Watson was forced to deal with more complicated technical problems when his men discovered an ore rich in gold, silver, and lead. The arrastra was incapable of tackling such rock, so Watson sold out to men who could provide the machinery and technical knowledge needed for a profitable operation. At first a Kansas City group purchased the property and planned to proceed with development, but they apparently accomplished little before deciding to dispose of the property.

In 1899, still another company was organized to work the Legal Tender. O. P. Matkin kept the mine in operation until at least 1904, producing a good income for himself and his brothers but little profit for the capitalists who invested in the mine. As at the Black Horse, local management and outside financial support successfully combined to operate the property.

Despite poor long-range income, hundreds of gold-seeking prospectors and capitalists swarmed into the Moreno Valley during the 1890s, necessitating the reestablishment of public transportation facilities. To meet the demand, the Springer and Moreno Valley Stage Line started daily runs on May 1, 1894. The passenger business was so large that the company had to run doubleheaders every other day to keep up with the demand; contracts from Wells Fargo Express and the United States Post Office Department were also lucrative. A competitive line, the Moreno Valley Stage and Freight Company, owned by H. H. Hankins, inaugurated coach and freight service before long. It did poorly at first, but when Hankins threatened to suspend operations, the residents of Springer raised $1600 to pull him through. Business soon improved, and Hankins prospered. In one month his coaches carried 221 passengers, each of whom paid $5 to make the rough and dirty ride from the railroad at Springer into the Baldy district.[4]

Most of those who came to the district ended up in Elizabethtown, which regained much of its old vigor and enthusiasm. The primitive quality which had characterized the town during its first boom period was considerably diminished. Newspapers reported fewer shootings, no lynchings, more church socials and dinner parties. Education, religion, and even the arts thrived. The first evidence of the town's new prosperity was the founding of a newspaper. The *Northern New Mexican Miner* first appeared in the early fall of 1896; publication continued uninterrupted until 1902.

Other evidence of prosperity appeared the following spring. Carpenters were busy building residences and business structures. When the population reached 1200 in June 1897, the old school building was bursting. The citizens demanded a new and larger one. The new building had been completed for the fall session of 1898. Three hotels did a good business: B. Nadock's Moreno Hotel, Herman Mutz's substantial Story Hotel (the remains of which still stand in the now abandoned town), and the Miner's Inn. In 1898 Weber and Ferry opened a meat market, which prospered in the bustling little town.

The residents of the city considered themselves to be very cosmopolitan when a Sunday school and an amateur dramatic society were established. So proud were they that some local composers wrote a poem, declaring their enthusiasm—and also demonstrating their poetic abilities:

> Read it here, Read it there
> Read it up and down
> You can see it everywhere,
> The boom has struck the town.

> Sound it from the housetops,
>   Paint it in the sky,
> E-town's boom has come to stay,
>   You know the reason why?
>
> We have the stuff—we have enough,
>   We're not the men to blow it,
> And we mind, it is the time
>   To let the wide world know it.[5]

The enthusiasm of the people of the Baldy district at the turn of the century marked a significant point in the history of the area. The vast sums of capital attracted to it by the Maxwell Land Grant Company would have to produce profits if prosperity were to continue. For this to happen, men interested in the mines would have to keep abreast of technological advances to extract greater quantities of gold from the big mountain and reduce costs. If they could achieve these goals, the Baldy district would retain its fame, and its boom would continue. If not, the area would soon sink into the class of broken, worthless, abandoned mining districts.

Modern Placer Mining at Baldy

Many miners looked to the introduction of large-scale, industrial placer mining as the panacea for E-town's troubles. Men like the Lynch brothers and Thomas Ritchie had profitably operated hydraulic systems on the slopes of the Moreno Valley for years. A big dredger with equipment to minimize water consumption and increase production would assure continued prosperity.

In 1894, Henry H. Argue and a group of Buffalo, New York, investors became interested in placering. Argue leased a tract of Moreno Valley land from the Maxwell company and negotiated with the Bucyrus Dredger Company for the installation of their large machinery. It was constructed on a steam-powered railroad car in order to move forward, scooping up, washing, and spitting out immense quantities of gravel. Relatively small amounts of water were used. It did not succeed, however, for expenses were too high and profits too low. After several attempts, the men abandoned the project, but the Argue company continued to operate conventional hydraulicking machinery for some time in an effort to recoup their losses.

Despite the failure of Argue's dredge, H. J. Reiling of Chicago decided to allow his newly developed dredging machine prove itself in the gravels of the Moreno Valley. Reiling organized the Oro Dredging Company and started construction in the fall of 1900. The huge boilers and hundreds of wheels, beams, and other parts were inched through the rugged Cimarron Canyon between the railhead and E-town. By August 1901, all was in place.

That day residents of Colfax County and visitors from all over the nation gathered on the flats below E-town for the dedication of the "Eleanor." Appropriately, H. J. Reiling opened the ceremonies:

> We have gathered here today to christen this boat and I have chosen the name of a lovely girl, one who is a precious stone, a diamond in her home. . . . I can name this boat the Eleanor, and know success is sure. . . . My associates and I have invested thousands of dollars here. If we succeed we know we will have your hearty congratulations; if we fail the regrets and sympathy of all. With such support we feel we can risk much to make this camp a success.

He then introduced Eleanor, Mrs. W. A. Maughey, "the loveliest pearl that fair Ohio had produced," who dedicated the cumbersome dredge as though it were a graceful steamship:

> With the authority given me by the powers that be, I christen thee, Eleanor. May thy wheels never turn without profit to thy owners; may there be no loss of gold to thy owners; may there be no leakage of water in thy seams. May harmony and success prevail.[6]

Soon after the conclusion of the festivities, the land-locked barge set out on its work. The dredge was successful from the first. By 1903 reports credited the little ship with taking out $750 to $1000 worth of gold a day and producing one-third of all the gold in the territory. The axiom that success can be as dangerous as failure soon proved true in the case of Moreno Valley dredging. Rather than move ahead conservatively, the Oro Dredging Company decided to expand into Colorado. They mortgaged the Eleanor to acquire additional capital. Reiling set off to run the new dredger. Growth proved disastrous, for after just one season of poor management and unprofitable gravel, the company found itself bankrupt. The machinery never operated again. The failure of a dredge operation to prosper marked the end of large-scale placer mining in the Moreno Valley and another step toward the decline of production in the district.

Into the Heart of Baldy:
The Deep Tunnel and Aztec Mines

Argue's perseverance in the dredge business was surpassed only by that of two brothers, Alexander T. and William P. McIntyre, who searched for the "mother lode" in Baldy Mountain for nearly forty years. In 1898 the *New Mexican Miner* proposed that some capitalists "tunnel . . . the mountain" and suggested a geological theory accounting for the richness of Baldy:

> Disregarding the learned and scientific ideas, and taking the common and accepted theory, there must be far richer and better leads than ever have been taken out in the Baldy region. . . . Where there is all this "smoke" . . . there is certain to be a great and hidden "fire."[7]

In the fall of 1900, the McIntyre brothers and Leroy Burt incorporated a company of their own, the Gold and Copper Deep Tunnel Mining and Milling Company. The company's plans were as formidable as its name. It would start at the top of Big Nigger

Gulch, above Elizabethtown, and bore 3000 feet into the mountain in a northeasterly direction, reaching a depth of 1800 feet. Work would continue from there until eventually a tunnel had been driven through the entire mountain. By November 1900, several "commodious" buildings had been erected and two shifts of miners put to work on the project. During that first winter the men labored with hand drills, but when the company's board of directors met in January, they voted to buy additional machinery and power drills to hasten work.

After a full year of operation, work on the deep tunnel slowed. The McIntyre brothers found it necessary to sell stock so that they could continue operations, virtually on a day-to-day basis. One brother usually stayed at the mine superintending work or serving as a consultant to some other company to meet expenses. The other went East, peddling shares of stock to keep the operation going.

The years between 1902 and 1908 were slow ones for the deep tunnel company and its determined promoters. On and on they plunged, deeper and deeper into the mountain. Still they found nothing of value. In July 1902, their hopes were high enough to predict that soon twenty "known" veins would be intersected. In addition, sufficient water flowed out of the mine that water could be sold to placer miners in the Moreno Valley. By 1908 the McIntyres were no longer able to attract sufficient capital to keep their labor force at work. From time to time some investor provided enough money to hire a gang to tunnel a few more feet, but it was to take twenty-five years before the tunnel would be completed all the way through Baldy Mountain.

While the deep tunnel company's employees were boring into Baldy from the west, others continued digging Aztec Ridge on the eastern slopes of the peak. After the failure of Sherman Sackett and the English development company in the mid-1890s, Colorado investors attempted to reactivate the Aztec. Unsuccessful at first, the Denverites interested a number of wealthy Chicago businessmen who organized the Baldy Gold Mining and Milling Company and promised to put $18,000 in development money into the area. "Professor" R. C. Wilson, noted for his ability to get work done, took over the superintendency and pushed development. Wilson sank a working shaft to 100 feet below the oldest previous workings and dug a crosscut tunnel at that level. The size of the mill was doubled to handle the $40-a-ton ore he retrieved. Another large body of high-grade ore was discovered in mid-winter, and by Christmas everyone at the Aztec was in "fine feathers." The mine closed for a few months during the worst of the winter, but during that period the mill was revamped to streamline the operation.

Activities in the village of Baldy rivaled those of its larger neighbor in the Moreno Valley for a few years around the turn of the century. In the fall of 1897, men from all over the district gathered there to watch a lightweight boxing match between two fighters named Sturbo and Connelly. Henry Buruel from the French Henry Mine served as timekeeper. The next spring residents of the village met after the sinking of the battleship *Maine* in Havana harbor to show their support of the war against Spain. After "spirited outbursts of patriotic speeches by the prominent citizens of the City of Baldy," a series of resolutions was passed in which the people "promised financial and physical" support for the nation. The enthusiasm was tremendous. "Never before in the history of our city's life," reported one Baldy resident, "has there been such a gathering of people." Undoubtedly the city could supply 1000 soldiers within two days. On a somewhat more sophisticated level, Virginia Keyes kept school in the little town, while the Reverend A. A. Hyde attempted to get a Methodist church started on land donated by the Maxwell Land Grant Company.

The 1899 mining season proved disastrous, however, and the Aztec operators went broke as fast as had the dredge men in the Moreno Valley. Everything went wrong. High development costs combined with poor lode returns overburdened the company with debt. When the eastern investors, wisely foreseeing financial collapse, refused to provide additional support, operations ceased. Before long the company was unable to make its mortgage payments and lost control of the mine, mill, and townsite. Between 1902 and 1907, A. B. Ward did intermittent prospecting and some minor development work in the mine. But he lacked financial backing and accomplished little. By 1908 everyone realized that the mine could be successfully managed only with the direct control and support of the Maxwell Land Grant Company. It alone could provide sufficient capital, local interest, and skilled management needed to produce a profit.

The year 1908 marked the temporary end of mining on Baldy's slopes. After the residents of Cimarron complained bitterly of water pollution in the Cimarron River, the Maxwell company ordered that all placer mining be suspended. Such a policy severely hampered the Moreno Valley, which had previously held on with its placers through rough periods of lode mining. That same year the Dutch company announced new land acquisition policies which required a miner to buy land script before he could locate any claims. The amount of capital thus needed before a man could even go out in search of a mine prevented many poorer miners from undertaking the task. The disappointment over the failure of a railroad to reach Elizabethtown and the inability of the dredge to continue profitable operations bled the district of capital.

As a result, by 1910 the eastern slopes of Baldy Mountain were quiet. Deep inside the mountain a little life occasionally stirred around the deep tunnel—but very little. In the Moreno Valley the hulk of the giant Eleanor rusted slowly away as the dirt and sand of the valley covered more and more of her. The partying moved from Baldy and Elizabethtown to Eagle Nest, near old Virginia City, where a new dam drew tourists and sportsmen from all over the West. At the headwaters of Ute Creek, the Aztec was vacant. Several decades would pass before a third and final revival of activities occurred at Baldy.

The Cimarroncito Mining District

It was only natural that some of the Baldy miners would cross the Cimarron Canyon and explore the tributaries of Cimarroncito Creek a dozen miles south of Baldy. The dacite porphyry found there resembled the minerals at Baldy; many miners assumed that the area was a continuation of the more famous mining field. As early as August 1868, miners took out placer claims along the Cimarroncito, but poor returns soon caused them to abandon the area and seek more profitable diggings. A year later, a lode miner laid out the Grey Eagle and Red Jacket quartz claims, but he, too, apparently found the area insufficiently rewarding and abandoned the claims without undertaking significant development.

Nothing further occurred in the mountains until the spring of 1880, when Thomas W. Knott and Charles L. Welles, who had done considerable prospecting throughout the region and owned several Baldy mines including the Black Horse, discovered gold in the upper reaches of the Cimarroncito. They reported that their find was only four feet beneath the ground; small chunks would be worth $100,000 if they could find a ton. The pair constructed a crude arrastra and filed claims on two mines, the Thunder and the Contention. A Cimarron newspaper which heard of the new discoveries dubbed the district "one of the most promising" and expressed hopes that Cimarron would soon benefit from its nearness to the mines.[8]

What the Cimarroncito district miners needed most was capital to develop their property and purchase expensive equipment necessary to process the ore. Money was forthcoming in the fall of 1881 when investors from Altoona, Pennsylvania, and Chicago visited the area and expressed an interest in acquiring the mines. Early in November, they bought the Thunder and the Contention for $15,000, and almost immediately ordered a fifteen-stamp mill. It did not take long for the rich ore which had attracted the easterners to disappear. Faced with rock worth only $5 to $10 a ton, the men soon suspended operations.

The resurgence of interest in mining on the Maxwell Grant during the 1890s stimulated increased activity along the Cimarroncito. The Four Creeks Mining Company, headed by Thomas W. Knott, who had prospected in the area fifteen years earlier, bought five claims in the district and began removing ore from them. Once again their success was brief; and the mines were put up for sale.

Many residents of Cimarron were optimistic about the future of mining along the Cimarroncito when they heard that a Colorado corporation, the Consolidated Verde Mining and Milling Company, had purchased the mining property there for a reported $100,000. The 91-acre tract was said to contain "one of the largest bodies of high grade ore in the west." A vein 35 feet wide contained rock valued at $100 a ton. Copper sulphide was the most common mineral, but there were also substantial quantities of gold, silver, and iron. The company announced that a few men would immediately begin work in the mine; many seemed certain that facilities for large-scale reduction and concentrating would soon be built in Cimarron to refine the ore. Most early work was done on the Thunder Mine, from which several carloads of ore were taken. To facilitate its transportation out of the mountains, a road was completed from the mines to Cimarron.

The greatest development was in the Contention and Thunder mines, both located in the immediate vicinity of Philmont's present Cyphers Mine Camp. Several hundred feet of tunneling had been completed in the Contention by the beginning of the new century, opening up extensive bodies of relatively high-quality ore. Because the mountain rose steeply above the mine entrance and the richest ores were found above the tunnel, promoters seem certain that a tremendous body of rich rock would be found. Considering that development had only begun, the chances for success seemed good. Even the experienced mineral seekers in the Moreno Valley were impressed with the Cimarroncito district. One E-town reporter wrote:

Without exaggeration it can be said here is a great mineral field, not so much with reference to the extent of the territory covered —although in the few months that have elapsed since prospectors began to come in, a large number of excellent prospects have been located—but the invariable richness of the ores together with the extent of the deposits make this camp one on which it will be well to keep an eye, as it is bound to rapidly come before the public as a great producer of gold and copper.[9]

The most important manager at Consolidated Verde's Cimarroncito operation was Charles Cyphers. Cyphers, after whom the Philmont camp in the heart of the district was named, is remembered by Cimarron people as "an old Mountain Goat." More than once he was reported to have carried 100 pounds or more in goods and supplies into camp on his back. Under the leadership of Cyphers, the Consolidated Verde Company continued to operate sporadically during the early years of the century. Plagued by low-grade ores with complex chemical structures which made milling difficult, the operation was never a great financial success. Cyphers remained optimistic, seemingly confident that someday the area would be a bonanza.

Cyphers and his associates apparently retained their rights in the district until June 1908, when the sale of the mines to the St. Louis and Cimarron Company was announced.

It has long been known that there are very rich ore deposits in this district, and many claims have been taken out and much development work has been done. But large quantities of ore have not been shipped out of this district.

The primary reason for the lack of exploitation was the poor quality of transportation facilities into the area. Now everything would change. Under the financial backing of some rich St. Louis men, the new company promised to speed up development, and Charles Cyphers would stay on as manager.[10]

The completion of the St. Louis, Rocky Mountain and Pacific Railroad into Cimarron greatly eased the transportation problem.

The mining men at Cimarroncito had assurances from the company that it would build a spur to their mines "as soon as we get enough ore out to make it advisable to expend the no small sum necessary to do so." If the mine turned out to be as great a producer as expected, the St. Louis company also planned to build a smelter in Cimarron. "I know the ore is there," the head of the mining company assured residents of Cimarron, "and I feel positive that under the management of Mr. Cyphers we will be shipping in large quantities within a month or two."

Despite their initial enthusiasm, the St. Louis owners did not find ore as rich as they had expected. No railroad spur was built, and no great loads of gold- and copper-bearing ore were extracted from the mountains along the upper Cimarroncito. Soon the area was virtually deserted. Only Cyphers remained. Finally in the 1920s he, too, abandoned the area, marking the end of all efforts to revitalize the district.

Today as a part of Philmont Scout Ranch, the Cimarroncito district has witnessed a new kind of activity. Boys from all over the nation visit the area to see what an old mining camp looked like. Charles Cyphers's old cabin has been transformed into a museum, where tools, bottles, and mining implements are displayed. Most of the mines, long ago abandoned, have caved in or been blasted shut to prevent injury to curious visitors. But the Contention mine is open, with newly installed supports to guarantee its safety. Every day dozens of boys tour the tunnel where men like Cyphers sought rich ore decades ago.

The last chapter in the story of the Cimarroncito mining district was written during the summer of 1961 when officials of Philmont employed mining experts to determine if there was any valuable ore left. The report substantiated suspicions which must have been long held by those who sought gold and copper in the area:

Copper mineralization is not substantial enough to be considered ore. . . . Gold and Silver, though occasionally high in value, are limited in scale; present economic conditions pro-

hibit a mining operation of even moderate size. Promise remains for a one- or two-man development, based on structural
suggestion, but large-scale exploration and development is not
within the realm of economic feasibility.[11]

XII

TRACKS,
TIES, AND TIMBER

Despite the apparent prosperity in the Philmont region at the beginning of the twentieth century, inadequate transporation facilities threatened to curtail continued development. Cattlemen found it difficult and expensive to send stock to Eastern markets. Fruit growers were confronted by increasingly complex problems in transporting their apples, pears, and cherries to consumers. Mining men required modern facilities to ship complicated ores and concentrated amalgams to distant smelters and to bring in heavy mining machinery. North of Cimarron in the Ponil country vast timber reserves could be exploited only if a practical means for carrying logs out of the mountains were secured. Without economical transportation, the area surrounding Philmont would soon sink into that class of broken, worthless communities which already cluttered the West. Railroads, everyone thought, would solve the transportation dilemma and assure continued prosperity. The people of northeastern New Mexico were determined that such roads would be built.

The St. Louis, Rocky Mountain and Pacific

It was not long before numerous companies were planning railroad construction into the region.[1] The Colorado and Southern Railroad, which controlled trackage into the timbered northern sector of the Maxwell Grant, announced early in 1899 plans to extend south to Ponil Park, less than twenty miles from the Baldy area and Cimarron. Even more promising was the Cimarron River and Taos Valley Railroad which said it would connect the town of Maxwell on the Santa Fe main line with Elizabethtown. Nothing resulted from any of these plans.

In July 1902, Thomas P. Harlan and Max Koehler of St. Louis arrived in northern New Mexico and declared their plans to build the New Mexico and Pacific Railroad from Raton to Elizabethtown. Eventually it would extend to the Pacific coast. When the conservative president of the Maxwell Land Grant Company, J. Van Houten, announced to area residents that the road definitely would be built, hopes for immediate construction suddenly increased. Even though financiers were duly impressed with the potential of the region, construction still did not begin.

Not until 1905 were the St. Louis men back in northern New Mexico. Reorganized as the St. Louis, Rocky Mountain and Pacific Railway Company, the men had diverted their interests from the gold mines and agricultural lands of the Cimarron area to coal beds near Raton. Work progressed slowly, and it was not until December 10, 1906, that the first train raced from Raton south through the coal fields of the Maxwell Grant into Cimarron.

For days before, ranchers, miners, Indians, and others poured into the little town to celebrate the arrival of the iron horse. Two local men set up anvils with gunpowder so placed as to explode with a tremendous noise when the giant locomotive came into sight. Soon a whistle was heard in the distance, and the flag-draped train pulled into Cimarron with a full load of dignitaries. From there the train continued west to Ute Park. Just as important to the economy of the Philmont area as the construction of the line was the location of railroad shops in Cimarron. A fully equipped roundhouse was well under construction by January 1907.

Despite their elaborate plans, railroad officials soon realized that there was insufficient passenger traffic between Cimarron and Ute Park to justify the regular scheduling of a train. The company therefore ordered a twelve-passenger gasoline-driven motor car in May 1907 to service the western end of the line. Open, but canopied and curtained to protect riders from the weather, the little car was the talk of Cimarron as it rolled toward Ute Park on an inaugural trip with several leading Cimarron residents aboard. In fifty minutes they reached Ute Park and returned to town in just over half an hour. The company was thrilled with its vehicle, which it immediately bought and put into regular operation over the line.

To stimulate business west of Cimarron, the company also arranged to open a resort in scenic Ute Park, where local Indians had once camped and where miners still prospected. Plans called for the immediate construction of a large pavilion with glass windows and porches to facilitate year-around enjoyment of the region's beauty. A lunch counter would serve light meals, and restrooms, "furnished with the utmost comfort and taste" would be available for relaxation. By the early summer of 1908, work had been completed, and the Ute Park resort officially opened. If the number of guests increased, the railroad promised to build an immense summer hotel, baseball diamonds, polo fields, tennis courts, and other facilities to accommodate them. The future of Ute Park looked bright.

Unceasing rumors that one of the large railroads was interested in buying the Rocky Mountain line were confirmed when the Atchison, Topeka, and Santa Fe Railroad company purchased the entire company. News of the sale was not all good, however, for the new owners immediately decided to service all the Rocky Mountain cars at its Raton shops. The Cimarron roundhouse facilities were abandoned and by early 1914 had been dismantled and moved to Raton.

A trip along the road to Ute Park was exciting in those days, even to the railroad men who made the journey day after day. Edward Mahoney, long an employee of the Swastika line, reported that business was always poor, making the trip sheer relaxation for railroad personnel:

I usually contrived to be out on the open observation platform, going up the Canyon from Cimarron, with my feet propped up on the brass railing . . . taking in the scenery and inhaling the odors of pine, sage, and good locomotive smoke—listening to the engine working up the two-percent grade, hearing the flanges squeal on the tight curves, and enjoying the sight and sound of a rushing mountain stream . . . which we crossed and recrossed many times between Cimarron and Ute Park.

When the big locomotive pulled into the Ute Park station in late afternoon, passengers found none of the imposing tourist facilities envisioned by the railroad. "There isn't much in Ute Park today, and there was even less 42 years ago," Mahoney recalled.[2] Despite the idyllic tranquility of the Ute Park railroad line, the absence of passenger and freight traffic on the road eventually resulted in the suspension of all service.

The Cimarron and Northwestern

The penetration of the Philmont area by the iron horse in the early days of the twentieth century made possible the exploitation of vast timber resources north of Cimarron.[3] There, in what is now the Philmont north-country, mountains were cut in numerous instances by canyons. Along the sides of these narrow valleys and reaching onto the mesas above them were thousands of acres of virgin timber. Ponderosa pine (often called western yellow pine) and Douglas fir (referred to as red spruce by the lumbermen) predominated. With the arrival of the railroad the value of that untouched lumber supply increased dramatically. Hundreds of newly opened coal mines near Raton required props to support their inner workings. Railroads were being built throughout northern New Mexico and southern Colorado; the Santa Fe, Colorado and Southern, and Rocky Mountain lines would all buy ties.

The canyons through which Ponil Creek and its several branches flowed were particularly inviting to lumbermen. Located only a few miles north of Cimarron, where production facilities might be readily constructed, the north, middle, and south forks of the creek were thickly blanketed with good timber. The arrival of a common carrier, the St. Louis, Rocky Mountain, and Pacific, in the area, provided for easy transportation of wood products throughout the nation. Most important, the right to cut these trees belonged to the Maxwell Land Grant Company and could thus be secured with relative ease.

One man seemed to be most aware of the possibilities for exploiting the timber reserve along the Ponil. He was Thomas Schomburg, who moved to Cimarron to start his own lumber and railroad businesses, the Continental Tie and Lumber Company and the Cimarron and Northwestern Railway Company. In organizing the companies, he received financial support from Frank Springer, the attorney with whom he had worked many years before, W. H. Delleker, who had been associated with the Rocky Mountain Timber Company, and others.

The Cimarron and Northwestern was incorporated in January 1907. To finance construction of the road and the purchase of equipment, the company issued $120,000 in common stock and an equivalent amount in bonds.

Local newspapers trumpeted the plans of the company to build from Cimarron thirty-six miles northwest through the Philmont region to Van Bremmer Park. The managers set about purchasing rights-of-way from local landowners, and soon chief engineer A. G. Allen was surveying the route. From the station grounds in "East Cimarron," the road crossed a corner of the William S. French ranch and traversed a 4000-foot dirt fill to reach the Chase orchard, where thirty fine apple trees went down in its path. From there the line continued in a northwesterly direction, hugging the edge of the canyon to avoid agricultural land, and entered the narrow, tree-lined North Ponil Canyon where it passed the sites later occupied by

Philmont's Indian Writings and Old Camp. In all, the road crossed the Ponil fifty-one times in twenty-two miles, and climbed 1400 feet with a maximum grade of two percent.

To facilitate communication, a telephone line paralleling the railroad was rushed to completion so that surveying, engineering, and grading crews might talk with each other and with the Cimarron headquarters. Everything was in readiness on March 23, 1907, when initial grading contracts were let to W. C. Whitescarver of Trinidad, Colorado. Soon he had dozens of men and teams at work in the Ponil Canyon. In Cimarron the station grounds and storage yards were also being readied. A large 50- by 100-foot warehouse was built and stocked with provisions for construction crews and timber contractors. Engineers laid out over a mile and one-half of yard tracks in such a manner that piles of lumber might easily be loaded onto outgoing cars. A station and mill site overlooked the entire yard.

Everyone in Cimarron clearly understood from the beginning that the Cimarron and Northwestern was designed solely to supply timber to the lumber mills. The Interstate Commerce Commission summarized:

> The carrier is virtually a plant facility for the transportation of the lumber mill products of the Continental Tie and Lumber Company. To supply the mills and bring out timber is the sole reason for the road's existence. When the timber is gone, the Continental Tie and Lumber Company, having no interest in cut-over lands, intends to close the road and take up the rails.[4]

To assure that its subsidiary showed reasonable financial returns, Continental Tie and Lumber contracted on April 1, 1907, to furnish enough timber traffic every year to fill 3600 railroad cars.

The initial purchase of equipment proved nearly sufficient for the life of the Cimarron and Northwestern. The single Baldwin locomotive bore the auspicious number "1." Five boxcars were bought to haul mine props, thirty-nine flat cars for lumber and logs, and one caboose to carry employees and any stray passengers who might ride the line. By June 13, 1907, company contractors had begun to lay track out of Cimarron, and six months later, on January 6, 1908, the Cimarron and Northwestern Railroad (the C and N) opened just over twenty-two miles of track from Cimarron through Philmont's north-country to Ponil Park.

Logging in Philmont's North-Country

All along the C&N route, foremen from the lumber company established timber camps. If there was a good-sized stand of timber in an area, a small sawmill might be built; if not, logs from several areas were taken to a centrally located mill. One of the largest camps was located at the intersection of Metcalf and North Ponil canyons near where Deputy Sheriff Metcalf had been ambushed during the settler's war. Another large settlement grew up at Ring, northwest of Ponil Park, and some ten miles north of Philmont. After each site had been selected, men were assigned to cut timber nearby. Usually they worked for neither the railroad nor the lumber company but received payment for the lumber delivered.

Some crews specialized in cutting mine props, which varied from 5 to 9 feet long, with 7- or 8-inch tops. Peeled red spruce was the most popular variety for mine entrances because it withstood the deteriorating effects of the mines better than the less expensive ponderosa pine. The biggest customer for props was the St. Louis, Rocky Mountain and Pacific Company which needed them for its huge coal mines near Raton. Because of the delicacy with which props had to be handled, cutting crews were usually small, consisting of two or three men, or even a family, working together. Many of the employees lived in the vicinity of their wood camps in crude cabins or lean-tos built of logs or culled lumber. The remains of many of these still dot the canyons of Philmont.

A second important product was lumber. Again cut by small independent crews working in the mountains, the logs were hauled to the nearest sawmill. If the distance was great, crews of men laboriously heaped the timber onto four-wheeled wagons; if not, a tree might be skidded off the back of a wagon or pulled by teams of horses or mules. After the lumber had been rough cut at the company mills at Ponil and Ring or at smaller independent mills scattered throughout the mountains, the lumber would be taken to the railroad and sent to Cimarron for finishing and drying.

Finishing work was done in the huge planing mill erected by the Continental Tie and Lumber Company while the railroad was being built into the mountains. A second planing mill in Cimarron, owned by the Cimarron Lumber Company, went into operation at about the same time. Small timber-cutting crews and mills, primarily in the Dean Canyon area, provided the large modern mill with plentiful quantities of lumber.

A third item produced in quantity was railroad ties. The men cut red spruce in the mountains and hewed it into ties by hand. Finished products were then taken to Cimarron where they could be reshipped to the Colorado and Southern at Trinidad or at Des Moines; the Santa Fe also bought many ties which it sent to Albuquerque for treating and seasoning. Rumors of immediate construction of a tie-treating plant at Cimarron circulated as early as 1907, but not until 1913 was the plant built. The tie-treating business was excellent. When the plant opened in the spring of 1915, Continental Tie and Lumber already had a contract for over 100,000 ties, which required two months to supply.

Within a very short time, however, officials of the lumber company decided that there was no longer sufficient timber along the existing railroad line and decided to extend it beyond Ponil Park. Under the direction of Guy H. Palmes, a young Colorado engineer, construction soon began on thirteen miles of new track from Ponil Park southwestward to Bonito, located just north of Philmont's Dan Beard Camp. Continental Tie and Lumber Company did all the work and retained ownership of the completed line. Soon Bonito became an important camp on the railroad. A large new mill employed 125 men with fifty teams and daily turned out 65,000 feet of lumber, enough to fill five railroad cars for shipment to Cimarron.

The railroad company's first years were the most profitable. Huge quantities of quality timber were available, providing large loads to be hauled from the mountain camps to Cimarron. In addition new track and equipment required little maintenance. As additional track was laid, however, expenses for repair and upkeep increased. Timber had to be hauled longer distances, increasing transportation costs. Moreover, then as now, frequent flash floods roared down the canyons, wiping out bridges, undermining fills, and causing general havoc along the company's lines.

Life must have been interesting in those lumber camps along the C&N line. Zenas Ward, who still resides in Cimarron and tells tales of the past to all who will listen, worked at the XA place along the North Ponil. He and other cowboys in the area often went to Metcalf to use the company's single-wire telephone to make weekend dates with Cimarron girls. The young lady Ward had a particular fondness for was Margaret Brooks, whom he married. Her father owned a prominent Cimarron mercantile establishment, and in her autobiography, Mrs. Ward described the scene as timber crews visited town: "The company had commissaries for the workmen but many of them began driving to Cimarron to trade. Pay day would see the wagons coming to town. The women and children sat on the floor of the wagon beds while the men occupied the seat."[5]

If people from Cimarron wanted to see what was going on in the lumber camps, they could ride the caboose to Ponil Park or beyond. The trip was especially interesting because the train crew often stopped along the way to hunt turkey or deer or to fish during lunch hour. Some of the loggers were colorful enough to leave a lasting image. Oldtimers remember that "Big Ike" Torrance seemed to have perpetual fishing fever and that Alex McElroy was renowned as the greatest teller of tall tales in the Ponil country.

The large volume of timber products sent from the mountains to Cimarron rapidly depleted the forests on the North Ponil. Instead of building railroads further into the mountains, the Continental Tie and Lumber decided to retreat down the canyon, abandoning and tearing up lines no longer in use. By mid-1916, Continental Tie retained only eight miles of track, much of which had been unused during the previous year. The close of 1920 showed a reduction to two miles, and a year later the lumber company was completely out of the railroad business. The company saved the rails it had torn out, however, for already it had plans to build into new timber tracts north of Cimarron.

On August 3, 1923, H. G. Frankenburger petitioned the Interstate Commerce Commission on behalf of the C&N to allow the abandonment of C&N tracks between South Ponil (where the North Ponil jutted off from the Ponil) and Ponil Park stations. "There is no further need of the line," he insisted, "as the available supply of timber in that territory is exhausted and no other tonnage can be obtained." Few passengers depended on the road, he pointed out, since the lumber industry provided ninety percent of the traffic. There were no cities, towns, or villages on that portion of the road which would be abandoned; only twenty inhabitants would remain once the timber camps closed. Late in August, the commission granted the request, leaving the C&N with only seven and one-half miles of track.[6]

During 1922 and 1923, Palmes again set to work at the task for which he was originally hired—designing, surveying, and supervising the construction of railroad lines. He started work at South Ponil and laid tracks for ten miles along the Middle Ponil to Philmont's Ponil Camp, then along the South Ponil to a point at the base of Wilson Mesa. Pueblano Camp is now located near the terminus of the railroad. The new line was not built as sturdily as the North Ponil route, because by now Continental Tie and Lumber was certain that only limited use would be made of the tracks before the timber supply was depleted and the line abandoned. They also knew that lavish construction would not pay long-term dividends. Because many of the rails had seen prior service on the North Ponil and because the company's Cimarron plant produced ties at a very low price, construction costs dropped considerably.

The timber potential of the new area rivaled that of Bonito or Ponil Park. Great stands of ponderosa pine, Douglas fir, and other marketable timber shaded the picturesque site. On top of Wilson Mesa, north of the river, were equally impressive stands of pine, but removing logs from the mesa presented a formidable challenge. Timber skids, flumes, and even overhead trams were contemplated to bring timber off, but Palmes finally designed a road up the mountainside. The first trucks ever used in the area hauled logs from the top of the mesa to the railroad below. Such an innovation could only point toward a future day when rubber-tired vehicles would put the iron horse out of the lumbering business.

In addition plans to develop logging areas along the South Ponil, Continental Tie extended its operations along the St. Louis and Santa Fe line in the Cimarron Canyon. A large mine-prop camp at Ute Creek was particularly important. Deer Lake Mesa, now part of Philmont, was cut off at this time, as were several other areas bordering the Cimarron River.

Fortunately, the company was unable to acquire timber rights along the South Ponil Canyon, leaving the trees for campers and hikers to enjoy today. And today, Scouts who choose to travel from Dan Beard or Ponil to Pueblano over Wilson Mesa follow the remnants of the steep logging road for some distance.

By June 1930, the timber supply in the area served by the C&N was gone. Past experience had shown its managers that long lines brought with them only increased expenses and diminished profit. Few advocated further extension of the road. Moreover, because of the Great Depression, the demand for lumber products dropped sharply. Capital was unavailable to finance construction. For these reasons, Frankenburger requested the Interstate Commerce Commission on June 3, 1930, for permission to abandon the remaining seven and one-half miles of track between Cimarron and South Ponil. He pointed out that 95 percent of the business of the railroad was furnished by the lumbering industry. When the line was abandoned, only ten ranch employees (presumably at Chase Ranch) would remain in the area. "It appears," replied the commissioners, "that the railroad has served the purposes for which it was built, and that no public convenience or necessity requires its continued operation." Permission to abandon was granted.[7]

The C&N ties were left in place, where many still remain. The rails were reportedly taken to San Francisco and sold to a Japanese industrialist who used them in preparing for the war unleashed by Japan in December 1941. The rolling stock was quickly disposed of, and the Cimarron and Northwestern Railway ceased to exist.

Boom in Cimarron

The construction of two railroads into the Cimarron area brought great prosperity to the little town in the opening decades of the twentieth century. For the first time in many years railroad employees, lumber company workers, and miners from Baldy built homes in the town. To handle such a demand, George Remley, Fred Whitney, and Charles Springer incorporated the Cimarron Townsite Company, obtained title to 225 acres on the north side of the Cimarron River, and began to sell lots. They planted hundreds of shade trees along the broad boulevards of "new town" and donated a whole block to be used as a baseball field.

Soon new buildings were under construction all over Cimarron. The Oxford Hotel opened with an elaborate supper in April 1907. Soon a modern theater with dressing rooms and scenery drops, began presentations. A group of local people organized their own telephone company, arranged for long-distance connections, and installed phones throughout the villages. When complaints of inadequate banking facilities arose, local businessmen soon founded the First National Bank of Cimarron, housed in a handsome two-story stone and brick building.

Cimarron's sporting enthusiasts organized the Cimarron Athletic

Club in the spring of 1909, and throughout the year sponsored numerous events including baseball games and polo exhibitions. Not to be outdone, a band of golfers laid out links just north of town and announced plans to build a clubhouse and other facilities.

Increased population also encouraged a religious revival. Catholic citizens, long without a meeting place, were urged by a Springer priest to build a house of worship. A Raton architect volunteered to design the building, and members of the parish pledged to make whatever sacrifices were necessary to enable its completion. Baptists also organized a church and rented a hall in which to conduct services. Methodists ran into trouble. No sooner had they completed construction of a new church than a windstorm completely destroyed the building. Undaunted by natural calamity, church members determined to rebuild and soon had a new structure ready for occupancy.

Two newspapers spread word of Cimarron's prosperity during the first decade of the century. The *Cimarron News and Press*, which appeared in January 1907, bore a masthead of the same type used by its namesake in the 1870s. A year later the *Cimarron Citizen*, owned by George Remley and closely associated with the townsite company, began publication.

The most significant addition to Cimarron during its years of great prosperity was a new water system. The project got under way in September 1907, when George H. Webster, Jr., manager of the Urraca ranch just south of Cimarron, received permission from the territorial engineer to appropriate water from Cimarroncito Creek to provide drinking water for the town. Three years passed before all arrangements had been perfected and Webster had organized the Cimarron Water Company. Construction proceeded rapidly as a dam on the Cimarroncito was rushed to completion and pipe laid to carry water from there into Cimarron. By the spring of 1911 the city could claim one of the finest water systems in New Mexico. During the years of railroad construction in Cimarron, the town had grown, improved, and prospered at a rate unknown for many decades. When the Rocky Mountain line abandoned its tracks in the early 1940s, the town and its economy suffered a serious decline. Many more years passed before such good times again typified the little town along the historic Cimarron River.

XIII

RANCHING IN
THE TWENTIETH CENTURY

Paralleling the development of railroads and highly capitalized mining during the first years of the twentieth century, ranching on Philmont changed dramatically after 1900. Symbolized in the death of Jesús Abreu in mid-1900 and the suicide of Francis Clutton just over a year later, the generation of pioneer ranchmen, who had driven off Indians and wolves, built fences, and installed the first windmills, disappeared. With them went the picturesque cattle drives, antigrant activities, and rustling which had typified their era. In addition many smaller ranches were amalgamated into larger spreads until, by the mid-1930s, a few huge ranches dominated all of the Philmont area.

In place of Abreu and Clutton came a new group of Eastern entrepreneurs typical of whom were Stanley R. McCormick, Charles Wood, and Waite Phillips. Far less dependent on their Philmont-area operations for earning a living, they were frequently more interested in obtaining recreation than profit from their New Mexico property. High-grade livestock continued to be important, but apple growing became increasingly profitable. Several men subdivided their land into family-sized farms which they offered for sale at high prices. Mustering capital in amounts previously undreamed of, they completed impressive construction projects which altered the traditional landscape. Elegant mansions housed the ranchers and their families in the lowlands along the Sangre de Cristos, and elaborate mountain retreats offered a sanctuary from the summer heat. Important irrigation projects such as Eagle Nest Lake and Webster Reservoir facilitated the increased production of alfalfa and the development of apple orchards even grander than those of the pioneer Chase family.

Northeastern New Mexico also began to attract national attention as visitors spread word of its beauty throughout the country. A few groups, including the first Boy Scout units in the area, began to camp among its vast woodlands, while the fame of such fishing streams as the Rayado and Agua Fria grew. When guests as famous as humorist Will Rogers, Vice-President Charles Dawes, and author Kenneth L. Roberts visited the region, additional publicity resulted.

McCormick and Webster's Urraca Ranch

The first of this new breed of rancher to put his stamp on the Philmont country was Stanley R. McCormick, youngest son of the famed reaper manufacturer Cyrus McCormick. Fearful that a respiratory ailment might incapacitate him, he joined Princeton classmate John W. Garrett of Baltimore in leasing, and later purchasing, Francis Clutton's 45,000-acre Urraca Ranch north of Cimarron. The ranch was soon stocked with a trainload of Arizona cattle and put into full operation. Garrett withdrew shortly, but McCormick bought additional land high in the mountains, which later became Philmont's rugged backcountry, until his spread comprised over 70,000 acres, much of which was prime grazing land.

For McCormick the principal value of the land was a retreat far from the bustle of industrial Chicago. Whenever possible, McCormick, often accompanied by friends or relatives, vacationed at the Urraca Ranch, hiking or fishing in nearby mountains or relaxing beneath the warm Western sun. Both Cimarron residents who witnessed the wealthy young Easterners riding through town in their open buggies and cowboys who were invited to parties to provide an authentic atmosphere were sometimes amused at the newcomers. But so much did the young businessman enjoy his visits that he soon drew up plans for a $100,000 residence to accommodate all his visitors.

Just as he seemed to have launched a successful career, he was stricken with an unusual mental disorder. Stanley McCormick's intellect remained unimpaired, his brother Harold insisted at hearings two decades later, but he sometimes suffered "an interruption between the process of his mind and the expression of his thoughts." Finally Stanley developed moods of complete apathy and indifference followed by "great outbursts which might become violent."

Katherine McCormick did all she could for her ailing husband. Hoping that the quiet serenity of the California coast might assist in his recovery, she moved to an estate named Riven Rock near Santa Barbara and employed a psychiatrist to take charge of his medical care. She decided to sell the New Mexico ranch, which was by now a constant source of loss and worry. Securing permission from Associate Justice John R. McFie of the Territorial Supreme Court, she disposed of the property to its competent manager, George H. Webster, Jr., for $125,000 in June 1910. Other measures assured continued income from young McCormick's additional holdings, estimated to be worth well over $10 million.

Although less colorful than McCormick, George H. Webster, Jr., contributed significantly more to the Urraca Ranch than had his predecessor. A builder as well as a promoter, he endeavored for fifteen years to develop the resources of the property, earning profit as well as satisfaction from his success. He was also active in politics, education, and agricultural societies and played an active part in the dramatic growth of New Mexico during the first decades of the century.[2]

No sooner had Webster arrived in Colfax County than he began to carry out a comprehensive program of improvements. First priority went to irrigation. During 1908, construction began on a dam

865 feet long and forty feet high to impound water from Cimarroncito Creek. It cost over $40,000 but provided water for irrigation of 1650 acres of rich bottomland, principally devoted to alfalfa. Webster called the facility Reservoir No. 1, but it is now called Webster Lake in his honor.

In the following years Webster continued to build additional but smaller irrigation projects. One major activity involved the construction of a "small reservoir" and the subdivision of a 1500-acre tract into small farms. Plots ranged from 20 to 160 acres; each purchaser would be able to build a home and have enough water for both domestic and agricultural purposes. Although local newspapers predicted that the land would find "ready sale," little if any was apparently disposed of.

Almost as significant as Webster's work in irrigation were his innovative agricultural endeavors. By 1915 he had planted over 400 acres of "the best commercial varieties" of apple trees on a large tract of land south of Cimarroncito Creek, and boasted that the Urraca Ranch had "perhaps the largest commercial orchard in the State." A plentiful supply of Mexican-American laborers to do the tedious picking assured that the endeavor would yield a profit. Moreover, careful experimentation and consultation with horticultural experts paid off. By 1915, when fifty-three of Webster's sixty-three entries won prizes at the Colfax County Fair, the Raton Range safely affirmed "that the apple exhibit from the Urraca orchards . . . was the finest ever made from any western orchard."

Neither did Webster neglect the cattle business. Over 1800 head of high-quality Herefords regularly grazed the ranch's 73,000 acres according to the long-established pattern of winter and summer ranges. To improve the system, Webster strung an additional 150 miles of fence. A Las Vegas rancher, who visited the property in September 1914, reported the range in a "most excellent condition, showing careful and skillful management." Webster was eager to improve his herd even further, so he offered to sell $80,000 in preferred stock to buy breeding stock.

Finally, he devoted considerable attention to developing the recreational resources of his property. He had it declared a state game preserve to protect the wild game and fish, stocked Reservoir No. 1 and other lakes with more than 500,000 eastern brook trout and steelhead, and introduced a number of elk into the high mountain country. To better enjoy the natural beauty of the area, he erected a "very attractive fishing lodge" at the intersection of the Rayado and Agua Fria creeks at the present Fish Camp. "The many natural lakes and picturesque mountain streams," Webster assured prospective stockholders in 1915, "render the Urraca Ranch one of the most fascinating, restful, and delightful camping grounds to be found anywhere."

Some of the first to camp on the Webster place were Boy Scouts. During the summer of 1916, Scout scribe Wayne Kellerman of Raton described his troop's plan to visit the property. After fishing, swimming, and boating at Reservoir No. 1, they hiked in to ranch headquarters where Webster offered a "spread" and a tour of his property. Other Scouts visited the area the following summer.[3]

Early in March 1917, a blazing fireplace ignited the old Clutton home where Webster and his wife lived. Within a few minutes, the entire building had been consumed. Only a few household goods could be saved, forcing the couple to move in with Frederick Whitney in Cimarron. A new house was soon constructed just south of the Cimarroncito, and is still used as the residence for the director of Philmont.

To newspaper readers who cared little about Boy Scouts or fires, the most spine-chilling news of the year arrived from Webster Lake in mid-April 1917. Some months before, Webster had hired a watchman named Lee Brown. Well liked by the other ranch hands, Brown lived quietly in the gate house near the reservoir until one day when two men, Frank Clough and his son, came to the ranch asking for him. Directed to the cabin, they waited to punish Brown for having broken up their family by his alleged immoral conduct with Mrs. Clough. The gatekeeper appeared at the cabin after finishing his chores, only to be knocked unconscious with a revolver and wired to the floor. The assailants then mutilated the naked man in what newspapermen called "the most dastardly crime in the annals of Colfax County." Fortunately, Brown was eventually able to stagger to the nearby Heck farmhouse and notify the police. The era of unpunished crime had passed, and authorities quickly arrested the pair and sent them to prison for many years.[4]

After 1917, Webster seemed to lose interest in developing the Urraca. A slump in agricultural prices and a tightening of credit following World War I no doubt contributed to a slowdown in construction. Webster also became increasingly involved in public affairs. As early as 1917, he represented Colfax County in a statewide taxpayer's association. In 1920, local Republicans chose him to run for the state legislature. Elected by an overwhelming majority, he represented the area so ably that he won the party's unanimous renomination two years later.

Suddenly on October 17, 1922, Webster withdrew from the legislative race, insisting that "personal business matters" would prevent him from attending the lawmaking sessions in Santa Fe. Perhaps frustrated by the failure of his first marriage, horrified by events at Webster Lake, or pressed to pay an increasingly burdensome debt, Webster decided to dispose of the Urraca Ranch. He first offered the ranch for sale in the spring of 1922. Waite Phillips—a Tulsa, Oklahoma, oilman, philanthropist, and rancher—had shown an interest and sent his manager Gene Hayward from Denver on an inspection tour. On April 25, 1922, Phillips purchased almost 44,000 acres including the Urraca and Rayado tracts for over $150,000. During the next year Webster apparently decided to dispose of all his holdings and leave the area; early in 1923 he sold Phillips the remaining 30,000 acres for nearly a quarter of a million dollars. The historic Urraca Ranch became Philmont.

Webster's influence at Philmont is still apparent. In addition to the lake that bears his name, many of his apple trees still stand, although unpruned and neglected, near the training center. His fishing lodge, taken over and remodeled by Waite Phillips, stood at to-day's Fish Camp.

While Webster constructed reservoirs and ditches on his Urraca property, even larger irrigation projects had been planned elsewhere in the Philmont area. The most important was the vast Eagle Nest Dam to harness the Cimarron River for the use of ranchers and farmers. Conceived and financed under the direction of rancher Charles Springer, it marked a high point in the development of water resources in northeastern New Mexico. The dam, which a half century later is still invaluable to agriculturalists and attracts fishermen and water sports enthusiasts from all over the Southwest, symbolized a new era in ranching.

Colonizing the Rayado

While Springer was supervising construction of the very successful Eagle Nest project, similar but less effective irrigation works were being planned in the Rayado area. A series of owners announced grandiose plans of development in hope of selling land to small farmers. None had the available capital or managerial ability of Springer, and little construction actually occurred. Their techniques were, however, typical of those used in the Southwest during the first quarter of the twentieth century.

A new era in the history of the Rayado Ranch began in April 1911, when the Abreu family sold their ranch to a company of Denver businessmen. Principals in the corporation were three brothers named Hagadorn. They planned to subdivide 5000 acres of the ranch into small farms averaging eighty acres. To assure adequate water for irrigation, the company would erect a series of reservoirs and an elaborate ditch system.[5]

Almost immediately the Hagadorns initiated a sales campaign throughout much of the United States. Brochures describing the Rayado received wide distribution. According to their publicity, the Rayado Colonization Company found many farmers interested in moving to New Mexico. In September 1913, the Hagadorns predicted that thirty Pennsylvania Dutch families would arrive the following spring. To accommodate them, homes, wells, barns, and other necessary facilities would be erected on each tract. This report must have been overly optimistic, however, for the following spring the number of dwellings under construction had been reduced to five. Still the demand for lumber was sufficient for the company to purchase its own sawmill which was put to work on the Upper Rayado, probably near where Philmont's Abreu Camp was later located. Contractors began building reservoirs in February 1914, promising completion by the time the summer rains began. Only one, Hagadorn Lake, was apparently completed. "Activities on the ranch have taken on new life," reported the Cimarron News, "and the present year promises unprecedented prosperity in the shape of substantial improvements and an increased influx of substantial farmers."

Although the statements of the Rayado company seem to have been grossly exaggerated and unreliable, some farmers evidently did purchase land and begin farming. The number may have increased after the Hagadorns devised a new plan whereby no down payment was required. Each settler would split his crop with the company until half of the price had been paid. Thereafter the farmer would finish buying his property through "easy installments." Most of the colonists lived on the mesa just north of the old Abreu headquarters.

Despite all Hagadorn's glowing predictions, it soon became evident that the climate and soil of the Philmont region were unsuitable for small agricultural enterprises. Most farmers discovered that they could not earn a living on the tiny plots they had contracted for. A few continued to make payments, but the majority simply abandoned the area and lost their investment. Their houses were deserted and soon after torn down. Today only a few cement foundations, visible along the road between Philmont's Camping Headquarters and Rayado, provide evidence of their presence. The only settler who left a lasting impression was Paul F. Zastrow, a

Russian immigrant who purchased just over 600 acres along Rayado Creek west of the Abreu home. Today a Philmont camp bearing his name (incorrectly spelled Zastro) is headquarters for Wood Badge courses attended by Scouters from all over the nation.

The next owner of the historic Rayado was the Chicago Livestock Company, financed by Illinois and Iowa investors. To manage the property they selected Charles E. Wood, who had previously run a stock farm in Iowa.[6] At first it seemed that their operation would differ little from Hagadorn's. Work on a second reservoir would be completed; additional colonists would be encouraged to settle in the Rayado area.

Soon colonization schemes were abandoned, however, and for the next six years Wood operated a diversified ranch not unlike that of the Abreu family. The main activity was raising high-quality Hereford cattle. An initial herd of 300 was quickly enlarged until it reached 1000. Numerous barns (many of them still being used), corrals, and other facilities were built around the old settlement. Wood also put 125 acres of the best irrigated land into alfalfa, most of which was fed to the livestock during the winter.

Wood developed two other major sources of income at Rayado. Since impressive stands of timber covered the tops of several nearby mesas, Wood moved a sawmill into the area and began turning out lumber in 1917. For five years it produced 8000 board feet a day. In addition, the Abreu orchards continued to produce excellent fruit.

Even though the Rayado Ranch had consistently paid good profits for the Chicago Livestock Company, it decided to abandon the enterprise in 1922. Two young stockmen, John and Frank Sauble, had been running cattle along the Sweetwater Valley just south of Philmont. They needed additional grazing land and showed an interest in the Rayado. At first they merely leased the property, but after a few months decided to buy. The Saubles apparently operated a general cattle ranch at Rayado. In 1929, however, the Oklahoma oilman who had purchased the Urraca Ranch and was rapidly expanding his holdings in northeastern New Mexico, bought them out. Thus the Rayado ended forever its independent existence and became a part of Waite Phillips's Philmont ranch.

Waite Phillips

No individual was more important to the history of the Philmont Scout Ranch than Waite Phillips. True, some men had a greater role in transforming the New Mexico frontier and many spent more time in the area. But because of the foresight and generosity of Phillips, the tract he owned became the property of the Boy Scouts of America. No longer the exclusive domain of the rich or the privileged, it was subsequently opened to young men and adults from across the United States.

Phillips rose from humble beginnings to become one of the wealthiest men in America. He was born on a farm in southwestern Iowa, near the village of Conway, on January 19, 1883. Endowed with an inherent love of nature, Phillips's boyhood interests lay in scouting the timbered creeks of that country. He attended the local public schools while at the same time helping with farm duties. With older brothers to take his place at the plow, Waite and his identical twin, Wiate, started West at the age of sixteen toward the "shining mountains." When his twin brother died during the summer of 1902 in Spokane, Washington, Waite returned home. Later he attended business school for a short time in Shenandoah, Iowa.

Phillips's business career began as bookkeeper for a Knoxville, Iowa, coal company. There he met and married Genevieve Elliot, daughter of the town banker. In 1906, however, Phillips moved to Bartlesville, Indian Territory, to join his two older brothers, Frank and L. E., in the oil business. By the time he left a decade later, he was very knowledgeable about petroleum. After a short stay in Arkansas, he began buying up oil leases around Okmulgee, Oklahoma, and within a few months his first strike came at Phillipsville. He rapidly bought up other properties, many of which proved exceedingly rich. "Almost overnight," one historian observed, "he became a millionaire." In 1924 Phillips sold out his accumulated properties for about $5 million and started a new enterprise, the Waite Phillips Company. During the following year, he "ate, slept, and drank the oil business." It all paid off in October 1925, when the New York investment house of Blair and Company purchased the Waite Phillips Company for $25 million. The following Christmas, Phillips rewarded his former employees with a $100,000 bonus.

In the meantime Phillips also expanded his investments in other businesses, especially in his hometown of Tulsa. Following the tradition set by his brother Frank, he invested in several banks, serving as Chairman of the Board of the National Bank and Trust Company of Tulsa for several years. In the heart of the city he began construction of the twenty-three-story Philtower office building in 1925; later a somewhat smaller edifice across the street known as the Philcade building was completed. As a residence for himself, Genevieve, and their two children, Elliott and Helen Jane, he erected a magnificent mansion, Philbrook, on the outskirts of the city. Frequently the family spent summers at the large ranch which Phillips acquired near Denver, Colorado.[7]

Phillips became interested in obtaining additional property in 1922, partly as an investment, but more because he wanted a larger and more spectacular area for recreation. Learning that George H. Webster might be interested in selling the Urraca, he sent Gene Hayward, his manager in Denver, to inspect the property. Hayward's report was enthusiastic. The ranch exactly suited Phillips's needs, so he completed the purchase in two major steps.

Almost immediately Phillips and his representatives began to enlarge his New Mexico holdings. Many of the plots were small, especially in the Rayado area where farmers were eager to dispose of their holdings. In addition to the farms of the Saubles, Hecks, and Chandlers, Phillips purchased major acreage from the Maxwell Land Grant Company, including land north of the Cimarron River and high in the mountains west of the Urraca Ranch. One small but important addition was the tiny eighty-acre Ladd orchard midway between the Urraca and Cimarroncito creeks along the old Santa Fe road. For $24,000 Phillips acquired the site of Philmont's Camping Headquarters. At first the Tulsa oilman planned to call his new ranch the Hawkeye, apparently in honor of his native state. Soon, however, it was changed to Philmont, combining his name and the word "mountain."

In addition to acquiring land, Phillips also undertook a development program even more impressive than Webster's. He insisted on the highest possible quality in his cattle herd and purchased large numbers of extremely expensive registered bulls. Corrals north of the Cimarroncito were either built or extensively remodeled to accommodate polo ponies. Phillips also designed and built a major ditch to carry water—sometimes via flumes—from the Cimarron River across the old Heck and Nash places to the enlarged alfalfa fields and apple orchards near his headquarters. Buildings were built or refurbished all over the ranch.

Phillips's most impressive project was a family mansion, designed by Kansas City architect Edward B. Delk, who had previously done Philbrook in Tulsa. The home, built in a southern Mediterranean style with many features similar to the Tulsa structure, was begun soon after the family returned from Europe in 1925. It contained two stories, with an exceptionally large living room, a huge master bedroom with sun porch, private rooms for the children and servants, and several guest rooms. A swimming pool and flower-bedecked patios added to the exterior beauty.

Phillips spared no expense in building the Villa Philmonte and other facilities to enhance the recreational value of the property. High in the mountains at the intersection of the Rayado and Agua Fria creeks, he began major renovations on Webster's cabin, transforming it into one of the most beautiful buildings in the area. A hunting lodge on the upper Cimarroncito, while simple, attracted many favorable comments from visitors. Phillips loved to ride horseback through the backcountry, so he built a series of trails covering most of the property. The most difficult followed the ridge of the Tooth of Time; in some places dynamite had to be used to carve a path through the solid rock. Phillips also stocked many of the streams on Philmont with trout; the number of deer increased dramatically, as did the elk, bear, and antelope. A few bighorn sheep were brought onto the property, as was a camel which soon became one of the curiosities of the neighborhood. The Philmont buffalo herd grew steadily, recalling the day when those shaggy beasts roamed the plains by the millions.

As Philmont became one of the showplaces of northeastern New Mexico, Waite Phillips began to invite many of his friends to enjoy its beauty. The most famous visitors arrived in the midsummer of 1927. Heading the party was United States Vice-President Charles Dawes. He was accompanied by John T. McCutcheon, famed cartoonist, and authors Kenneth L. Roberts and Ben Ames Williams. The highlight of the visit was a trip to Phillips's magnificent fishing camp along the Rayado. A chef and butler had been sent ahead to make sure that the guests were properly cared for. Shower baths, hair mattresses, epicurean meals, and the like were provided.[8] Sometime later, aviator Wiley Post and Will Rogers also visited Philmont.

Phillips was not content, however, merely to entertain guests at his New Mexico ranch or lead a life of leisure. An advocate of Andrew Carnegie's "Gospel of Wealth," he strongly believed it to be the responsibility of those who acquired riches to share them with others. "Real philanthropy," he once wrote, "consists of helping others, outside our own family circle, from whom no thanks is expected or required." As one newspaper later pointed out, he lived by those words: "Benevolence was the distinguishing characteristic of Waite Phillips. As embodied in his life, it was the path of duty." During the 1930s Phillips began to make numerous philanthropic contributions. Late in September of 1938, Phillips offered his beautiful Philbrook estate to the Tulsa community. Many predicted that the home, with its expensive furnishings and magnificent art collection, would become the cultural focus of Oklahoma.[9] Little did the citizens of Oklahoma realize that within a few months Phillips would make another donation of national significance to the Boy Scouts of America, and that his vast New Mexico ranch would be turned into a paradise for scouting.

XIV

THE END
OF BALDY MINING

At the same time that men like Webster and Phillips were developing their ranches along the edge of the Sangre de Cristos, Colfax
County miners renewed their search for gold on the slopes of Baldy
Mountain. They knew that there was still a tremendous store of
precious metal locked inside the great geological vault. But how,
they wondered, could it be profitably extracted? A shortage of water
in the Moreno Valley had doomed all but the richest placer grounds.
Giant dredges like the *Eleanor* seemed incapable of earning sustained profits. Mine and mill operators with insufficient technical
knowledge and practical experience had brought tremendous losses
to all but a few investors on both sides of Baldy. Elusive veins inside
the mountain had evaded the McIntyre brothers' deep tunnel mine.
After the promoters of the once renowned Aztec Mine failed to make
a profit, many experts predicted that the Baldy district was on a
one-way track to abandonment.

Excitement on Aztec Ridge

The Maxwell Land Grant Company, having never lost faith in the
ability of its mines to produce, hoped to invalidate these cheerless
predictions of failure. Its resurrection of the Aztec Mine in 1909

opened the third and final act in the drama of Baldy mining. The Dutch corporation employed J. T. Sparks to superintend miners at the headquarters on Ute Creek. To provide technical advice, the company hired Charles A. Chase, a well-known Colorado mining engineer. It was probably on his recommendation that Sparks sank four shafts, identified numerically, at intervals of 75 feet along Aztec Ridge just above Baldy Town. Shaft number four struck a contact formation ore body late in 1911. Sparks probed from the initial find, but was able to extract only meager quantities of low-grade ore. Because of high development costs, expenses exceeded returns by nearly $25,000. Sparks also was said to be drinking excessively, and in April 1914, J. Van Houten, the company president, fired him.[1]

Van Houten immediately put Ernest V. Deshayes, a mining engineer who had worked as assayer and surveyor under Sparks, in charge of operations, but warned him that unless promising ore was uncovered within three months, the company would discontinue operations at the mine. Coordinating geological diagrams and maps, Deshayes calculated that a second contact formation should be 300 feet below the old Aztec level. A new tunnel intersected the expected formation; it did not appear to contain values, but as a matter of routine, Deshayes sent samples to the assayer:

> That afternoon [Deshayes recalled years later] the assayer looked me up and handed me the assay returns on the samples. To my amazement the return on the simple shale was a value in gold of nearly three thousand dollars per ton. I told the assayer that there must be a mistake for that sample was ordinary shale. Well, he replied, if that was just shale it was the most valuable shale I ever heard of.[2]

The amount of rock was relatively small, but the lode was so rich that the Maxwell company's profits surged upward. The total Colfax County gold production jumped from $15,588 in 1913 to $350,745 in 1915.

Rapid development in mine and mill generated increased activity at the little town perched high on the western slope of Baldy Mountain. So many families arrived at Baldy Town that the Maxwell company was unable to accommodate them and some lived in tents. Because everyone aspired to work in the mines, construction men were scarce. In July 1916, the Maxwell company contracted with a Cimarron builder to erect a hotel to relieve the desperate housing shortage. Many years later, even after the hotel was demolished, its tall, thin chimney stood as a Baldy landmark until a heavy winter wind toppled it in the late 1960s.

Despite his mining success, Deshayes refused to take advice from either Maxwell company president Van Houten or Charles A. Chase, both of whom were paid to give it. By late in 1916 the rich ore body was nearly gone; the area where it had been found was thoroughly explored without success. Deshayes proposed that test drilling be done on the Ponil slopes of the ridge in hope of finding rich ore further down the horizontal contact formation. Van Houten opposed the plan, insisting that a long tunnel be driven from the northwest or Ponil side to intersect the contact. Deshayes objected loudly to the Dutchman's plans, and in September 1917 submitted his resignation.

The Deshayes administration had proved the value of having scientifically trained personnel to run the Aztec. While he was still at the mine, Van Houten hired Edward H. Perry and Augustus Locke, trained mining consultants from California, to make a thorough geological study of the mine and propose a plan for its operation. The pair completed their work in the fall of 1916 and shortly thereafter submitted a report which made specific recommendations as to where shafts and tunnels should be driven to encounter rich ore. These studies assisted later superintendents in developing the underground workings at the Aztec.

World War I created formidable difficulties for the managers of the Baldy mines. Certain necessary materials were in short supply; labor was scarce; prices were prohibitively high. Maxwell company officials were strongly anti-German and insisted that their employees agree with their sentiments. Contributions to the Red Cross, investment in Liberty bonds, and a generally pro-British fervor were prerequisite to success at the Aztec.

By the time Douglas Muir took over management in the spring of 1918, rich ore bodies had become more and more expensive to exploit. Costs in the mill had risen to $10.07 a ton, while mine development prices simultaneously surged to almost $16 a foot for nearly 1000 feet of work. Whereas it had previously been profitable to work low-grade ore deposits, by 1918 only the richest could be handled profitably. Increased costs, plus the failure of Muir to find any new ore bodies reduced net profits from the Aztec.

Frustrations of Baldy Mining

Excitement at the Aztec obscured all other activities in the Baldy district. The McIntyre brothers continued their work in pushing a tunnel completely through the mountain. Forced to stop work in 1908 for lack of funds, the valiant and determined pair pushed on two years later. By 1912 they had issued and sold $200,000 worth of stock as their original charter authorized and had spent all the money. Burdened with nonassessable shares, the McIntyres had no choice but to increase their capitalization and sell more stock. They did. Fourteen years later an additional $90,000 had gone by the board.[3]

In the years that followed, the brothers sold just enough stock to pay for driving their tunnel further into the heart of the mountain. They remained consistently optimistic, always certain that they would soon encounter those elusive veins. The men never struck it rich. But even after William died in April 1930, his brother Alex continued the project alone.

Two years after "Billy's" death, employees of the deep tunnel company appeared at the headwaters of South Ponil Creek, just above Philmont's Copper Park Camp, and started work on a second tunnel, designed to intersect the first one deep inside Baldy. The completion of the new project would be the culmination of the long crosscutting work. Four years later, when workmen broke through the rock, the two tunnels were centered within an inch of each other. Although it was still possible even then to walk straight through Baldy from one side to the other, no rich veins intersected the walkway. The Deep Tunnel Gold Mining and Milling Company had been a colossal failure, exhausting the money of many investors and the lives of William and Alex McIntyre.

Placer miners were less patient than investors in the deep tunnel fiasco. Although many mining journals announced in 1915 that "a sum equal to $300,000" would be spent in working Moreno Valley placers that year, production statistics gave no evidence of that much activity. Sluicers took just over $16,000 worth of precious metal out of Colfax County placers in 1916. Never again during the next two decades did production for any year exceed $10,000.

Across the mountain in Ute Creek, a series of small placer companies started up in the early 1920s. The first, Ute Gold Mining Company, was incorporated in September 1921. Five years later it was bankrupt. In April 1926, R. G. Mullen, who promoted a large number of mining ventures in the district, incorporated Ute Creek Gold Placer Company and planned to buy some placer grounds at a foreclosure sale. During 1927 Mullen's group actively placered with a 1000-yard steam shovel. The company apparently lasted only a short time. A third typically short-lived firm was the Baldy Mountain Placer Company, organized in September 1922 and dissolved in September 1925. Today the hikers from Baldy toward Miranda Camp or Ute Park pass pile after pile of rocks, all that remains to show where these uniformly unsuccessful endeavors were carried out.

Also founded in 1922 was the Aztec Extension Gold Mines Company. It seemed as harmless as the rest until an unusually humorous letter from Frank D. Desmond, president of the company, exposed it as the most glaring example of promotional deceit ever perpetrated in the Baldy district. Desmond responded to a query from the New Mexico Corporation Commission as to the status of the company:

> I was Pres[ident] of the Aztec Extension Gold Mines Company because I had put the most money in it, and I was quite sure that it was a "going" concern, until I learned that it had "gone." They told me it was a "good buy," but they must have spelled it "g-o-o-d b-y-e." . . .
> So it appears that the Aztec Extension Gold Mines company has been dissolved into that non-assessable spirit world of dreams and hopes and paper returns of perverted "hunks."
> If you should decide that the corporation is non-existent, so be it. Yesterday is now a dream and tomorrow is only a vision. As far as I know the company did nothing except what it did to me. Hopes, thrills, delusions, then the transformation into doubt, dismay, and despair. Regret, yes. Remorse? Ah, no. You know the old saying . . . there's one born every minute, and two or three to sell him some stock.[4]

Part of the proposal made to Desmond involved leasing an unnamed mine, probably the Aztec, which was deserted when the Dutch owners suspended work. The town of Baldy presented a "forlorn appearance of complete abandonment" when a state appraiser visited it in 1921. He examined the mine, described the hazardous prospects of trying to reopen it, and appraised the famous mine's value at "zero."[5] Others were more optimistic. The first of the tenants to try bringing life back to Baldy was the Aztec Gold Mines Company, incorporated in 1921 with an initial capitalization of $1 million. Robert G. Mullen was chief promoter. Even though the company reported gold production of $20,000 a month during the last half of 1922, it was in perilous financial condition when the newly rebuilt mill was severely damaged by fire May 24, 1923. Unable to raise sufficient capital to reconstruct it, the corporation dissolved itself and cancelled the lease.

Mullen, never easily discouraged, quickly raised new financial support and incorporated the Rosita Gold Mining and Milling Company in October 1923. They rebuilt the mill in 1924, apparently increasing its capacity. A year later 150 men were at work. Persistent quarreling among the owners, a reported lack of sobriety by Mullen, and the absence of rich ore contributed to the failure of the Rosita company. In February 1926, the Maxwell Land Grant Company decided it had put up with the unsatisfactory operation of the mine long enough and cancelled the contract with Mullen.

Last Years of the Aztec

It soon became apparent that the Dutch company once again planned to open the mine itself.[6] After the completion of initial exploratory work under Frank C. Bowman, the Maxwell company began to rehabilitate the mill, installing a second Lane Chilean grinder and flotation equipment. After about a year on the job, Bowman was dismissed and replaced by Alvis F. Denison, who had been mine foreman. High costs prompted the Maxwell company's representatives to close the mill soon after, but they did permit Denison to retain a small crew to continue searching for rich bodies inside the mountain. He evaluated maps of the workings and decided that there should be a large area of good rock on the north or Ponil side of the ridge. As Van Houten had come to the same conclusion earlier, Denison received permission to run several exploratory raises off the main Ponil tunnel, paying particular attention to areas where sandstone and shale were in contact. It was there, he knew, that intrusive, gold-bearing ore should be found. He was consistently disappointed, however, and never uncovered paying rock.

Denison, like several of his predecessors, recommended that a thorough geophysical study of the Aztec area be made to take advantage of technological developments since the last survey. Van Houten contacted the Radiore Corporation of Los Angeles which sent a crew to Baldy to undertake the work. One casing they left behind can still be seen in Copper Park. Radiore found several spots which could be prospected successfully and pointed them out to the mine managers. The best was on the Ponil side of the ridge. In addition, Denison obtained a portable compressor and diamond drills to do exploratory work of his own. His only discovery was a copper ore deposit beneath Copper Park, again on the north side of the Aztec. A tunnel to reach this area had been driven 100 feet into the mountain when Denison resigned in the spring of 1930 to operate his father's Arkansas manganese mine. His replacement was James P. McMenemy, who continued work on the "H" Tunnel under Copper Park.

On April 30, 1930, Van Houten cabled the mine manager to cease all work except on the main tunnel. Soon the American stockholders of the Maxwell company ordered even that project halted. On June 1, the mine closed, and Baldy Town was virtually deserted. The Maxwell company could not and would not subsidize expensive exploration in the midst of worldwide economic distress.

Little other activity enlivened the Baldy district during the Great Depression. In 1920 the state appraiser reported that no mine but the Aztec had any "presumption of value." In the Moreno Valley only a few prospectors sinking a single shaft were found; no other evidence of activity showed around the nearly deserted village of E-town. A decade later the Aztec produced a mere $248, which constituted the total gold production of a district once renowned as one of the best in the Rocky Mountains. All appearances indicated that a quarter of a century of relative prosperity at the Aztec had done little to brighten dark prospects.

In 1932 Matt W. Gorman, formerly Baldy Town assayer, negotiated a lease with the Maxwell company for the Aztec. He immediately attempted to repair the neglected Lane Chilean mills and the power plant, but had little success. Gorman was unable to finance capital outlays himself, but within a year he was able to obtain backing from Van Houten. No doubt the Dutchman was more easily persuaded to invest in the project after President Franklin D. Roosevelt announced that the government would buy gold at a standard price of $35 an ounce. With profits assured, the pair agreed that Van Houten would provide the capital while Gorman directed work on the mountain. Profits were to be shared equally. The new partners immediately disposed of the long-obsolescent crusher and brought in the first ball mill ever used in the district.

By the spring of 1935 the Maxwell company directors realized that with the high price of gold, they could earn better profits from the Aztec because of its ability to invest in better equipment and advance cash for underground development. On April 10, 1935, the Dutch company cancelled Gorman's lease, agreeing to a new one by which he would manage the Aztec as an employee. The modernization program continued at a more rapid rate. Inside the ridge, Gorman discovered ore bodies six to fifteen feet below the contact zone where ore had usually been located. By breaking through floors of tunnels dug by Denison, Gorman's men were able to locate substantial quantities of valuable rock, though it was not as rich as earlier finds.

In spite of increased production, the Aztec failed to return profits as anticipated. Necessary purchases of machinery in 1935 brought about a net loss of $19,000; the Aztec added only $6000 to the company's coffers during the next twelve months. Mill repairs and water shortages indicated to company managers that only slim profits could be expected for 1937.

Directors of the Maxwell company, suspecting incompetence among the American operators, decided to send a Dutch engineer with considerable mining experience in Indonesia, Victor J. Van Lint, to New Mexico to assist Van Houten. Like Chase before him, Van Lint was very critical of Aztec operations. The assaying was not properly done; ore cars, rails, and pipe were in short supply. The diesel engine which powered compressors at the Ponil entrance lacked sufficient power, he complained. Although maps of individual segments of the Aztec had been drawn, he found that no one had ever unified them so as to demonstrate general geological patterns inside Aztec Ridge. Van Lint also warned that friendships rather than business principles had dictated the personnel practices. As a result many mine employees were incapable of handling their jobs.

Because of his outspoken criticism and European mannerisms, Van Lint quickly gained the intense dislike of almost all the mine employees. Many refused to have social relations with him or his family. They accused him of expecting the impossible. Unable to accustom himself to the lack of enthusiasm among local Spanish-American workers, Van Lint was said to have treated them like Indonesian savages. The Dutchman's lack of familiarity with specific mining problems also did little to earn him the respect of his more learned critics.

Van Lint and Gorman continued to disagree violently about the operation of the Aztec. Van Lint even accused his foreman of dumping rich ore into waste piles and running worthless rock through the mill to make him look bad before his superiors. The long hostilities ended in the spring of 1938 when Van Lint refused to renew Gorman's contract and ordered him out of camp. Simultaneously he fired several others whom he felt were allied with Gorman.

Development on the Ponil slope of the mine had failed to uncover any new ore pockets. To guarantee sufficient ore to keep the crushers running, several leased mines including Pippert's Montezuma were taken over, and their ore was also fed into the Baldy mill. An increasing quantity of dump ore, from which Van Lint hoped to remove enough gold which had been lost from previous milling to be profitable, was remilled. When the Fair Labor Standards Act became law on June 25, 1938, the company was forced to pay its miners an hourly wage of twenty-five cents, with additional amounts for time in excess of forty hours; operational expenses further increased. Many residents suspected that after the usual winter shutdown in 1939 the Aztec would never reopen. Hanson and Van Lint made a thorough examination of the property, however, and recommended that exploration continue the following spring.

The plan was approved, and the mine and mill started on April 1,

1940. During the next six months, only 1698 tons of Aztec ore went through the mill; some 17,500 tons of old ore were reworked. By fall Van Lint realized that the Aztec had become a liability to the company. After Nazi armies overran Holland in May 1940, he was certain that the Dutch stockholders could not operate a mine which did not even meet expenses. Subsequently the mine and mill ceased to operate on September 1, 1940. Two weeks later the little town was once more virtually abandoned. By early 1941 houses were demolished, mill machinery sold, and rails, pipe, and everything else of value hauled away. The Aztec mine had closed forever.

Death of the Baldy District

Just over Aztec Ridge from Baldy Town was the French Henry mine, worked sporadically by C. H. Anderson in 1937. In September of that year a group of wealthy men organized a company, one of the few entirely speculative ventures in the history of the district, to open it.[7] Included among the promoters were the most distinguished businessmen in New Mexico. Colonel Raymond L. Harrison, Albuquerque automobile parts dealer, was the principal sponsor. Within a short time the group was joined by Clinton P. Anderson, influential Albuquerque insurance executive and prominent Democratic Party politician. He subsequently served as United States secretary of agriculture and senator from New Mexico. Relying solely on the evaluation of a "local engineer of sorts who could do surveying," these men entered the mining business. On July 5, 1938, the French Henry Mining and Milling Company received its incorporation papers.

Matt W. Gorman, who had left the Aztec just previously, was employed as resident manager. He quickly purchased milling machinery, including a 50-ton ball crusher and a "host of mechanical devices for separating the gold from the crude ore," at a cost of about $200,000. In addition, Gorman erected a log building for the officers to stay in while visiting the mine and several other structures for employee residences, storage facilities, and the like along the banks of the South Ponil.

The Albuquerque investors soon realized that they had been duped. The ore recovered was not at all like that which they had been shown; some suspected that their mine had been salted with ore from the Aztec. Anderson hired James B. Tenney to make a thorough study of the French Henry. His report confirmed suspicions that the property was worthless. He recommended that development work cease immediately to avoid larger losses. There was no chance of profitable exploitation. Fortunately, the speculators were able to recover about two-thirds of their investment by selling machinery. The closing of the French Henry marked just one more instance of the failure of Baldy lode mines to produce the satisfactory dividends which might rescue the district from an increasingly dismal situation. The old structures later became Philmont's French Henry Camp.

In the Moreno Valley opposite Elizabethtown, small placer mining activities continued for two years during the early 1940s. For example, two Ohioans, Floyd Fuller and Gilbert Monroe, decided to invest in New Mexico placer mining. Joined by several other Ohio businessmen, they incorporated the Fullroe Company on October 17, 1940. Since placering with sluice boxes or by spraying great quantities of water on a gravel bank was no longer profitable, they located the most modern machinery. Most important was a huge revolving screen which separated worthless rocks from the sand and gravel which might contain flakes of gold. The machine pumped the remaining muddy mixture onto a large flat table where corduroy riffles caught precious minerals just as sluice boxes had done, three-quarters of a century earlier at the same site. A gasoline-powered shovel with drag line, deep-well pump, tractor, light plant, bulldozer, and truck completed the necessary equipment. In all it cost about $25,000. Operations continued for eight months producing small but satisfactory returns.[8]

The active entrance of the United States into World War II marked the end of all significant mining on Baldy. A few lone prospectors may have sluiced small quantities of precious metal from the Moreno Valley, but never in the last twenty years has the amount exceeded $500.[9] The people who once lived in Elizabethtown have moved to Eagle Nest, where fishermen, winter sports enthusiasts, and sightseers support a small year-round population. In the south end of the Moreno Valley, a ski resort, Angel Fire, attracts many additional people to the region. One author who visited the now abandoned capital of the Baldy district wrote:

> E-town was deserted when I visited it, and the wind blew in cutting blasts across its treeless streets. On the crown of one low hill is a church, built of stained and weathered boards; on the top of another hill is the cemetery. . . . Tall sagebrush hides many of the foundation holes, in which debris and fragments of sun-tinted lavendar glass lie jumbled together. . . . E-town may come alive in summer, when fishermen and tourists roam the mountains and cattlemen drive their herds into the fertile valley and up the slopes of Old Baldy, but in February it is only a rattling husk.[10]

Late in 1962 new hope for life at Baldy was injected by the purchase of 10,098 acres of land on the eastern slopes of the great mountain by the National Council of the Boy Scouts of America. By then, even the Maxwell Land Grant Company had concluded that there was no chance for profitable mining operations. For a mere $196,520, Tacoma, Washington, lumber executive Norton Clapp purchased the area and all rights for the Scouts. It would be incorporated into Philmont Scout Ranch so that "the historic mining sites and rugged mountains and lakes [would be] available for exploration by our youth." The sale included the Aztec Mine, which had produced over $4 million in gold since its discovery in 1868.

XV

A PARADISE FOR SCOUTING

After 1938 the historic land along the eastern edge of the Sangre
de Cristo Mountains of northeastern New Mexico assumed a special
role in the history of the American West. The presence of Indians,
Spanish explorers, Santa Fe traders, miners, and cattlemen had already contributed much to its color and legend. But when Waite
Phillips deeded large tracts of his magnificent estate to the Boy
Scouts of America, the property entered a new and very different
era. A veritable camping paradise was developed for Scouts, attract-
ing boys and their leaders from all over the United States. Across the
nation Philmont became synonymous with high adventure. The
process by which Phillip's wilderness ranch was transformed into
Philmont Scout Ranch provides a dramatic conclusion to the
colorful history of the region.

Phillips's First Donation

No sooner had Oklahoma oilman Waite Phillips decided to give his
spacious Philbrook home to the citizens of Tulsa than he began to
consider the possibility of other gifts which would have an even
greater impact. He chose the Boy Scouts of America. As early as 1934

he had contacted the youth group through its regional Scout executive, James P. Fitch. A preliminary investigation was made, but four years passed before Phillips felt ready to make a definite move.

Late in the summer of 1938, the Tulsa businessman wrote National Scout President Walter Head to suggest once again that he might be willing to give the Boy Scouts a 35,000-acre tract in the mountains of New Mexico. So that they could inspect the property, Phillips invited a committee of Scout officials to visit the ranch as his guests. From the start, Head and James E. West, Chief Scout Executive, wondered how such a camp would fit into their program. The very thought of a vast New Mexico property seemed foreign to Scouting's traditional mode of operation. How could such an establishment be financed? Would it conflict with the national policy of promoting council ownership of such facilities? Despite their misgivings, however, the Scouts in New York felt compelled at least to inspect the acreage offered them.[1]

West appointed a special committee of three men, all experts in camp management and design, whom he sent to Philmont. L. L. McDonald, national director of camping and later camp chief for the Boy Scouts' Schiff Scout Reservation in New Jersey; Ray H. Bryan, assistant director of the Scouts' engineering service; and regional executive James P. Fitch were assigned to make a thorough study of the proposal. For five days, accompanied by Phillips or his manager, they rode over much of the 300,000-acre ranch. Special attention went to the Ponil Canyon country, which had been proposed as a campsite. Skepticism soon gave way to enthusiasm. Conversation centered on the real possibility of establishing a great national Boy Scout camp in New Mexico.

No sooner had the Scout Executives returned East than Phillips made a "definite written confirmation" of his earlier oral offer: if the National Council of the Boy Scouts of America accepted his proposal on or before November 1, 1938, he would donate 35,857 acres of land together with $50,000 for developing and improving it.

His only requirement was that the gift be used "for the benefit of the members of the Boy Scout organization."

Phillips also elaborated his thoughts as to how the property might be used. The junction of the Middle and South Ponil creeks, he wrote, seemed a logical place for the headquarters. From there trails built toward Bear and Dean canyons and North Ponil Creek would provide access to the entire tract. To assure year-round communication, he recommended that the state be encouraged to take over road maintenance from Cimarron. He also suggested that the area be designated as a game preserve so the visiting Scouts could view the deer, turkey, grouse, and other wildlife in the area. Although insisting that these suggestions were in no way binding, Phillips, probably after initial talks with the Scout leaders, even suggested that the new camp be named "Philturn," combining the first part of his name with the word "turn," symbolic of every Scout's obligation to do a daily good deed. "Philturn Boyscout Park," he thought, might be suitable.

In New York a bustle of activity followed receipt of Phillips's letters. Scout officials began a quiet canvass of local councils to determine if the proposed camp would be of use in their programs. Armed with evidence of need, Head and West strongly urged the National Council to accept Phillips's offer when it met in New York on October 20. The Council ratified the proposal, thanked Phillips, and set forth an outline of the role of the New Mexico camp in Scouting's overall program. "Here, deep in the heart of the primitive forest where wildlife abounds and nature's wonders challenge the imagination," a resolution proclaimed, "those Scouts whose experience and training have qualified them for this adventure in the wilderness will be able to have the experiences of our pioneer forefathers who established the traditions and the historical background of this high country." One month later, November 28, 1938, Waite and Genevieve Phillips deeded what was officially named "Philturn Rockymountain Scoutcamp" to the Boy Scouts of America.

Philturn Rockymountain Scoutcamp

Once they had acquired the vast New Mexico tract, Scout officials were faced with the challenge of developing it into an exemplary camp. Every decision made during the following months established precedent. Engineers and architects designed buildings and facilities to fit the unique demands of a Western ranch. There were miles of trails to be laid out and built over rugged sandstone cliffs. Phillips having provided the funds for construction, West, Arthur A. Schuck, and everyone else in the Boy Scout organization enthusiastically proclaimed the property's potentials and set about to make sure they were realized. To direct the new property, West chose B. B. Dawson, the Nebraska Scout executive.

Dawson conceived of Philturn as a "he-man" wilderness camp. In keeping with Phillips's suggestion, a central headquarters would be established where groups might be checked in and out, purchase supplies and equipment, and obtain information as to the location of possible campsites throughout the property. Once groups left base camp, however, they would be entirely on their own. The director would have no responsibility for programs but merely make source materials available to the units. A major part of Dawson's program involved the establishment of qualifications for attendance: minimum requirements of leadership, campcraft experience, age, and even rank should be established. Once the boys had proved themselves and received the necessary approval, they would be permitted to use the camp and its facilities with as few restrictions as possible. The "pampering" prevalent in many dude ranches and private camps should be avoided at all costs. "What about the boy?" Dawson asked. What would he think of a trip to Philturn? "You have only to gather one or a dozen about you and point to the possibilities," the new director wrote West, "then read your answer in the sparkle of their eyes."

Thousands of Scouts were already looking forward to visiting Philturn by the time Dawson arrived in January 1939. Much work remained to be done, especially at the base camp, named Five Points because of its location at the intersection of five main canyons. Aided by Ray Bryan and others from the Scout engineering service, Dawson supervised the design and construction of three troop camping sites near the headquarters. A small cabin soon provided temporary accommodations for the director, while a commissary building was provisioned with food and supplies which groups might require. Horses and burros had been purchased and would soon be arriving. In the backcountry, troop sites consisting of cooking shelters and fireplaces took form in Dean Canyon, at Stony Point high atop the ridge north of Five Points, and near the old C&N terminus at Pueblano. Encouraged by Scout leaders, the Raton Chamber of Commerce, and Phillips himself, the State of New Mexico agreed to maintain the twelve miles of dirt road from just outside Cimarron to Five Points.

Although the camp had not been scheduled to open until June 12, 1939, the first Scouts arrived in late March. That summer ninety-nine boys from Texas, Kansas, Louisiana, and Oklahoma stayed for a full twelve days, taking part in such varied activities as gold panning and wildlife study. Some even examined the Indian petroglyphs in North Ponil Canyon. Ninety additional Scouts camped at Philturn for shorter periods, while another 300 visitors registered at Dawson's makeshift office. In all 1863 camper days were spent at the property that first season. Although small by comparison with later years, attendance that first year encouraged the camp's promoters. Philturn was on its way.

Fall brought a flurry of construction as Scout leaders rushed to complete new buildings before winter set in. Most important was a main lodge to house the kitchen, dining room, director's office, and secretary's quarters. The structure, built of Oregon white cedar, included a beautiful rock porch and fireplace which set the pattern for other permanent facilities. Despite cold weather, carpentry work went rapidly, and by January 1940, the main lodge was virtually complete. Meanwhile, the director's residence, a guest house, three stone shelters, and a shower house were also being erected to supplement the facilities built the previous year.

The 1940 season brought in more boys from all over the nation. "For every Scout or Leader who attended during the 1939 season, more than four attended during the season of 1940," Director Dawson boasted in some promotional literature. "There must be something out there, fellows, that will bear looking into if you are in search of the real old-timer type of Western adventure."

Naturally some problems also developed during the first two camping seasons. Many groups failed to prepare adequately for their visit. Too often a few boys loaded into their Scoutmaster's car and headed for New Mexico without advance planning or preparation. Some even failed to notify Dawson that they were coming. Many seemed unfit to partake of Philturn's high-adventure activities. Just as serious were Dawson's shortcomings. Although he was an excellent outdoorsman and Scouter, administration was not his strong point. Financial records and reports received inadequate attention because the director preferred to hike a new trail or repair a water line. When Bryan and others visited from the New York office, they devoted much of their time to straightening out accounts so that Schuck, West, and Barclay would know what was happening at Philturn. Sometimes letters from the Chief Scout Executive went unanswered. Moreover, Dawson often dictated policy without consulting his superiors. Insisting that certain requirements be met before a group hit the trail, he once sent a whole troop back home because they lacked sufficient camping experience. National Scout officials became greatly displeased because of such actions.

Even though he certainly realized the problems involving Dawson's leadership, Waite Phillips was more concerned about other matters. His visits to Philturn were often limited by business activities in Tulsa or on Philmont itself. Phillips began to consider how the facilities might be made available to more Scouts and their leaders. "It seems to me," Phillips later wrote to West, "that great benefit could be derived from having these facilities used in the fall and spring, and even in the winter by Scoutmasters and Scout Directors." Such visits, he said, would not only acquaint these men with the camp, but also enable them to inspire the Scouts with whom they worked.

Phillips then invited Dawson and his wife to dinner at the Villa Philmonte to talk about needed improvements at Philturn. He recommended construction of a longhouse to be located west of the trading post building near the mouth of Horse Canyon. The structure would house summer employees, but during the winter it might accommodate Scoutmasters for the training Phillips had proposed. A rough plan which Phillips and Dawson developed provided a simple but comfortable layout for men who did not care to camp outside and yet wanted to feel that they were living close to nature. To finance this and several other projects, Phillips offered to pay one-half of all costs.

In New York, West and his associates thoroughly examined Phillips's suggestions, calling Dawson East to confer about details. Besides the longhouse and a new director's home agreed to by Phillips, another major camp would be built at the old corral location. Five new outlying sites were to contain log cabins; a health lodge would provide needed medical facilities. The total estimated cost grew to $22,000, of which Phillips agreed to pay half. Construction soon began, and by the time Scouts arrived for the 1941 season, the new facilities were almost finished.

The year 1941 witnessed further growth in attendance. For reasons beyond anyone's control, however, the number still reached only half of the estimated 2000. Heavy rains forced cancellation of several early schedules, and industrial demands brought on by the war in Europe forced some leaders to cancel their vacations. Some older boys who had planned to visit Philturn took advantage of the war to secure high-paying jobs.

On August 17, 1941, Philturn's most famous group reached the New Mexico camp. Unlike many groups, the six boys led by the

Scout executive Samuel D. Bogan had long prepared for their trip. Besides practicing camping skills and acquiring necessary equipment, they had trained with Yale University experts in archaeology. This then was no ordinary troop. Calling themselves the Philturn Archaeological Expedition, Bogan and his boys had set out to explore the prehistoric ruins of the North Ponil Canyon. After two days of preparation and instruction at Five Points, the Scouts loaded their equipment into a chuckwagon and set out with Billy Wetzel for their destination. In the ten days that followed, intensive excavation yielded numerous valuable items which were deposited at Yale's Peabody Museum until they were returned to Philmont years later. As Bogan reported in his fascinating book, *Let the Coyotes Howl*, the group's efforts thoroughly substantiated Dawson's appraisal that this was "a good outfit, one of the best."

During the summer of 1941, as well as the two preceding it, Waite Phillips frequently visited Philturn. Sometimes he arrived on his horse "Old Gus" and rode quietly through the campsites watching Scouts at work. Perhaps he stopped to ask how the boys were enjoying themselves, but never was his identity revealed. On other occasions he would ask Dawson, Bryan, or someone else at the camp to join him; they talked as he pointed out a new trail through some part of the ranch. More often he arrived in a car, parked it opposite one of the troop shelters, and quietly observed activities for fifteen, twenty, or thirty minutes before driving off.

Philmont Becomes a Scout Ranch

Concrete indication of Phillips's reaction to Philturn came late in September 1941 when the Tulsa oilman asked to meet with leading Scout officials at the earliest possible date. On October 4, he outlined in great detail his plan to give the Boy Scouts of America an additional 90,000 acres of land contiguous to Philturn. The donation included the beautiful Villa Philmonte, a ranch administration complex, livestock headquarters, several mountain lodges, and some of the most beautiful grazing land and inspiring wilderness country in the entire Rocky Mountain West. Moreover, Phillips advised the astonished Scout officials that he might also give them his twenty-three-story Philtower office building in Tulsa to finance the development and operation of the Scouting wilderness camp in New Mexico.

At Phillips's suggestion, West appointed Schuck to visit the ranch and the building to familiarize himself with all that the gift involved and to make a complete report to the National Council. Departing almost immediately, Schuck visited the ranch October 8-11 and inspected the Tulsa building on the 12th.[2]

Schuck's first consideration was the ranch operation of Philmont. Whereas Philturn had functioned as a wilderness camp, the new property would provide boys from throughout the nation with an opportunity to see an operating Western ranch. Although the maintenance of the ranch would thus have been justified as a program feature even if it only broke even, the ranch also provided an annual income estimated at nearly $5000. This would continue because Phillips planned to include, in addition to the Philmont land, an inventory of livestock valued in excess of $50,000. Philturn experience had demonstrated the special appeal of horses in a camping program. "Last year," Schuck recalled, "we had 284 boys at Philturn at one time and only 52 horses." By acquiring additional horses, plus breeding stock with which to raise an even larger herd, the program would be significantly supplemented. Assurance of proper management for the vast ranch came when Roy Cartwright agreed to continue as superintendent, even at a reduced salary.

More important than the ranching potential of Philmont was its appeal as an excellent recreational and camping area. If it were properly developed, Phillips's ranch might become the wilderness mecca for Scouts from all over the country. Ideally situated roads, trails, riding facilities, and lodges would accommodate whatever plan of development was adopted. Some buildings seemed suitable for adult training; still others might be made available for vacationing Scout executives; professional Scouts who had retired or were in poor health could live at the ranch, contributing to its program and development as they were able. In short, Schuck concluded, the acquisition of the property would make "a tremendous contribution to the quality of the Scouting program, in addition to giving boys and men a very valuable experience."

Turning his attention to the Philtower building, Schuck presented an equally glowing report. He described it as excellent; rental of nearly all the office space assured steady income. "There is no building of its size," he concluded, "that could be any finer, more practical, or complete in its arrangements. . . . It is far superior to the majority of the so-called first class office buildings in many of our larger cities." The estimated 1941 profits before depreciation totaled over $150,000.

In all his negotiations with Scout officials, Phillips stressed the idea that boys should be able to visit the property regardless of their financial status. To facilitate such a plan, he suggested that senior Scouts earn all or part of their vacation by assisting in such projects as trail building, timber and brush clearing, land improvement, and game control.

In explaining why he was giving the property to the Scouts, Phillips insisted that no other reason need be given than his desire to benefit American youth. Although Philturn's success had encouraged his plan for making a second donation larger than the first, his motivation was no doubt more complicated than he professed. Years later, Phillips further expanded his thoughts in a short history of the ranch:

> Having secured much benefit in all ways, beyond that of financial returns, for myself and family from its development and operating activities, it seemed to be following a natural sequence to make it available, for similar purposes, to the many instead of the few. That decision has given me considerable satisfaction—certainly more than if retained or sold for restricted purposes and less beneficial.[3]

All he hoped was that the institution thus created might "inspire and train boys in the virtues of faith, initiative, self-reliance, resourcefulness, and courage."

Once Scouting's leading officers had approved his several proposals, Waite Phillips addressed President Walter W. Head on December 11, 1941, formally offering the Philtower and 91,358 acres of Philmont ranch to the Scouts. His only requirement was that the Scouts continue to pay "their just portion of local and state taxes on that part of the assets and operations devoted to competitive commercial purposes." Phillips also reiterated his beliefs regarding the role of the ranch. Especially in light of the Japanese attack on Pearl Harbor four days earlier, he noted that one of America's most important tasks was training its youth. "The Boy Scouts of America has the most efficient plan and organization to do such work," he concluded. "The environment of a well-developed Mountain Ranch is the best place to achieve this objective." Pursuant to the recommendations of Head, West, and Schuck, the National Council voted at its December 18 meeting to accept Phillips's offer. On December 30, 1941, Philmont Scout Ranch was born.

Beginnings of Philmont Scout Ranch

Everyone in the New York Scout office realized the enormous task ahead. More than three times as large as Philturn, the 127,000-acre property presented problems far more complex than its predecessor.[4] Instead of one small camp, dozens of buildings and campsites dotted the land. The magnificent Villa Philmonte, the fishing and hunting lodges, the historic adobe complex at Rayado, and the cow camps sprinkled through the mountains required constant maintenance. Moreover, the prospects of operating a 23-story office building concerned many Scouts. Never before had the organization taken on the task of real estate management.

On Phillips's recommendation, Clyde King was selected as managing director of the new Scout properties. Louis R. Moses remained as Philtower manager, and Cartwright continued as ranch super-intendent.

Concerned about administration at the camp, Dr. Elbert K. Fret-well, the new Chief Scout Executive, appointed a committee to consider the problem. They concluded that effective operation of the properties could best be achieved by coordinating the ranch and camp under one manager. To fill the new position, the personnel division of the Scouts recommended Minor Huffman, an assistant regional executive in Dallas. Dawson remained as camp director until his resignation in March 1944. To aid in overseeing the vast complex, a new subcommittee of the National Council was charged with supervising Phillips's properties. Made up of volunteers experienced in property management, ranching, and other associated fields, the group met four times annually to review developments and suggest long-range policies.

During the next four years World War II affected Philmont's development. Transportation restrictions limited attendance to boys from nearby areas. Adult leaders often found it impossible to accompany boys on extended trips, and many young men either served in the military service or worked at defense plants near their homes. Despite such problems, attendance gradually increased from 1315 in 1942 to more than 1600 in 1946, the first year after wartime travel restrictions were lifted.

During the war, the camp's facilities were made ready for those who would come later. East of the Villa Philmonte (uniformly called the "Big House" by the Scouts) a bunkhouse was completed in 1943. It could accommodate ninety-six men for adult conferences or training sessions. Inside the building, the old servants' quarters were torn out and converted into a large dining room which would seat 120. Despite travel restrictions, these facilities received heavy use. The old Ladd home (termed the Carson place by Phillips) became headquarters for the camping department. What had previously been a stable became a mess hall; another stable was turned into an assembly hall. Additions were made to the old chicken house so Scouts could stay in it overnight. As many as 200 campers a day could be served at headquarters. Anticipating the day when the program would attract 10,000 senior Scouts and hundreds of adults for training conferences, Joseph Bishop, director of the Scout engineering service, spent several weeks at Philmont planning future construction.

Development work also took place in the mountains of the backcountry. Five Points, now renamed Ponil Camp, initially served local councils, but it was also the main entrance into the northern part of the ranch. Other base camps at Phillips's Cimarroncito hunting lodge, Abreu (west of Rayado at the mouth of the Rayado Canyon), and Carson-Maxwell (old Rayado) served as starting points for groups heading into the mountains. Shelters and fireplaces were constructed at several of these locations.

Philmont personnel also underwent change during the early years. When Cartwright resigned as ranch superintendent in 1943, he was replaced by Leo Gates, a longtime employee of Phillips, who made several changes in the livestock operations. He sold Phillips's registered sheep and bought some grade cattle. Thus it was hoped that visiting Scouts would be able to get a better idea of what a working ranch was like. More hay and alfalfa were also planted to feed the ranch's increased number of horses and pack animals. Large crops of apples were obtained from the old Webster orchards. In later years Ira Stevens, Bill Heck, and Richard Bergquist filled the important post of ranch superintendent.

New names also appeared on the camping department roster. When Clyde King resigned as properties manager in Tulsa, Pliney Powers, a deputy chief Scout executive, assumed general management responsibilities for the ranch and building. Huffman and others at Philmont now reported to the Scout executive through Powers. In March 1946, James P. Fitch, who had served as Region IX executive for more than a quarter of a century and been involved in much of the early development at Philmont, was named manager of Phillips's properties. Initially he was to live in Tulsa and provide direction for both Philtower manager Moses and ranch manager Huffman. At the end of the year Fitch moved his office to Philmont, where he served as general manager until his retirement in 1949. Then Powers reassumed his old responsibilities.

A number of men had direct charge of the camping program after Dawson's resignation. Huffman himself managed the activities during 1944, but by fall Fred Patton accepted the job and began to plan for the following season. Ill health forced his resignation a year and a half later. Fermor Spencer Church, whose Los Alamos Ranch School had been taken over by the government when it began atomic research north of Santa Fe, accepted leadership of the camping department on a temporary basis. During his two-year tenure many innovations were introduced. In addition to the older training and work program, a new backpacking experience was made available to older Scouts.

By the time Huffman resigned late in 1946, Philmont had established its reputation as the top camping area in the Boy Scout program. Thousands of boys who had taken part in its activities went home describing the rugged excitement they had found in the mountains of New Mexico. More came every year. The foundation had been laid for an adult program which could strengthen Scouting across the nation by preparing Scouters to do a better job. Moreover, physical facilities around the Villa Philmonte, at the new Camping Headquarters, and in camps throughout the vast property were ready to handle the additional senior Scouts who would use them during the years that followed.

Development of Philmont's Program

To direct the camping department, Boy Scout officials next selected George Bullock. During Bullock's administration, thousands of campers flocked to New Mexico to take part in its many varied activities. Emphasis on the lore of the Southwest permeated every program: Kit Carson, Charles Beaubien, and Lucien Maxwell came alive on mountain treks and at old mining camps. Phillips's dream of boys earning their way through work saw fulfillment in the Ranch Pioneering Trek. Adult Scouters from all over the United States began to think of Philmont as the center for training activities. Bullock instituted several treks offering different routes and programs.[5] Most popular were the north- and southbound expeditions. Originally boys in the twelve-day program pulled burros over sixty-two miles of trails crossing the most rugged country on Philmont. The establishment of new camps extended the trails to eighty-one miles. After a shakedown at headquarters, northbound groups spent a day at the Carson-Maxwell Camp. Next morning they hiked a few miles north to a new Olympia Camp for a day of basic training. High country stops at Abreu and Rayado fishing lodges preceded the climb to Clear Creek Mountain, "the top of Philmont." After a day of rest at Cimarroncito, boys continued north to Harlan Camp, named after the promoter of the St. Louis, Rocky Mountain and Pacific Railroad. A hike up Turkey Creek Canyon past Black Jack's Hideout the next day took boys into Dean Camp. The following morning they reached Bent, just up-canyon from Ponil. "You'll remember your Northbound," Bullock wrote prospective hikers, "as long as you remember the fun and adventure and beauty of mountains." Southbound expeditions followed an identical route, starting at Ponil and finishing at Carson-Maxwell.

For those wishing a shorter trip, Philmont offered Kit Carson Treks starting in 1947. Backpacking all the way, Scouts arranged schedules lasting eight to fifteen days and visiting such mountain camps as Urraca Cow Camp (now Black Mountain), Crater Lodge, Rincon Bonito (now Beaubien), and Porcupine. In later years the Stockade, "a rugged log structure reminiscent of the blazing frontier of Kit's own time," served as the starting and the ending camp.

Boys especially attracted to horses registered for the Cavalcade, seven days astride a sure-footed mountain pony leading a packhorse. At night there were stops at many of Philmont's most scenic camps, where tents were already erected to assure a dry bed and warm night.

Unsurpassed views led to fond memories of an exciting Western visit. The "big one" was the Wagon Train Trek, 21 days of adventure that covered the entire property. Eating off an authentic Western chuckwagon, riding horseback along narrow mountain trails, fishing in one of a dozen rushing trout streams, pioneering, and burro packing—the Wagon Train had them all. Although it followed approximately the same route as the shorter expeditions, the Wagon Train stopped longer at the more interesting points. An added horseback ride took Scouts into North Ponil Canyon to visit the Indian Writings. A night at Pueblano along the South Ponil assured unsurpassed adventure and beauty. Then on the long-remembered final night, buffalo steaks appropriately ended an adventure in Western living.

Several more specialized opportunities appealed to individual boys rather than whole troops or posts. Directly related to the earlier Philmont Service Corps was the Ranch Pioneering Trek. Just as Waite Phillips had wished, a select number of boys explored vocational opportunities in ranching and farming through actual agricultural work. For the first three weeks they were headquartered at the ranch department barns along the Urraca engaging in such typical cowboy activities as irrigating, haying, driving livestock, and repairing fences. The last seven days were spent hiking and camping along Philmont's mountain trails. During the Thanksgiving holidays, a special mountain lion hunt gave older Scouts an opportunity to stalk wild game. Christmas vacation brought Operation 10, an exciting adventure in the snow-covered Rockies.

Such a variety of popular programs brought increased attendance necessitating additional facilities. In 1948, only 2275 boys and leaders visited Philmont, but three years later the number had nearly quadrupled to 8402. New camps such as Porcupine, Black Mountain, Beaubien, Dean, Harlan, Stockade, and others opened.

The Scouts also restored Kit Carson's long-abandoned Rayado home in 1949, and during the next two years developed an extensive museum complex there. One of the most popular additions was a mine in the old Cimarroncito district. Almost immediately Scouts flocked from all over the country to visit the new Cyphers Camp. While boys began to think of Philmont as a mecca for fun and rugged adventure, their leaders learned that the property also offered extensive Scout training. Starting in the late 1940s, more and more men attended Philmont conferences. Numbers increased rapidly in 1949 with the completion of the Wood Badge lodge at Zastro, located on the Rayado River between Abreu and Carson-Maxwell camps.

Because of the program's initial success, the Philmont Training Center opened in the summer of 1951 under the direction of William L. Lawrence, the Scout national director of volunteer training.[6] A tent city housing 100 had been constructed near the Villa so that volunteer Scouters could bring their wives and children, thus combining a Western vacation with valuable instruction. An auditorium-cafeteria complex was added west of the Villa. With such new facilities available, Philmont's Volunteer program offered eighteen courses in 1952; a total of 777 men and nearly 1000 family members attended.

The Volunteer Training Service also developed courses for younger Scout leaders. The popularity of Junior Leader Training grew rapidly, especially after it was moved to new quarters at historic Rayado. A smaller Conservation Training Program also developed.

Although Philmont seemed to be flourishing, problems soon became evident to national Scout leaders, especially Arthur A. Schuck, Chief Scout Executive. General manager Pliny Powers spent most of his time in New York and gave little direct supervision to certain aspects of the Western operation. The Philtower building badly needed modernization to keep up with new developments; tenants used so much electricity, for instance, that fans had to be turned on the master switches to prevent fire. If something were not done, rentals and income would surely decline. Moreover buildings and other facilities at Philmont were similarly deteriorating. Rewiring and repairs were needed in many older structures, and several new service buildings were required.

In an attempt to remedy this situation, Schuck turned to his old co-worker Ray H. Bryan, who as assistant director of the engineering service had played an important role in developing Philturn's physical facilities. Bryan assumed the newly created post of assistant to the chief Scout executive and general manager of Phillips's properties on September 1, 1953.[7]

Assisted by Charles T. Rosenfield, a local contractor employed as maintenance superintendent, Bryan immediately undertook a program of physical plant improvement. A complete evaluation of the Villa Philmonte showed the need for extensive repairs there. Crews soon renovated and enlarged warehouse facilities, while the ranch administrative complex received much needed additions. New commissary-staff buildings were going up in many mountain camps to assure better use of the entire property. In Tulsa, Bryan ordered the expenditure of $25,000 for Philtower improvements, including extensive rewiring. Long-range plans were developed for continuing renovation of the building.

Policy revisions in the camping department began in 1954 after George Bullock resigned to become Scout executive of the Kit Carson Council, Albuquerque. His replacement was Jack L. Rhea, formerly an assistant director of the volunteer training service. Aware that increasing attendance demanded simpler, more flexible scheduling procedures, Bryan and Rhea abolished the old system of treks. Instead, expeditions (as groups visiting the ranch were now called) were registered for a twelve-day visit. While at camping headquarters or at one of several starting areas, the members of each expedition planned an itinerary which took them to whatever camps offered them the most appealing features. Lengthy horseback trips and chuckwagons were abandoned, although each boy received a half-day ride. Burros were available in the northern portion of the ranch. Some Scouts preferred to stay off the beaten paths, camping several nights in unstaffed trail sites; others followed much the same routes as Bullock's old treks. Specially trained rangers were employed to assist the Scouts acclimate during their first few days on the ranch. In the backcountry camps, new program features appealed to every Scout. One of the most interesting was archaeology at Indian Writings in the North Ponil Canyon. The program was carefully managed to assure scientific precision, but it also enabled boys to participate in actual excavation and the discovery of skeletons, house ruins, and artifacts which greatly aided scientists in describing the prehistoric civilizations of the area. The National Rifle Association assisted in developing marksmanship programs at several camps, with rifle ranges at Pueblano, Sawmill, or Cimarroncito proving especially popular. After acquisition of the Baldy tract, programs were developed which described the history of the area, explained the technology of mining, and enabled visitors to explore old mines and pan for gold. A visitor to Clear Creek, for example, found bearded staff members working for the Rocky Mountain Fur Company who showed them how to use a Pennsylvania long rifle, stalk small game, or set traps, while at Black Mountain the staff demonstrated the crafts and skills used in the nineteenth century, and at Head of Dean and Miner's Park the Maxwell Tie and Lumber Company conducted contests in log splitting, crosscut sawing, pole climbing, and log rolling. Horses continued to be important, with short rides available at several locations, and, beginning in 1975, a twelve-day horseback Cavalcade offered for older boys. As the Boy Scouts invited girls to become members, Philmont offered co-ed expeditions into the backcountry, employed women rangers and other staff members, and offered unique "Mountain Women" programs for exceptional individuals.

Increasing annual attendance gave evidence that the new activities appealed to Scouts. Whereas in 1954, 7,404 Explorers, older Scouts, and their leaders attended the national camp, eight years later the number exceeded 11,000. After eight years, Jack Rhea left after the 1962 season, succeeded by A. J. "Skipper" Juncker.

Attendance surpassed old records for two consecutive years prior to Juncker's untimely death in the spring of 1965. Joe Davis, an enthusiastic veteran Scouter from Chicago, directed the camping program from 1965 through 1974, a period of exceptionally rapid growth: enrollment reached 16,000 in 1970 and an all-time high of 18,853 in 1974. John Shutt replaced Bryan as General Manager late in 1970, serving until his retirement in 1974, when veteran ranch superintendent William C. Littrell assumed overall responsibility for Philmont's multi-faceted activities. Joe Hawkins, who had previously assisted Juncker and Davis and worked at Schiff Scout Reservation, directed backcountry programs through the 1976 season, when he was succeeded by Floyd Knutsen.

Steady growth and program improvement required the construction of new facilities. The Ernest Thompson Seton Memorial Library and Museum, a magnificent Pueblo-styled building donated by Mississippi businessman L. O. Crosby, opened in 1966 to display the collections of one of Scouting's founders. In 1975, a new headquarters dining hall, contributed by I. A. O'Shaughnessy of St. Paul, Minnesota, accommodating up to seven hundred at one sitting, opened, and the old dining room became an expanded trading post. New housing facilities for campers and staff were constructed at headquarters, the old horse barns were relocated further to the south, and, so that vehicle traffic into the backcountry could be reduced or eliminated, some roads were closed and centralized mountain commissaries were built at strategic locations.

The ranch department undertook expanded activities under Superintendent William C. Littrell after 1954. The department supervised conservation and forestry activities as well as livestock management and farm production. Little lumbering went on after early contracts with Roy Cartwright expired in the early 1940s until it became evident to Littrell and Bryan that limited cutting would be necessary to harvest overmature and diseased trees which hindered new growth. In addition, such activities would provide improved access to remote areas and funds for other needed conservation work. On the recommendation of experts in forestry and conservation, Scout officials contracted for restricted cutting at Miners Park, on Urraca Mesa, and in Buck Creek and Sawmill canyons. Minimum erosion damage, preservation of water supplies and young timber, and brush cleanup were required. The logging program was financially successful, but because the lumbermen never fully complied with contract stipulations, Philmont pledged greater caution in undertaking future lumbering activities.

Littrell also supervised wildlife management activities, maintaining large populations of deer, bear, elk, and other game animals so that Scouts could observe them while hiking and camping. If experts determined that the number of animals had grown too large, limited hunting was permitted by Nimrods, a group of about 150 carefully selected businessmen and Scouters who contributed toward game management expenses.

Littrell's department also preserved Philmont as an operating ranch, not only so that boys could see agricultural operations but also to earn a profit. In keeping with these objectives, Phillips's initial herd of 278 herefords grew slowly to over 500 head. Because of intense competition in raising registered livestock, however, Philmont emphasized its commercial herd, although the quality remained high, ranch cattle occasionally won prizes at local fairs, and Littrell was frequently honored by the New Mexico Cattlemen's Association. When Littrell became General Manager, Robert C. Knox, veteran head of the ranch's cattle department, became ranch superintendent.

Less colorful but no less important than what goes on at Philmont were the operations of the Philtower building in Tulsa, which continued to subsidize camping activities. To assure rental income, expansion and modernization go on constantly, so that even with ultra-modern buildings competing with it for tenants, Philtower has maintained a consistently high occupancy rate. Under the management of John Ellington, structural repairs, the installation of recorded music, high-speed elevators, expanded parking facilities, and office renovation have made this possible. Large accounting firms, oil drilling concerns, petroleum geologists, lawyers, and retail merchants are among those who find it desirable to maintain offices at the Philtower address. Each year an income of about $100,000 was available for Philmont expenses or deposited in a reserve fund that grew to over $1,250,000. The money was invested so that one day the fund could become Philmont's source of income. When the building celebrated its fiftieth birthday in 1976, it could still be characterized as "an ageless tribute to Tulsans who treasure quiet richness enhanced with dignity."

Waite Phillips moved for a short time to the nearby home of his friend John J. Nairn after giving part of his ranch to the scouts. The remainder of the property was purchased by McDaniel and Sons, a Somerton, Arizona ranching concern which owned it until August 1970. Phillips moved with his wife to Los Angeles. As he grew older he visited his belvoed New Mexico less frequently, and poor health prevented his presence in 1960 when Arthur A. Schuck renamed Clear Creek Mountain after him. A heart flare-up in December 1963 further strained Phillips's vigor and energy, and on January 27, 1964, Scouts learned that one of their greatest benefactors had died in his Los Angeles home. His will included funds so that underprivileged boys could attend the Scout ranch, and his son Elliott has continued the elder Phillip's interest in the property by serving on the Philmont Ranch Committee.

Looking back young Phillips must have been pleased with the results of his father's benevolence. Because of his generosity, a part of the famed Beaubien and Miranda Grant had become a world-famous youth center. Boys from all over the United States and other parts of the globe who had never visited a ranch or seen the mountains could undertake an unforgettable wilderness adventure amid unexcelled scenic beauty and historic spots. Adults came to study youth leadership and improve their scouting skills at the Villa Philmonte. In Philmont Scout Ranch at Cimarron, New Mexico, Waite Phillips had left an enduring monument.

NOTES

CHAPTER I

1. G. D. Robinson, et al., *Philmont Country: The Rocks and Landscape of a Famous New Mexico Ranch*, U.S. Geological Survey Professional Paper 505 (Washington, D.C.: Government Printing Office, 1964), passim; Nevin M. Fenneman, *Physiography of the Western United States* (New York: McGraw-Hill Book Co., 1931), pp. 40-47, 92-132.

2. L. C. Graton, "Colfax County," in Waldemar Lindgren, L. C. Graton, and C. H. Gordon, eds., *The Ore Deposits of New Mexico*, U.S. Geological Survey Professional Paper 68 (Washington, D.C.: Government Printing Office, 1916), pp. 91-97.

3. R. F. Daubenmire, "Vegetational Zonation in the Rocky Mountains," *Botanical Review*, vol. 9 (June 1943), pp. 343-71; R. A. Rydberg, "Vegetative Life Zones in the Rocky Mountain Region," *New York Botanical Garden Memoirs*, v. 6 (1916), pp. 477-99; G. A. Pearson, *Forest Types in the Southwest as Determined by Climate and Soil*, U.S. Dept. of Agriculture Technical Bulletin 247 (Washington, D.C.: Government Printing Office, 1931), pp. 14-133.

4. Susan S. Magoffin, *Down the Santa Fe Trail and Into Mexico, 1846-1847* (New Haven: Yale University Press, 1962), p. 76.

5. Vernon Bailey, *Life Zones and Crop Zones of New Mexico*, U.S. Dept. of Agriculture, Biological Survey, North American Fauna No. 35 (Washington, D.C.: Government Printing Office, 1913), pp. 40-52; Vernon Bailey, *Mammals of New Mexico*, U.S. Dept. of Agriculture, Biological Survey, North American Fauna, No. 53 (Washington, D.C.: Government Printing Office, 1931).

6. "Answers of Augustus Storrs of Missouri to Certain Queries . . . ," *Senate Executive Document No. 7*, 18th Cong., 2d sess., p. 5.

7. Lewis H. Garrard, *Wah-to-yah and the Taos Trail* (Norman: University of Oklahoma Press, 1955), p. 156; *Colfax County Stockman* (Springer), Sept. 3, 1890, p. 4; Sept. 26, 1902, p. 3; *Santa Fe Daily New Mexican*, Sept. 3, 1890, p. 4; *Raton Reporter*, Oct. 5, 1913, p. 1.

8. *Raton Range*, Nov. 13, 1914, p. 1.

9. *Colfax County Stockman*, Jan. 31, 1891, p. 1; *Springer Times*, June 29, 1928, p. 1.

10. *Santa Fe New Mexican*, Sept. 23, 1898, p. 2; Jan. 9, 1899, p. 2; *Las Vegas*

CHAPTER II

1. H. M. Wormington, Ancient Man in North America (Denver: Museum of Natural History, 1957), pp. 247-60; Waldo R. Wadel, Prehistoric Man on the Great Plains (Norman: University of Oklahoma Press, 1961), pp. 54-88.
2. H. M. Wormington, Prehistoric Indians of the Southwest (Denver: Museum of Natural History, 1959), pp. 27-105.
3. Material in this section is drawn from "Summaries of Archaeology Reports," mimeographed volume, Seton Library, Philmont Scout Ranch; Sam Bogan, Let the Coyotes Howl: A Story of Philmont Scout Ranch (New York: G. P. Putnam's Sons, 1946); Eugene Lutes, "A Marginal Prehistoric Culture of Northeastern New Mexico," El Palacio, vol. 66, no. 2 (April 1959), pp. 59-68; Fred Wendorf, "The Archaeology of Northeastern New Mexico," El Palacio, vol. 67, no. 2 (April 1960), pp. 59-60; Frank Alpers, "Surface Surveys of Prehistoric Ponil River Sites," El Palacio, vol. 70, no. 4 (Winter 1963), pp. 36-42; and Galen Baker, "The Archaeology of the Park Plateau in Southeastern Colorado," Southwestern Lore, vol. 30, no. 1 (June 1964), pp. 1-18.
4. Alan Skinner, "Lizard Cave: A Rock Shelter in Northeastern New Mexico," El Palacio, vol. 70, no. 2 (Autumn 1964), pp. 22-29.
5. Lutes, "Marginal Prehistoric Culture," pp. 59-61.
6. Michael A. Glassow, "Report of the Ninth Season's Activities," mimeographed pamphlet (1964).
7. Galen R. Baker, "Attempts at Relative Age Determination of Petroglyphs in the Park Plateau of the Pueblo-Plains Periphery" (Paper presented to the Society for American Archaeology, November 1964).

CHAPTER III

1. George E. Hyde, Indians of the High Plains from the Prehistoric Period to the Coming of Europeans (Norman: University of Oklahoma Press, 1959), pp. 4-7; Dolores A. Gunnerson, "The Southern Athabascans: Their Arrival in the Southwest," El Palacio, vol. 66 (1956), pp. 346-65; James H. Gunnerson, "Apache Archaeology in Northeastern New Mexico," American Antiquity, vol. 34 (January 1969), pp. 23-39; and Albert H. Schroeder, "Shifting for Survival in the Southwest," New Mexico Historical Review, vol. 43 (October 1968), pp. 301-03.
2. Morris E. Opler, "A Summary of Jicarilla Apache Culture," American Anthropologist, n.s., vol. 38 (April-June 1936), pp. 202-23; and his "Myths and Tales of the Jicarilla Apache Indians," Memoirs of the American Folklore Society, vol. 31 (1938), esp. pp. 210-19; and H. Clyde Wilson, "Jicarilla Apache Political and Economic Structures," University of California Publications in Archaeology and Ethnology, vol. 98 (1964), pp. 339-50.
3. Gunnerson, "Apache Archaeology," pp. 30-35.

4. Pliny Earle Goddard, "Jicarilla Apache Texts," *Anthropological Papers of the American Museum of Natural History*, vol. 8 (1911), esp. pp. 242-69.

5. Marvin K. Opler, "The Southern Ute of Colorado," in Ralph Linton, ed., *Acculturation in Seven American Indian Tribes* (New York: D. Appleton-Century Company, 1940), pp. 119-206; Albert H. Schroeder, "A Brief History of the Southern Utes," *Southwestern Lore*, vol. 30 (1965), pp. 53-78; and Hyde, *Indians of the High Plains*, pp. 52-55.

6. Hyde, *Indians of the High Plains*, pp. 52-57.

7. Clark Wissler, "The Influence of the Horse in the Development of Plains Culture," *American Anthropologist*, n.s., vol. 16 (1914), pp. 1-25.

8. This section is drawn from Albert H. Schroeder, *A Study of the Apache Indians: Part II, The Jicarilla Apaches* (Santa Fe: n.p., 1958); Alfred B. Thomas, *After Coronado: Spanish Exploration Northeast of New Mexico, 1696-1727* (Norman: University of Oklahoma Press, 1935); William E. Dunn, "Spanish Reaction Against the French Advance Toward New Mexico, 1717-1727," *Mississippi Valley Historical Review*, vol. 2 (1915), pp. 348-61; and Michael A. Glassow, "A Consideration of the Routes of Early Eighteenth Century Spanish Expeditions through Northeastern New Mexico," unpublished manuscript.

CHAPTER IV

1. William H. Goetzmann, *Army Exploration in the American West, 1803-1863* (New Haven: Yale University Press, 1959), pp. 30-42; and W. Eugene Hollon, *The Lost Pathfinder: Zebulon Montgomery Pike* (Norman: University of Oklahoma Press, 1949), pp. 90-142.

2. Josiah Gregg, *Commerce of the Prairies*, Max L. Moorhead ed. (Norman: University of Oklahoma Press, 1954), pp. 10-11.

3. Quoted in Goetzmann, *Army Exploration*, p. 43; H. M. Chittenden, *The American Fur Trade of the Far West*, 2 vols. (New York: Barnes and Noble, 1935), vol. 2, pp. 563-83.

4. "The Journals of Captain Thomas Becknell," *Missouri Historical Review*, vol. 4 (January 1910), pp. 65-84; *Petition of Sundry Inhabitants of the State of Missouri* . . . , House Executive Document No. 79, 18th Cong., 2d sess., p. 6.

5. Kenneth L. Holmes, "The Benjamin Cooper Expeditions to Santa Fe in 1822 and 1823," *New Mexico Historical Review*, vol. 37 (April 1963), pp. 139-44.

6. F. F. Stephens, "Missouri and the Santa Fe Trade," *Missouri Historical Review*, vol. 10 (July 1916), p. 233.

7. This section is based on Gregg, *Commerce of the Prairies*; R. L. Duffus, *The Santa Fe Trail* (New York: Longmans, Green and Co., 1930); Max L. Moorhead, *New Mexico's Royal Road* (Norman: University of Oklahoma Press, 1958); and John E. Sunder, ed., *Matt Field on the Santa Fe Trail* (Norman: University of Oklahoma Press, 1960).

8. Moorhead, *New Mexico's Royal Road*, pp. 96-97.

9. Sunder, *Matt Field*, pp. 160-63.

10. Kate L. Gregg, *The Road to Santa Fe* (Albuquerque: University of New Mexico Press, 1952), pp. 126-28.

11. "Samuel Chambers, a naturalized citizen, petition to the territorial deputation asking permission to settle on the Rio del Ponil. Refused. November 10, 1830," Document No. 220, Twitchell Archives, U.S. Bureau of Land Management, Santa Fe.

12. A recent thorough study is David Weber, *The Taos Trappers* (Norman: University of Oklahoma Press, 1971).

13. Elliott Coues, ed., *The Journal of Jacob Fowler* (New York: Francis P. Harper, 1898), pp. 144-45.

CHAPTER V

1. This chapter originally appeared as two articles in *New Mexico Historical Review*: "The Beaubien and Miranda Land Grant, 1841-1846," vol. 42, no. 1 (January 1967), pp. 27-47; and "Rayado: Pioneer Settlement in Northeastern New Mexico, 1848-1857," vol. 46, no. 1 (January 1971), pp. 37-56.

CHAPTER VI

1. Irving Howbert, *Memories of a Lifetime in the Pike's Peak Region* (New York: G. P. Putnam and Sons, 1925), pp. 170-71.

2. Ibid., testimony of Calvin Jones in *Transcript of Record of Charles Bent et al., vs. Guadalupe Miranda et al.* (Santa Fe: Voz del Pueblo Print, 1894), p. 157.

3. *Transcript of Title of the Maxwell Land Grant Situated in New Mexico and Colorado* (Chicago: Rand McNally & Co., 1881), pp. 3-4, 25.

4. W. A. Keleher, *The Maxwell Land Grant: A New Mexico Item*, 2nd ed. (New York: Argosy-Antiquarian, 1964), pp. 40-41.

5. *Transcript of Title of Maxwell Land Grant . . . .*, pp. 30-34.

6. 1850 manuscript census for New Mexico in *Santa Fe Weekly Gazette*, Aug. 13, 1861, p. 1.

7. The material about Arny is adapted from Lawrence R. Murphy, *Frontier Crusader: William F. M. Arny* (Tucson: University of Arizona Press, 1972), pp. 102-12.

8. Material on Indian Agency affairs is drawn from the Reports and Letters Received, Office of Indian Affairs, New Mexico Superintendency, R. G. 75, National Archives; and the annual reports of the Secretary of the Interior, 1861-65.

9. *Transcript of Title of Maxwell Land Grant*, pp. 29-44.

10. Carleton to George I. Campbell, Aug. 25, 1866, in *District of New Mexico Letters*, vol. 16, pp. 571-72, R. G. 98, National Archives.

CHAPTER VII

1. *History of New Mexico* (Los Angeles: Pacific States Publishing Company, 1907), 2:954.

2. *Santa Fe Weekly Gazette*, June 27, Nov. 30, 1867; June 20, 1868, p. 2;

Rossiter W. Raymond, Statistics of Mines and Mining in the States and Territories West of the Rocky Mountains (Washington, D.C.: Government Printing Office, 1870), pp. 388-89.

3. Jim B. Pearson, The Maxwell Land Grant (Norman: University of Oklahoma Press, 1961), pp. 16-17; Santa Fe New Mexican, June 8, 1867, p. 2.

4. Fayette A. Jones, New Mexico Mines and Minerals (Santa Fe: New Mexican Printing Company, 1904), p. 142; Pearson, Maxwell Land Grant, pp. 17-18; Mining and Scientific Press (San Francisco), Feb. 8, 1868, p. 87.

5. Jones, New Mexico Mines, pp. 142-43.

6. Santa Fe Weekly Gazette, June 1, 1867, p. 2.

7. Ibid., July 6, July 13, 1867, p. 2.

8. Ibid., June 16, July 13, 1867; April 18, 1868, p. 2.

9. Ibid., June 29, July 13, 1867, p. 2; Jones, New Mexico Mines, p. 144.

10. Mining and Scientific Press, Jan. 18, 1868, p. 39; Santa Fe Weekly Gazette, Feb 13, 1868, p. 4; April 18, 1868, p. 2.

11. Santa Fe Weekly Gazette, July 13, 1867, p. 2.

12. Ibid., Nov. 30, 1867; Jan. 18, 1868, p. 2.

13. Ibid., Nov. 30, 1867; Jan. 1, 18, Feb. 7, 29, April 18, 1868, p. 2.

14. Ibid., Jan. 16, Feb. 1, 1868, p. 2; Daily New Mexican, June 23, July 14, 1868, p. 1.

15. Mining and Scientific Press, Jan. 11, 1868, p. 22; Jones, New Mexico Mines, p. 144; Pearson, Maxwell Land Grant, pp. 41-42.

16. Raymond, Statistics of Mines, pp. 391-93.

17. Santa Fe Weekly Gazette, Nov. 30, 1867, p. 2.

18. Ibid., Nov. 28, 1867, p. 2; Raymond, Statistics of Mines, pp. 384-85; Daily New Mexican, Sept. 23, 1870, p. 1.

19. Santa Fe Weekly Gazette, June 20, Aug. 1, 1868, p. 2; Daily New Mexican, June 20, July 21, 1868, p. 2.

20. Raymond, Statistics of Mines, pp. 384-88; John A. Collinson and W. A. Bell, The Maxwell Land Grant (London: Taylor and Co., 1870), pp. 10-12.

21. Raymond, Statistics of Mines, pp. 387-88.

22. Scientific Press, April 2, 1870, p. 213; Daily New Mexican, Nov. 30, 1868, p. 1.

23. Raymond, Statistics of Mines, p. 388.

24. Tom Hilton, Nevermore, Cimarron, Nevermore (Fort Worth: Western Heritage Press, 1970), pp. 21-24; Daily New Mexican, June 23, 1868, p. 2; July 14, 1868, p. 1.

25. Santa Fe Weekly Gazette, Feb. 6, March 13, 1869, p. 2; Daily New Mexican, March 27, 29, April 14, 1870, p. 1.

26. Daily New Mexican, March 27, 1870, p. 1; Thomas Harwood, History of New Mexico Spanish and English Missions, 2 vols. (Albuquerque: El Abogado Press, 1908), p. 173.

27. Porter A. Stratton, The Territorial Press of New Mexico, 1834-1912 (Albuquerque: University of New Mexico Press, 1969), pp. 6, 265.

28. Daily New Mexican, Dec. 29, 1870; July 17, 1871, p. 1.

29. C. M. Chase, The Editor's Run in New Mexico and Colorado (Montpelier, Vt.: Argus and Patriot, 1882), p. 62.

CHAPTER VIII

1. Paul A. F. Walter, *Banking in New Mexico Before the Railroad Came* (New York and Santa Fe: Newcomen Society in North America, 1955), p. 8.
2. Henry G. Inman, *The Old Santa Fe Trail* (Topeka: Crane & Co., 1916), pp. 377-78.
3. *Transcript of Record of Charles Bent et al. vs. Guadalupe Miranda et al.* (Las Vegas: La Voz del Pueblo Print, 1894), pp. 158-59, 255.
4. *Cimarron News and Press*, Aug. 19, 1880, p. 1.
5. Inman, *Old Santa Fe Trail*, p. 376; *Transcript of Record of Charles Bent*, pp. 122, 155.
6. For the location of manuscript materials relative to the Cimarron agency used throughout this chapter, see ch. VI, note 8.
7. *Transcript of Title of the Maxwell Land Grant* (Chicago: Rand McNally & Co., 1881), pp. 60-61.
8. Correspondence on survey and title questions is in *Records of the Surveyor General on New Mexico Land Grants*, Federal Land Office, Santa Fe, Microfilm Roll 14.
9. J. B. Chaffee, *The Beaubien and Miranda Grant in New Mexico and Colorado* (New York: n.p., 1869), 8 pp.
10. *Transcript of Title of the Maxwell Land Grant*, pp. 62-68.
11. Thomas Harwood, *History of New Mexico Spanish and English Missions*, 2 vols. (Albuquerque: El Abogado Press, 1908), pp. 89-90.
12. Nelson A. Miles, *Personal Recollections and Observations* (Chicago and New York: The Warner Co., 1897), pp. 182-84.
13. W. A. Keleher, *The Maxwell Land Grant: A New Mexico Item*, 2nd ed. (New York: Argosy-Antiquarian, 1964), pp. 60-65.

CHAPTER IX

1. Harold H. Dunham, *Government Handout: A Study in the Administration of the Public Lands, 1875-1891* (New York: Columbia University Press, 1941), pp. 221-22.
2. *Santa Fe Daily New Mexican*, Sept. 17, Oct. 28, 1870; Jan. 17, April 15, 17, 21, 1871; April 2, 1873—all p. 1. Luff to J. H. Hanker, Oct. 24, 1870, and telegrams to Clendenin are in the J. W. Arrott Collection, New Mexico Highlands University, Las Vegas, N.M.
3. *Santa Fe Daily New Mexican*, Sept. 18, 1875, p. 1; Harwood, *History of New Mexico*, 1:204, 262-69.
4. F. Stanley, "O. P. McMains: Champion of a Lost Cause," *New Mexico Historical Review*, vol. 24 (Jan. 1949), pp. 1-11; Harwood, *History of New Mexico*, 1:299-303.
5. *Santa Fe Daily New Mexican*, Nov. 5, 9, 1875, p. 1; Aug. 28, 1877, p. 2; and Harwood, *History of New Mexico*, 1:269-75.
6. *Santa Fe Daily New Mexican*, Jan. 11, Feb. 8, April 25, May 16, 25, June

12, 1876—all p. 1. Agnes Morley Cleaveland, *Satan's Paradise* (Boston: Houghton Mifflin Co., 1952), pp. 65-66, 74.

7. *Santa Fe Daily New Mexican*, Jan. 17, June 16, 1876, p. 1; Aug. 8, 1876, p. 2; Aug. 29, 1877, p. 1. Harwood, *History of New Mexico*, 1:272-74.

8. For the location of this and subsequent manuscripts from the surveyor general's office, see ch. VIII, note 8.

9. Dunham, *Government Handout*, pp. 226-31; Thomas L. Karnes, *William L. Gilpin* (Austin: University of Texas Press, 1970), pp. 326-27; Pearson, *Maxwell Land Grant*, pp. 75-76.

10. Pearson, *Maxwell Land Grant*, pp. 94-111.

11. *Transcript of Record, U.S. vs. Maxwell Land Grant Co., et al.*, Supreme Court of the United States, October term 1886, no. 974, R. G. 267, National Archives, Washington, D.C.

12. *121 U.S. Reports*, 327 ff.; Dunham, *Government Handout*, pp. 236-37; Keleher, *Maxwell Land Grant*, pp. 109-11.

13. Pearson, *Maxwell Land Grant*, pp. 112-34.

CHAPTER X

1. Chase, *The Editor's Run*, p. 62; *Santa Fe Daily New Mexican*, July 6, 1895, p. 1.

2. *Santa Fe Daily New Mexican*, Nov. 10, Dec. 22, 1893, p. 1; Dec. 15, 1895, p. 1; Sept. 23, 1898, p. 2.

3. Ibid., Aug. 24, 1891; July 27, 1896—p. 1; *Stock Grover and Farmer* (Las Vegas), June 1, 1889, p. 1; April 18, 1891, p. 2.

4. *Las Vegas Daily Optic*, Jan. 25, 1882, p. 1; Jan. 14, 1885, p. 4; *Stock Grower and Farmer* (Las Vegas), Feb. 2, 1889, p. 2.

5. Manuscript diary in Bancroft Library; land transactions mentioned in this chapter are recorded in the Colfax County Courthouse, Raton.

6. Taped interview, June 27, 1960, Seton Library, Philmont; Harwood, *History of New Mexico*, 1:212-13.

7. *Cimarron News and Press*, May 27, 1880, p. 2; *Las Vegas Daily Optic*, July 1, 1887, p. 3; *Colfax County Stockman*, Aug. 8, 1891, p. 1; Nov. 24, 1894, July 6, 1895, June 7, 1902, p. 3; *Raton Range*, July 5, 1900, p. 2; July 10, 1914, p. 1.

8. *New Mexico News and Press* (Raton), Nov. 26, 1881, p. 1.

9. *Cimarron News and Press*, April 7, May 19, 1881, p. 1.

10. *Las Vegas Daily Optic*, Feb. 11, March 12, Oct. 23, 1885, p. 4; "Letterbook 1," pp. 51-53, 96, H. M. Porter Papers, Colorado State Historical Society, Denver.

11. *Las Vegas Daily Optic*, April 26, May 11, Nov. 5, 1887, p. 4; *Stock Grower and Farmer* (Las Vegas), May 21, Aug. 20, 1887, June 29, 1889, p. 3; Pearson, *Maxwell Land Grant*, p. 144.

12. *Colfax County Stockman*, Sept. 14, 22, Oct. 6, 13, 1894, p. 3.

13. Ibid., Dec. 8, 1894, p. 3; William French, *Further Recollections of a Western Ranchman* (New York: Argosy-Antiquarian, 1965), pp. 480-82.

14. *Colfax County Stockman*, Dec. 28, 1901, p. 3.

15. Chase, *Editor's Run*, pp. 47-49; *Raton Reporter*, Jan. 27, 1892, Dec. 31, 1914, p. 4; Charles F. Coan, *History of New Mexico*, 2 vols. (Chicago and New York: American Historical Soc., 1925), 2:440-42.

16. *Las Vegas Daily Optic*, Jan. 30, 1886, p. 2; Paul Ton, "Henry Miller Porter" (unpublished Ph.D. dissertation, University of Denver, 1969), pp. 190-324.

17. Ton, "Henry Miller Porter," pp. 404-30; Chase, *Editor's Run*, pp. 88-92; *Raton Range*, April 29, 1892, p. 4.

18. Coan, *History of New Mexico*, 2:505-07; F. Stanley, *The Grant That Maxwell Bought* (Denver: World Press, 1950), p. 233; *Raton Range*, June 16, 1909, p. 2; Nov. 21, 1922, p. 1.

19. *Springer Sentinel*, July 10, 1901, p. 1; *Colfax County Stockman*, March 10, June 16, 1900, p. 3; May 19, 1901, p. 2; *Raton Range*, July 18, 1901, p. 2; Nov. 18, 1913, p. 2.

20. Leon Noel, "The Largest Estate in the World," *Overland Monthly*, 2nd ser., vol. 12 (Nov., 1888), pp. 481-88.

CHAPTER XI

1. *The Gold Mines of the Moreno Valley and Ute Creek Districts, Colfax County, New Mexico* . . . (Chicago: Poole Brothers, 1894).

2. Correspondence between Lynch, V. S. Shelby, Robert C. Beatie, Sackett, and T. B. Catron, Catron Collection, Zimmerman Library, University of New Mexico, Albuquerque; *Stearns-Roger Manufacturing Company v. Aztec Gold Mining and Milling Company, et al.*, 14 New Mexico 300; Pearson, *The Maxwell Land Grant*, p. 181.

3. Unless otherwise noted, information in this chapter is drawn from the following newspapers: *Santa Fe Daily New Mexican*, *New Mexican Miner* (Elizabethtown), *Mining Reporter* (San Francisco), *Mining and Scientific Press* (San Francisco), *Engineering and Mining World* (Denver).

4. *Santa Fe Daily New Mexican*, April 30, May 5, 1894; Dec. 4, 1896; March 29, April 10, July 16, 1897—all p. 1.

5. *New Mexican Miner*, June 2, 1897, p. 1.

6. Manville Chapman, "The Eleanor of E-town," *New Mexico Magazine*, November, 1937, pp. 20-22, 47. Pearson, *Maxwell Land Grant*, pp. 197-98.

7. *New Mexican Miner*, Oct. 21, 1898, p. 1.

8. In addition to newspapers, this section is based on Jim B. Pearson, "The Elizabethtown-Red River Area: A New Mexico Gold Story" (unpublished Ph.D. dissertation, University of Texas), 1955.

9. *Elizabethtown Mining Bulletin*, Jan. 18, 1900, p. 1.

10. *Cimarron Citizen*, June 24, 1908, p. 1.

11. Report of the Denver Golden Corporation, Program Department, Philmont.

CHAPTER XII

1. In addition to local, contemporary newspapers, this section is based on Pearson, *The Maxwell Land Grant*; Henry E. Bender, Jr., "St. Louis, Rocky

Mountain and Pacific Ry., A History," *New Mexico Railroader*, vol. 4, no. 4 (April 1962); "Locomotives and Equipment of the St. Louis, Rocky Mountain, and Pacific Ry.," *New Mexico Railroader*, vol. 4, no. 5 (May 1962); and "The Line and Facilities of the St. Louis, Rocky Mountain & Pacific Ry.," *New Mexico Railroader*, vol. 4, no. 6 (June 1962).

2. Edward Mahoney, "Rocky Mountain and Santa Fe," *New Mexico Railroader*, vol. 4, no. 7 (July 1962), p. 3.

3. This section is based on local newspapers, on interviews and correspondence with Thomas Schomburg and Guy H. Palmes, and on Interstate Commerce Commission, *Annual Report on the Statistics of Railways* . . . , 1910-21.

4. *Decisions of the Interstate Commerce Commission*, vol. 106, p. 562.

5. Margaret Ward, *Cimarron Saga* (Pampa, Texas: Pampa Print Shop, 1959), p. 71.

6. *Decisions of the Interstate Commerce Commission*, vol. 82, pp. 217-18.

7. Ibid., vol. 166, pp. 391-92.

CHAPTER XIII

1. For additional information and documentation on McCormick, see Lawrence R. Murphy, "Stanley R. McCormick: The Youngest Reaper," *California Historical Society Quarterly*, vol. 48, no. 2 (June 1969), pp. 113-23.

2. Information on Webster was derived from contemporary local newspapers, legal documents filed in the Colfax County Courthouse at Raton; and "The Urraca Ranch, Cimarron, Colfax County, New Mexico," an undated brochure in the Seton Library at Philmont.

3. *Raton Reporter*, July 25, 1916, p. 1; *Cimarron News-Citizen*, July 5, 1917, p. 1.

4. *Cimarron News-Citizen*, April 17, June 7, 1917, p. 1; *Raton Reporter*, April 17, 1917, p. 1.

5. Newspaper accounts, deeds, and excerpts from a Rayado Colonization Company advertisement in the Seton Library were used for this section.

6. A letter from Ira Wood, son of Charles E. Wood, provided much of this information, as did local newspapers.

7. For biographies of Phillips, see Clarence B. Douglas, *The History of Tulsa, Oklahoma* (Chicago: S. J. Clarke Co.), vol. 3, pp. 708-09; Joseph B. Thoborn and Muriel H. Wright, *Oklahoma: A History of the State and Its People* (New York: Lewis Historical Publishing Company, 1929), vol. 4, pp. 812-13; *National Cyclopedia of American History* (New York: James T. White Co., 1930), vol. 30, p. 180; *New York Times*, Oct. 25, 1925, p. 29; Dec. 11, 1925, p. 11; Dec. 22, 1925, p. 10. The author also benefited from seeing Phillips's notes for an autobiography, provided him by Elliott W. Phillips.

8. *New York Times*, July 8, 1927, p. 17; *Raton Reporter*, Dec. 19, 1927, p. 1; Kenneth L. Roberts, "Hardships of New Mexico," *Saturday Evening Post*, vol. 200 (Dec. 10, 1927), pp. 10-11, 48, 52, 54, 57.

9. Waite Phillips, *Epigrams* (privately printed, 1964), p. 7; *Tulsa World*, Oct. 6, 1938, p. 1; Oct. 8, 1939, p. 1; Jan. 28, 1964, p. 5; Jan. 29, 1964, p. 4.

CHAPTER XIV

1. This section is based on Pearson, *Maxwell Land Grant*, pp. 250-51; Charles A. Chase and Douglas Muir, "The Aztec Mine, Baldy New Mexico," *American Institute of Mining Engineers Transactions*, vol. 48 (1923), pp. 270-81; Willis T. Lee, "The Aztec Gold Mine, Baldy, New Mexico," *U.S.G.S. Bulletin No. 620* (Washington, D.C.: Government Printing Office, 1916), pp. 330 ff.

2. Ernest V. Deshayes to author, Oct. 24, 1964.

3. For information on the completion of the deep tunnel, see Pearson, *Maxwell Land Grant*, pp. 244-47; Hazel Cooke Upshaw, "Deep Tunnel Mine," *New Mexico Magazine*, vol. 28 (March 1950), pp. 23, 43. The author also interviewed Bill Brewster and received a lengthy letter from Alvis F. Denison.

4. Frank J. Desmond to New Mexico Corporation Commission, undated letter in Aztec Extension Gold Mines folder, Corporation Commission Records, State Records Center, Santa Fe.

5. J. R. Finley, *Report of the Appraisal of Mining Properties in New Mexico, 1921-1922* (Santa Fe: Catholic Publishing Co., 1922), pp. 69-70.

6. In addition to Pearson, *Maxwell Land Grant*, pp. 254-64, this section is based on interviews with J. W. Leitzell, Matt Gorman, Vernon Hanson, Bill Brewster, and Victor J. Van Lint; Leitzell, Gorman, and A. F. Denison also provided information in letters to the author.

7. Information on the French Henry was provided in letters from Clinton P. Anderson, Barney Cruz, Jr., and W. A. Keleher.

8. The author secured information on Fullroe, Inc., in letters from Floyd C. Fuller, Charles F. Johnson, Jr., and Barney Cruz, Jr., and in interviews with Gorman and Van Lint. Also see *Janey V. Fullroe* (47 New Mexico 423).

9. Muriel S. Wolle, *The Bonanza Trail* (Bloomington: Indiana University Press, 1953), p. 33.

10. *Raton Range*, Dec. 17, 1962, p. 1.

CHAPTER XV

1. This section is based largely on unpublished correspondence between Phillips and Scout officials and Dawson in the collection of Ray H. Bryan; the author has also benefited from letters and/or interviews with Arie W. Poldervaart, Minor Huffman, Ray H. Bryan, and B. B. Dawson. Information was also obtained from the *Annual Report of the Boy Scouts of America*, 1938, and a pamphlet titled "A National Senior Scout Wilderness Camp" in the Philmont files.

2. Schuck's report and other material on the Phillips proposal are in "Philmont Scout Ranch" folder, Bryan collection.

3. Waite Phillips, "History of the Southwest and Philmont Ranch," manuscript in Philmont Scout Ranch files.

4. This section is based on material in various issues of *Annual Report of the Boy Scouts of America*, plus letters and reports provided by Minor Huffman.

5. Brochures describing the various programs are in the Philmont Scout Ranch files.

6. A letter from William L. Lawrence to the author supplemented material in the Scouts *Annual Report*.

7. This section is based largely on interviews and letters to the author from Ray H. Bryan.

8. An interview with William C. Littrell provided the bulk of material for this section.

SELECTED BIBLIOGRAPHY

MANUSCRIPT SOURCES

Alexander, Eveline Thorp. Unpublished diary in the Bancroft Library, University of California, Berkeley.

Arrott, James W. Collection of materials pertaining to Fort Union, New Mexico, at New Mexico Highlands University, Las Vegas, N.M.

"Baldy Mountain Placer Company" file, Corporation Commission records, State Records Center, Santa Fe.

Bryan, Ray H. Collection, New Brunswick, N. J.

Catron, Thomas B. Collection, Zimmerman Library, University of New Mexico, Albuquerque.

Colfax County Records and Deed Books. County Recorder's Office and storage room, Raton, N.M.

Denver Golden Corporation. Unpublished report on the Thunder Mine. Program department files, Philmont Scout Ranch.

Desmond, Frank J. to New Mexico Corporation Commission, n.d., in "Aztec Extension Gold Mines" folder, Corporation Commission records, State Records Center, Santa Fe.

District Court Records. Colfax County Court House, Raton, N.M.

Gorman, Mat. Collection of Baldy mining materials. Trinidad, Colo.

Huffman, Minor. Collection of Philmont material, Roswell, N.M.

McGavran, Harry G. Collection of materials relating to Charles Beaubien and the early history of Philmont in the possession of Harry G. McGavran, Jr., Los Alamos, N.M.

Mexican Archives of New Mexico, State Records Center, Santa Fe.

Office of Indian Affairs. Letters Received, New Mexico Superintendency, R. G. 75, National Archives, Washington, D.C.

Office of Indian Affairs. Records, New Mexico Superintendency. R. G. 75, National Archives, Washington, D.C.

Phillips, Waite. Unpublished notes for an autobiography in the collection of Elliott W. Phillips, Valmora, N.M.

Surveyor General. Records of New Mexico Land Grants. Bureau of Land Management Archives, Federal Building, Santa Fe.
"Transcript of Record," *U.S. v. Maxwell Land Grant Co., et al.* Supreme Court of the United States, October term, 1886. Unpublished manuscript in R. G. 267, National Archives, Washington, D.C.
Twitchell, Ralph, E. Archival collection on New Mexico Land Grants. Bureau of Land Management, Federal Building, Santa Fe.
U.S. Army. District of New Mexico, Letters. R. G. 98, National Archives, Washington, D.C.
U.S. Army. Letters Received, Ninth Military Department. R. G. 94, National Archives, Washington, D.C.
U.S. Army. Orders, Ninth Military Department. R. G. 98, National Archives, Washington, D.C.
U.S. Army. Return of Troops at Rayado, New Mexico, Records of the Office of the Adjutant General, R. G. 94, National Archives, Washington, D.C.

PERSONAL TESTIMONIES

Interviews with the following individuals provided much valuable information. Unless otherwise noted, they were conducted by the author. Narciso M. Abreu interviewed by Harry G. McGavran, July 1960 (tape recording, Seton Library); Mrs. Gertrude Alpers, August 1965; Frank Alpers, Jr., August 1965, 1970; William Brewster, August 28, 1963; Mrs. Ruby Burch, August 1965; Ray H. Bryan, August 23, 1966; B. B. Dawson, June 10, 1964; Robert W. Evans, June 9, 1964; Narciso Federici, August 27, 1963; Matt W. Gorman, September 1, 1964; Vernon Hansen interviewed by William R. Craig, March 5, 1964; J. W. Leitzell, August 22, 1963; Mrs. R. C. Loomis, July 1965; William C. Littrell, August 16, 1966; Elliott W. Phillips, July 1969; Thomas W. Schomburg, June 9, 1964; Mrs. Adelina Abreu Valdez interviewed by Harry G. McGavran, July 1960 (tape recording, Seton Museum); Victor J. Van Lint, December 21, 1963; George Whyte, August, 1966.
The following individuals provided information to the author through written correspondence: Narciso M. Abreu, Clinton P. Anderson, Ray H. Bryan, Barney Cruz, Jr., Alvis F. Denison, Ernest V. Deshayes, Floyd C. Fuller, William A. Keleher, J. W. Leitzell, Guy H. Palmes, Victor J. Van Lint, and Ira V. Wood.

LEGAL CASES

Janey v. Fullroe (47 New Mexico 423)
Stearns-Roger Manufacturing Company v. Aztec Gold Mining and Milling Company, et al. (14 New Mexico 300)
U.S. v. Maxwell Land Grant Company, et al. (121 U.S. Reports 325)

NEWSPAPERS

Cimarron Citizen, 1908.
Cimarron News and Press, 1875-77, 1907-08.
Cimarron News-Citizen, 1916.
Colfax County Stockman (Springer), 1898-1924.
Daily New Mexican (Santa Fe), 1868-1900.
Engineering and Mining Journal (Chicago), 1900-07.
Globe (Washington, D.C.), 1841-43.
Las Vegas Daily Optic, 1881-87.
Las Vegas Morning Review, 1899.
Mining and Engineering World (Denver), 1910-18.
Mining and Scientific Press (San Francisco), 1868-1900.
Mining Reporter (Denver), 1899-1901.
Mining World (Denver), 1905-15.
New Mexican (Santa Fe), 1867-68.
New Mexican Miner (Elizabethtown), 1897-1902.
New Mexican News and Press (Raton), 1881.
Raton Daily Range, 1900-63.
Raton Reporter, 1910-29.
Santa Fe Weekly Gazette, 1866-70.
Santa Fe Weekly New Mexican, 1866-70.
Springer Sentinel, 1901.
Springer Times, 1928.
Springer Tribune, 1950-68.
Stock Grower and Farmer (Las Vegas), 1889-91.
Tulsa Tribune, 1938, 1964.
Tulsa World, 1938, 1964.

GOVERNMENT DOCUMENTS

Annual Report of the Boy Scouts of America, 1937-70.
"Answers of Augustus Storrs of Missouri to Certain Queries Upon the Course, Present State, and Future Prospect of Trade and Intercourse between Missouri and the Internal Provinces of Mexico. . . ." Senate Exec. Doc. 7, 18th Cong., 2 sess.
Bailey, Vernon. Life Zones and Crop Zones of New Mexico. U.S. Department of Agriculture, Biological Survey, North American Fauna No. 35, 1913.
————. Mammals of New Mexico. U.S. Department of Agriculture, Biological Survey, North American Fauna No. 53, 1931.
Interstate Commerce Commission. Decisions.
————. Report on the Statistics of Railroads in the United States. 1910-26.
Lee, Willis T. The Aztec Gold Mine, Baldy, New Mexico. United States Geological Survey Bulletin No. 620, 1910.

Lindgren, Waldemar, L. C. Graton and C. H. Gordon. *The Ore Deposits of New Mexico.* United States Geological Survey Professional Paper No. 68, 1916.

Pearson, G. A. *Forest Types in the Southwest as Determined by Climate and Soil.* United States Department of Agriculture Technical Bulletin No. 247, 1931.

"Petition of Sundry Inhabitants of the State of Missouri. . . ." *House Exec. Doc.* 79, 18th Cong., 2 sess.

Raymond, Rossiter W. *Statistics of Mines and Mining in the States and Territories West of the Rocky Mountains.* 1870. 1872.

"Report of the Secretary of the Interior," 1861-71.

"Report of the Secretary of War," 1850-52.

Robinson, G. D., et al. *Philmont Country: The Rocks and Landscape of a Famous New Mexico Ranch.* U.S. Geological Survey Professional Paper 505, 1964.

U.S. Department of the Interior, Bureau of Mines. *Minerals Yearbook.* 1934-1942. Washington, D.C.: Government Printing Office, 1934-42.

THESES AND DISSERTATIONS

Kelsey, Harry, Jr., "Clay Allison, Gunfighter," unpublished Master's thesis, University of Denver, 1954.

McCullough, James I. "The Maxwell Grant," unpublished Master's thesis, New Mexico Normal University, 1931.

Minge, Ward Allen. "Frontier Problems in New Mexico Preceding the Mexican War, 1840-1846," unpublished Doctoral dissertation, University of New Mexico, 1965.

Pearson, Jim B. "The Elizabethtown-Red River Area: A New Mexico Gold Story," unpublished Doctoral dissertation, University of Texas, 1955.

Ton, Paul. "Henry Miller Porter: Merchant, Private Banker, and Cattleman, 1858-1917," unpublished Doctoral dissertation, University of Denver, 1969.

ARTICLES

Alpers, Frank H., Jr., "Surface Surveys of Prehistoric Ponil River Sites," *El Palacio*, vol. 70, no. 4 (Winter 1963).

Atherton, Lewis E. "Business Techniques in the Santa Fe Trade," *Missouri Historic Review*, vol. 24 (April 1940).

Baker, Galen, "The Archaeology of the Park Plateau of Southeastern Colorado," *Southwestern Lore.* vol. 30, no. 1 (June 1964).

Bender, Henry E., Jr., "The Line and Facilities of the St. L. RM & P Ry.," *New Mexico Railroader*, vol. 4, no. 6 (June 1962).

———. "Locomotives and Equipment of the St. Louis, Rocky Mountain and Pacific Ry.," *New Mexico Railroader*, vol. 4, no. 5 (May 1962).

————. "St. Louis, Rocky Mountain and Pacific Ry.," A History," *New Mexico Railroader*, vol. 4, no. 4 (April 1962).

Chase, Charles A. and Douglas Muir. "The Aztec Mine, Baldy, New Mexico," *American Institute of Mining Engineers Transactions*, vol. 58 (1923).

Daubenmire, R. F. "Vegetational Zonation in the Rocky Mountains," *Botanical Review*, vol. 9 (June 1943).

Dunham, Harold H. "Lucien B. Maxwell: Frontiersman and Businessman," *Denver Westerners' Brand Book*, vol. 5 (March 1949).

————. "New Mexican Land Grants with Special Reference to the Title Papers of the Maxwell Grant," *New Mexico Historical Review*, vol. 30 (1955).

Dunn, William E. "Spanish Reaction Against French Advance Towards New Mexico, 1717-1727," *Mississippi Valley Historical Review*, vol. 11, no. 3 (December 1915).

Felty, Paul, and Larry Murphy. "Bonanza on Old Baldy Mountain," *Boys' Life*, June, 1965.

Gett, J. Ralph. "The Rayado Ranch," *Western Empire: The Development Magazine*. No date.

Goddard, Pliny Earle. "Jicarilla Apache Texts," *Anthropological Papers of the American Museum of Natural History*, vol. 8 (1911).

Gunnerson, Dolores A. "The Southern Athabascans: Their Arrival in the Southwest," *El Palacio*, vol. 56 (1956).

Gunnerson, James H. "Apache Archaeology in Northeastern New Mexico," *American Antiquity*, vol. 34 (January 1969).

Holmes, Kenneth L. "The Benjamin Cooper Expedition to Santa Fe in 1822 and 1823," *New Mexico Historical Review*, Vol. XXXVII (April 1963).

Howell, Joseph Jr. "Piñon and Juniper Woodlands of the South-West," *Journal of Forestry*, vol. 39 (1941).

"The Journals of Captain Thomas Becknell from Boone's Lick to Santa Fe and from Santa Cruz to the Green River," *Missouri Historical Review*, vol. 4 (January 1910).

Lecompte, Janet. "The Manco Burro Pass Massacre," *New Mexico Historical Review*, vol. 41 (1966).

Lutes, Eugene. "A Marginal Prehistoric Culture of Northeastern New Mexico," *El Palacio*, vol. 66 (April 1959).

Murphy, Lawrence R. "The Beaubien and Miranda Land Grant, 1841-1846," *New Mexico Historical Review*, vol. 62, no. 1 (January 1967), pp. 27-47.

————. "A Philmont Story," *Scouting Bulletin of the Catholic Committee on Scouting*, vol. 48, no. 2 (June 1969).

————. "Rayado: Pioneer Settlement in Northeastern New Mexico, 1848-1857," *New Mexico Historical Review*, vol. 46, no. 1 (January 1971).

————. "Stanley R. McCormick: The Youngest Reaper," *California Historical Society Quarterly*, vol. 48, no. 2 (June 1969).

Noel, Leon. "The Largest Estate in the World." *Overland Monthly*, 2nd s. vol. 12 (November 1888).

Opler, Morris E. "A Summary of Jicarilla Apache Culture," *American Anthropologist*, N. S. vol. 38 (April-June 1936).

————. "Myths and Tales of the Jicarilla Apache Indians." *Memoirs of the American Folklore Society*, vol. 31 (1938).

Ray, I. L., and J. F. Smith, Jr. "Geology of the Moreno Valley, New Mexico," *Geological Society of America Bulletin*, vol. 52 (1941).

Roberts, Kenneth L. "The Hardships of New Mexico," *Saturday Evening Post*, vol. 200 (December 17, 1927).

Rydberg, R. A. "Vegetative Life Zones in the Rocky Mountain Region," *New York Botanical Garden Memoirs*, vol. 6 (1916).

Schroeder, Albert H. "A Brief History of the Southern Utes," *Southwestern Lore*, vol. 30 (1965).

————. "Shifting for Survival in the Southwest," *New Mexico Historical Review*, vol. 43 (October 1968).

Skinner, Alan. "Lizard Cave: A Rock Shelter in Northeastern New Mexico," *El Palacio*, vol. 71, no. 2 (Autumn 1964).

Smith, J. F., and L. L. Ray, "Geology of the Cimarron Range, New Mexico," *Geological Society of America Bulletin*, vol. 54 (1943).

Stanley, F. "O. P. McMains: Champion of a Lost Cause," *New Mexico Historical Review*, vol. 24 (January 1949).

Stephens, F. F. "Missouri and the Santa Fe Trade," *Missouri Historical Review*, vol. 10 (July 1916) and vol. 11 (July 1917).

Taylor, Morris F. "A New Look at an Old Case: The Bent Heirs' Claim in the Maxwell Grant," *New Mexico Historical Review*, vol. 43 (1968).

Walter, Paul A. F. "Dr. Frank Springer," *New Mexico Historical Review*, vol. 2 (1927).

————. "New Mexico's Pioneer Bank and Bankers," *New Mexico Historical Review*, vol. 21 (1946).

Wendorf, Fred. "The Archaeology of Northeastern New Mexico," *El Palacio*, vol. 67, no. 2 (April 1960).

Wilson, H. Clyde, "Jicarilla Apache Political and Economic Structures," *University of California Publications in Archaeology and Ethnology*, vol. 98 (1964).

Wissler, Clark. "The Influence of the Horse in the Development of Plains Culture," *American Anthropologist*, N.S. vol. 16 (1914).

BOOKS

Anderson, Eugene C. *The Metal Resources of New Mexico and Their Economic Features Through 1954.* New Mexico School of Mines Bulletin No. 39. Socorro: New Mexico School of Mines, 1957.

Bogan, Sam. *Let the Coyotes Howl: A Story of Philmont Scout Ranch.* New York: G. P. Putnams' Sons, 1946.

Bolton, Herbert E. *Coronado: Knight of Pueblos and Plains.* Albuquerque: University of New Mexico Press, 1949.

Brooks, Clinton E. and Frank D. Reeve, eds., *Forts and Forays: James A. Bennet, a Dragoon in New Mexico, 1850-1856.* Albuquerque: University of New Mexico Press, 1948.

Carter, Harvey L. *"Dear Old Kit," The Historical Christopher Carson.* Norman: University of Oklahoma Press, 1968.

Casson, Herbert N. *Cyrus Hall McCormick: His Life and Work.* Chicago: A. C. McClurg and Co., 1909.

Chaffee, J. B. *The Beaubien and Miranda Grant in New Mexico and Colorado.* New York: n.p., 1869.

Chase, C. M. *The Editor's Run in New Mexico and Colorado.* Montpelier, Vt.: Argus and Patriot Book and Job Printing House, 1882.

Chittenden, Hiram M. *The American Fur Trade in the Far West.* 2 vols., New York: Barnes and Noble, 1935.

Cleaveland, Agnes Morley. *Satan's Paradise, From Lucien Maxwell to Fred Lambert.* Boston: Houghton Mifflin Co., 1952.

Cleland, Robert G. *This Reckless Breed of Men.* New York: Alfred A. Knopf, 1952.

Coan, Charles F. *A History of New Mexico.* 3 vols., Chicago and New York: American Historical Society, Inc., 1925.

Collinson, John A. and W. A. Bell, *The Maxwell Land Grant Situated in Colorado and New Mexico.* London: Taylor and Company, 1870.

Colton, Ray C. *The Civil War in the Western Territories.* Norman: University of Oklahoma Press, 1959.

Conard, Howard L. *"Uncle Dick" Wootton.* Chicago: W. E. Dibble and Company, 1890.

Duffus, R. L. *The Santa Fe Trail.* New York: Longmans, Green and Company, 1930.

Dunham, Harold. *Government Handout: A Study in the Administration of the Public Lands, 1875-1891.* New York: Columbia University Press, 1941.

Emmett, Chris. *Fort Union and the Winning of the Southwest.* Norman: University of Oklahoma Press, 1965.

Fenneman, Nevin M. *Physiographic Provinces of the Western United States.* New York: McGraw-Hill Book Co., 1931.

Field, Matthew C. *Matt Field on the Santa Fe Trail,* ed. John E. Sunder. Norman: University of Oklahoma Press, 1960.

Finley, J. R. *Report of the Appraisal of Mining Properties of New Mexico, 1921-1922.* Santa Fe: Printer of the Catholic Publishing Company, 1922.

Fowler, Jacob. *The Journal of Jacob Fowler.* ed. Elliott Coues. New York: Francis P. Harper, 1898.

French, William. *Further Recollections of a Western Ranchman*. ed. Jeff C. Dykes. New York: Argosy-Antiquarian Ltd., 1965.

Gerrard, Lewis H. *Wah-to-yah and the Taos Trail*. Norman: University of Oklahoma Press, 1955.

Glasscock, G. B. *Then Came Oil*. New York: Bobbs-Merrill Co., 1938.

Goetzmann, William H. *Army Exploration in the American West, 1803-1863*. New Haven: Yale University Press, 1959.

The Gold Mines of the Moreno Valley and Ute Creek Districts Colfax County, New Mexico, an Illustrated Sketch of the Scenery and Geological Features of that Prosperous Region to be reached via the Atchison, Topeka and Santa Fe Railroad. Chicago: Poole Brothers, 1894.

Greever, William S. *The Bonanza West: The Story of the Western Mining Rushes, 1848-1900*. Norman: University of Oklahoma Press, 1962.

Gregg, Josiah. *Commerce of the Prairies*. ed. Max L. Moorhead. Norman: University of Oklahoma Press, 1954.

Gregg, Kate L. *The Road to Santa Fe*. Albuquerque: University of New Mexico Press, 1952.

Guide to the Maxwell Grant—1¾ Million Acres in New Mexico and Colorado, Reliable Information to Land Seekers—Cheap Land on Easy Terms—10,000 Farms for Sale in the Serene, Sunny Clime of Colorado and New Mexico. Chicago: Rand McNally and Company, n.d.

Hannum, Anna P. ed. *A Quaker Forty-Niner: The Adventures of Charles Edward Pancoast on the American Frontier*. Philadelphia: University of Pennsylvania Press, 1930.

Harwood, Thomas. *History of New Mexico Spanish and English Missions*. 2 vols., Albuquerque: El Abogado Press, 1908.

Hilton, Tom. *Nevermore, Cimarron, Nevermore*. Fort Worth: Western Heritage Press, 1970.

History of the Famous Don Diego Hotel and Its Famous Founder. Springer, N.M.: Tribune Press, n.d.

History of New Mexico: Its Resources and People. 3 vols., Los Angeles, Chicago and New York: Pacific States Publishing Company, 1907.

Hollon, W. Eugene. *The Lost Pathfinder: Zebulon Montgomery Pike*. Norman: University of Oklahoma Press, 1949.

Howbert, Irving. *Memories of a Lifetime in the Pike's Peak Region of Colorado*. New York: G. P. Putnam and Sons, 1925.

Hutchinson, William T. *Cyrus Hall McCormick*: 2 vols., New York: D. Appleton-Century Company, 1935.

Hyde, George. *Indians of the High Plains from the Prehistoric Period to the Coming of Europeans*. Norman: University of Oklahoma Press, 1959.

Inman, Henry A. *The Old Santa Fe Trail*. Topeka: Crane and Co., 1916, repr. Minneapolis: Ross and Haines, 1968.

Jennings, Jesse D. and Edward Norbeck, eds. *Primitive Man in the New World.* Houston: Rice University by the University of Chicago Press, 1964.

Jones, Fayette Alexander. *New Mexican Mines and Minerals. . . . Being an Epitome of the Early Mining History and Resources of New Mexican Mines.* Santa Fe: New Mexican Printing Company, 1904.

Karnes, Thomas L. *William L. Gilpin: Western Nationalist.* Austin: University of Texas Press, 1970.

Keleher, William A. *The Maxwell Land Grant: A New Mexico Item.* Santa Fe: Rydal Press, 1942, repr. New York: Argosy-Antiquarian Ltd, 1964.

———. *Turmoil in New Mexico, 1846-68.* Santa Fe: The Rydal Press, 1953.

Lambert, Oscar D. *Stephen B. Elkins.* Pittsburgh: University of Pittsburgh Press, 1955.

Lasky, Samuel G. and Thomas Wootten. *The Metal Resources of New Mexico and Their Economic Features.* Socorro: New Mexico School of Mines, 1933.

Lavender, David. *Bent's Fort.* Garden City, N.Y.: Doubleday and Co., 1954.

Linney, Charles E., Fabian Garcia, and E. C. Hollinger, *Climate As it Affects the Crops and Ranges of New Mexico.* New Mexico Agricultural Experiment Station Bulletin 182, State College, N.M.: New Mexico State College, 1930.

McCall, George A. *New Mexico in 1850: A Military View.* ed. Robert W. Frazer. Norman: University of Oklahoma Press, 1968.

Magoffin, Susan S. *Down the Santa Fe Trail and Into Mexico, 1846-1847.* ed. Stella M. Drumm. New Haven: Yale University Press, 1962.

Miles, Nelson A. *Fighting on the Plains.* New York: Harper and Brothers, 1911.

———. *Personal Recollection and Observation of General Nelson A. Miles.* Chicago and New York: The Warner Co., 1897.

Moorhead, Max L. *New Mexico's Royal Road.* Norman: University of Oklahoma Press, 1958.

New Mexico Bureau of Immigration. *The Mines of New Mexico.* Santa Fe: New Mexican Printing Company, 1896.

Oosting, Henry J. *The Study of Plant Communities.* San Francisco: W. H. Freeman and Co., 1958.

Opler, Marvin K. "The Southern Utes of Colorado," in Ralph Linton, *Acculturation in Seven American Indian Tribes.* New York: D. Appleton-Century Co., 1940.

Pearson, Jim Berry. *The Maxwell Land Grant.* Norman: University of Oklahoma Press, 1961.

Phillips, Paul C. *The Fur Trade.* 2 vols., Norman: University of Oklahoma Press, 1961.

Phillips, Waite. *Epigrams.* ed. Elliott W. Phillips. n.p.: privately printed, 1964.

Porter, H. M. *Autobiography of Henry M. Porter.* Denver: World Press, 1932.

———. *Pencillings of a Western Pioneer.* Denver: World Press, 1929.

Sabin, Edwin L. *Kit Carson Days.* 2 vols., New York: Press of the Pioneers, 1935.

Schroeder, Albert H. *A Study of the Apache Indians: Part II, The Jicarilla Apaches.* Santa Fe, 1958.

A Sketch of the Gold Mining Camps and Mining Regulations of the Maxwell Land Grant. n.p.: 1896.

Souvenir of the Great Elizabethtown Gold and Copper Mining District. Elizabethtown: New Mexican Miner, 1902.

Stanley, F. *Fort Union, New Mexico.* Denver: World Press, n.d.

————. *The Grant that Maxwell Bought.* Denver: World Press, 1952.

————. *One Half Mile from Heaven or the Cimarron Story.* Denver: World Press Publishing Company, 1959.

Stratton, Porter A. *The Territorial Press in New Mexico, 1834-1912.* Albuquerque: University of New Mexico Press, 1969.

Tassé, Joseph. *Les Canadiens de L'Ouest.* Montreal: n.p., 1878.

Thoburn, Joseph B., and Muriel H. Wright. *Oklahoma: A History of the State and Its People.* New York: Lewis Historical Publishing Company, 1929.

Thomas, Alfred B. *After Coronado: Spanish Exploration Northeast of New Mexico, 1696-1727.* Norman: University of Oklahoma Press, 1935.

Ton, Paul. comp., *An Index to the Henry Miller Porter Papers.* Denver: State Historical Society of Colorado, 1968.

Transcript of Record of Charles Bent et al. vs. Guadalupe Miranda et al. Santa Fe: Voz del Pueblo Print, 1894.

Transcript of Title of the Maxwell Land Grant Situated in New Mexico and Colorado. Chicago: Rand McNally and Co., 1881.

Twitchell, Ralph E. *Leading Facts of New Mexican History.* 2 vols., Cedar Rapids, Iowa: Torch Press, 1912, repr. Albuquerque: Horn and Wallace, 1962.

Wadel, Waldo R. *Prehistoric Man on the Great Plains.* Norman: University of Oklahoma Press, 1961.

Walter, Paul A. F. *Banking in New Mexico Before the Railroad Came.* New York and Santa Fe: Newcomen Society in North America, 1955.

Ward, Margaret. *Cimarron Saga.* Pampa, Texas: Pampa Print Shop, 1959.

————. *Cousins by the Dozens.* Pampa, Texas: Pampa Print Shop, 1965.

Weber, David J. *The Taos Trappers.* Norman: University of Oklahoma Press, 1971.

Wolle, Muriel S. *The Bonanza Trail.* Bloomington: Indiana University Press, 1953.

Wormington, H. M. *Ancient Man in North America.* Denver: Museum of Natural History, 1957.

————. *Prehistoric Indians of the Southwest.* Denver: Museum of Natural History, 1959.

MISCELLANEOUS

Glassow, Michael A. "A Consideration of the Routes of Early Eighteenth Century Spanish Expeditions Through Northeastern New Mexico, with an Evaluation of the Ethnohistorical Data Concerning Jicarilla Apache Settlement Patterns of the Contact Period," unpublished manuscript in the files of Dr. Glassow, University of California, Santa Barbara.

"Philbrook Art Center," descriptive booklet obtained from the center in Tulsa.

"Philmont Scout Ranch Soil and Water Conservation Plan," mimeographed book in the files of Philmont Scout Ranch, Cimarron.

Philmont Scout Ranch, *Summaries of Archaeology Program.* Mimeographed reports in the files of Philmont Scout Ranch, Cimarron.

"A Plan for Multiple Use Through Resource Conservation Development, Philmont Scout Ranch and Explorer Base," mimeographed book in the files of Philmont Scout Ranch, Cimarron.

"The Urraca Ranch, Cimarron, Colfax County, New Mexico," undated brochure, Seton Library, Philmont.

INDEX